"[This is] a book that goes t the nature of the church. An ambitious, even breathtaking, undertaking: brilliantly conceived, thoroughly engrossing, and thought provoking from first to last."

Dr. Leonard Sweet
Best-Selling Author
E. Stanley Jones Professor of Evangelism, Drew University
Visiting Distinguished Professor, George Fox University
Chief Contributor to Sermons.com

"With our origins in a renewal movement within the Church of England, and several branches emerging from internal renewal efforts as we matured, the broad Wesleyan family of churches share the pressing need of an adequate ecclesiology—one that owns and celebrates our strengths as 'movement,' while reclaiming central aspects of the continuity and wisdom of the church through the ages. This volume is an important contribution to this effort, which will be of help to the whole family!"

Dr. Randy L. Maddox
William Kellon Quick Professor of Wesleyan and Methodist Studies
Duke Divinity School, Durham, North Carolina

"This volume is a gift not only to the Church of the Nazarene but also to the entire Wesleyan family. Faithfully rooted in John Wesley's theology and practice, biblically informed, and ecumenical in breadth, these essays provide profound insight into the nature of the church and its implications for worship, community, formation, mission, and polity. It deserves to be widely read and deeply pondered."

Dr. Henry H. Knight III
Donald and Pearl Wright Professor of Wesleyan Studies
Saint Paul School of Theology, Overland Park, Kansas

"One of the most neglected conversations in our denomination centers on what we mean by 'church.' Professors Leclerc and Maddix have edited an excellent array of essays that seek to remedy our lack of attention to ecclesiology from a variety of perspectives and disciplines. I am pleased to commend this resource to anyone who cares deeply about the future of the Church of the Nazarene."

Rev. Philip R. Hamner
Senior Pastor
Overland Park, Kansas, Church of the Nazarene

"Drs. Leclerc and Maddix have provided the resource on a Wesleyan understanding of the 'church' many of us have said for years should be written. As they state in the introduction, I have also been a part of conversations expressing the need of an adequate ecclesiology. I am very pleased to have this volume for myself and to recommend it to all of our ministers. Although written with educational settings in mind, it is a wonderful resource for everyone in ministry, lay and clergy alike. The authors have not intended to write as a 'final word' on the subject, but they have given to us a truly defining look at the 'church' in a time [when] it is desperately needed."

Dr. Stephen Borger
Intermountain District Superintendent
Church of the Nazarene

ESSENTIAL CHURCH

a wesleyan ecclesiology

Diane Leclerc
&
Mark A. Maddix
Editors

BEACON HILL PRESS
OF KANSAS CITY

Copyright 2014 by Beacon Hill Press of Kansas City

ISBN 978-0-8341-3242-9

Printed in the
United States of America

Cover Design: Nathan Johnson
Interior Design: Sharon Page

Unless otherwise indicated, all Scripture quotations are from the *New Revised Standard Version* (NRSV) of the Bible, copyright 1989 by the Division of Christian Education of the National Council of the Churches of Christ in the USA. All rights reserved.

Scripture quotations marked CEB are from the *Common English Bible* (CEB), copyright 2011. All rights reserved.

Scripture quotations marked NIV are from *The Holy Bible, New International Version*® (NIV®). Copyright © 1973, 1978, 1984, 2011 by Biblica, Inc.™ Used by permission. All rights reserved worldwide.

Library of Congress Cataloging-in-Publication Data
Essential church : a Wesleyan ecclesiology / Diane Leclerc and Mark A. Maddix, editors.
   pages cm
  Includes bibliographical references.
  ISBN 978-0-8341-3242-9 (pbk.)
  1. Wesleyan Church—Doctrines. 2. Church. I. Leclerc, Diane, 1963- editor of compilation.
  BX9995.W45E87 2014
  262'.07—dc23
                                             2014006165

10 9 8 7 6 5 4 3 2 1

ESSENTIAL CHURCH

a wesleyan ecclesiology

Diane Leclerc
&
Mark A. Maddix
Editors

BEACON HILL PRESS
OF KANSAS CITY

Copyright 2014 by Beacon Hill Press of Kansas City

ISBN 978-0-8341-3242-9

Printed in the
United States of America

Cover Design: Nathan Johnson
Interior Design: Sharon Page

Unless otherwise indicated, all Scripture quotations are from the *New Revised Standard Version* (NRSV) of the Bible, copyright 1989 by the Division of Christian Education of the National Council of the Churches of Christ in the USA. All rights reserved.

Scripture quotations marked CEB are from the *Common English Bible* (CEB), copyright 2011. All rights reserved.

Scripture quotations marked NIV are from *The Holy Bible, New International Version*® (NIV®). Copyright © 1973, 1978, 1984, 2011 by Biblica, Inc.™ Used by permission. All rights reserved worldwide.

Library of Congress Cataloging-in-Publication Data
Essential church : a Wesleyan ecclesiology / Diane Leclerc and Mark A. Maddix, editors.
     pages cm
   Includes bibliographical references.
   ISBN 978-0-8341-3242-9 (pbk.)
   1. Wesleyan Church—Doctrines. 2. Church. I. Leclerc, Diane, 1963- editor of compilation.
   BX9995.W45E87 2014
   262'.07—dc23
                                                                                                   2014006165

10 9 8 7 6 5 4 3 2 1

To
Dr. Timothy Thomas, who introduced Mark to the
Church of the Nazarene,
and Dr. Steve Seamands, who taught him the
historical theologies of the church

and

Dr. Rob L. Staples, an example to Diane of how to be
a true theologian of the church,
and Dr. Floyd T. Cunningham, my brother and my example
of true devotion to the church

CONTENTS

Contributors
11

1. Introduction: Wesleyan Ecclesiology
Diane Leclerc and Mark A. Maddix
15

Part 1: The Church at Its Core
27

2. The Church: The Event of the Kingdom of God
Eric Severson
29

3. Trinitarian Identity: The Church's True Foundation
Henry W. Spaulding II and Henry W. Spaulding III
37

4. Putting Christ in His Place:
Ecclesiology and Christology in the Nazarene Tradition
Mark H. Mann
48

5. Mission Possible:
The Importance of the Spirit in Wesleyan Ecclesiology
Diane Leclerc
62

6. Tradition at Its Best: The Classical Marks of the Church
Tim J. Crutcher
75

7. Cultural Correlation: The "Postmodern" Marks of the Church
Deirdre Brower Latz
84

Part 2: The Church's Essential Functions
95

8. The Church at Worship
Jeffrey T. Barker
97

9. The Church's Sacraments
Brent Peterson
107

10. The Church's Proclamation
James N. Fitzgerald
115

11. The Church as Confessional Educator:
A Catechetical Approach to Christian Education
Mark A. Maddix
124

12. The Church as Formational Fellowship
Dean G. Blevins
138

13. The Church as Egalitarian Liberator
Kristina LaCelle-Peterson
147

14. The Church of Compassion and Justice
Stephen Riley
156

15. The Church as a Witnessing Community
David Busic
167

Part 3: The Church as Organized Organism
177

16. The Body of Christ: A Theology of Ecclesial Relationships
Richard P. Thompson
179

17. The Priesthood of All Believers: A Theology of Laity
Rebecca Laird
189

18. Unifying the Church:
A Theological Understanding of Ordination
Brent Peterson
199

19. The "Designated Reader":
An Ecclesiological Metaphor for Pastoral Leadership
Jeff Crosno
209

20. Pastoring Pastors: A Functional Theology of Superintendency
Jeren Rowell
219

Notes
229

CONTRIBUTORS

Rev. Jeffrey T. Barker, D.Min. (Candidate), Associate Professor of Practical Theology, Eastern Nazarene College, Quincy, Massachusetts; Pastor, Bethel Church of the Nazarene, Quincy, Massachusetts
Jeffrey Barker currently serves as both a local church pastor and associate professor of practical theology at Eastern Nazarene College. He holds degrees from Eastern Nazarene College (B.A.), Nazarene Theological Seminary (M.Div.), and Boston University (STM).

Rev. Dean G. Blevins, Ph.D., Professor of Practical Theology and Christian Discipleship, Nazarene Theological Seminary, Kansas City, Missouri
Dr. Blevins served as president of the Religious Education Association and professor of Christian education at Trevecca Nazarene University. He holds a Ph.D. in theology and personality from Claremont School of Theology. With more than twenty years of teaching in Christian education and practical theology, Dr. Blevins serves as editor of *Didache: Faithful Teaching* and coordinates clergy education for the Church of the Nazarene in the United States and Canada.

Rev. David Busic, D.D.S., General Superintendent, Church of the Nazarene, Lenexa, Kansas
David Busic served as senior pastor of three churches; his most recent was Bethany First Church of the Nazarene, Bethany, Oklahoma. In 2011 he became the ninth president of Nazarene Theological Seminary. During the Twenty-Eighth General Assembly of the Church of the Nazarene in 2013, he was elected the fortieth general superintendent. He and his wife, Christi, have three grown children: Megan, and husband, Joel Cantwell; Benjamin, and wife, Alicia; and Madison.

Rev. Jeff Crosno, D.Min., Pastor, Spokane Valley Church of the Nazarene, Spokane, Washington
Jeff Crosno previously served large congregations in the Kansas City, Portland, Pasadena, and Chicago metro areas and has earned doctorates from Nazarene Theological Seminary and Princeton Theological Seminary.

Rev. Tim J. Crutcher, Ph.D., Associate Professor of Theology and Church History, Southern Nazarene University, Bethany, Oklahoma
Tim Crutcher has been teaching at Southern Nazarene University for ten years, prior to which he taught at Africa Nazarene University. He holds degrees from Nazarene Theological Seminary and the Catholic University of Louvain and is the author of *The Crucible of Life: The Role of Experience in John Wesley's Theological Method*.

Rev. James N. Fitzgerald, Ph.D., Pastor, Trinity Church of the Nazarene, Duncanville, Texas
James Fitzgerald serves as the senior pastor of Trinity Church of the Nazarene in Duncanville, Texas. He received his Ph.D. in homiletics from Vanderbilt University and has taught at Trevecca Nazarene University, Southern Nazarene University, Northwest Nazarene University (online), and Nazarene Theological Seminary.

Rev. Rebecca Laird, D.Min., Associate Professor of Christian Ministry, Point Loma Nazarene University, San Diego, California
Rebecca Laird is associate professor of Christian ministry and practice at Point Loma Nazarene University in San Diego, California. She is coeditor with Michael Christensen of a trilogy of writings from Henri Nouwen: *Spiritual Direction: Wisdom for the Long Walk of Faith*, *Spiritual Formation: Following the Movements of the Spirit*, and *Discernment: Reading the Signs of Daily Life*. She is author of *Ordained Women in the Church of the Nazarene: The First Generation*.

Rev. Dr. Deirdre Brower Latz, Ph.D., Principal, Nazarene Theological College, Manchester, United Kingdom
Deirdre Brower Latz has been involved in pastoral ministry since 1993 and theological education since 2000. She has pastored churches in Bristol and Manchester, United Kingdom. Her Ph.D. from Manchester is in practical theology, and exploring issues of how the church engages with urban poverty and social justice from a Wesleyan perspective continues to be a keen area of interest. Alongside this she continues to reflect on how the church responds to its context.

Rev. Diane Leclerc, Ph.D., Professor of Historical Theology, Northwest Nazarene University, Nampa, Idaho
Diane Leclerc has published many articles and six books, including *Discovering Christian Holiness: The Heart of Wesleyan Holiness Theology* (2010) and *Spiritual Formation: A Wesleyan Paradigm* with Mark Maddix (2011). She has served as president of the Wesleyan Theological Society and is a member of the Wesleyan-Holiness Women Clergy Society. She pastored a Nazarene congregation in Maine and served as the first pastor of a new church plant in Boise, Idaho. She is married and has a teenage son.

Rev. Mark A. Maddix, Ph.D., Professor of Practical Theology and Christian Discipleship; Dean, School of Theology and Christian Ministries, Northwest Nazarene University, Nampa, Idaho
Mark Maddix served in pastoral ministries for twelve years and in teaching ministry for the last fifteen years. He also served as the president of the North American Professors of Christian Education (NAPCE). He has published many articles and coauthored five books, including *Discovering Discipleship: Dynamics of Christian Education* (2010) and *Spiritual Formation: A Wesleyan Paradigm* (2011). Mark is a frequent speaker on topics of Christian discipleship, spiritual formation, and online education. He is married to his wife, Sherri. They have two grown children, Adrienne Maddix Meier and Nathan Maddix.

Rev. Mark H. Mann, Ph.D., Associate Professor of Theology, Director of the Wesleyan Center, Point Loma Nazarene University, San Diego, California
: Mark Mann is an ordained minister in the Church of the Nazarene and, in addition to his responsibilities at PLNU, serves as an associate pastor at Peace River Christian Fellowship (Nazarene), a community aspiring to be an authentic expression of the body of Christ in Ocean Beach, California.

Rev. Brent D. Peterson, Ph.D., Associate Professor of Theology, Northwest Nazarene University, Nampa, Idaho
: Brent Peterson has over fifteen years of pastoral experience in Kansas City and Chicago and has also completed his sixth year at NNU. Brent teaches in the area of theology and specifically focuses on ecclesiology, worship, and sacraments. He also teaches a Sunday school class at Nampa First Church of the Nazarene.

Rev. Kristina LaCelle-Peterson, Ph.D., Associate Professor of Religion, Houghton College, Houghton, New York
: Kristina LaCelle-Peterson teaches church history at Houghton College, as well as courses that deal with Christian conceptions and practices of justice. She did her doctoral work at Drew University in theological and religious studies with an emphasis on nineteenth-century revivalism and radical reform movements. Before she began college teaching she pastored a church in Rochester, New York. Her first book is *Liberating Tradition: Women's Identity and Vocation in Christian Perspective*.

Rev. Stephen Riley, Ph.D. (Candidate), Assistant Professor of Old Testament, Northwest Nazarene University, Nampa, Idaho
: Stephen Riley is currently living his dream of teaching Old Testament at Northwest Nazarene University as he finishes his dissertation through Southern Methodist University. Prior to coming to NNU, he and his wife, Sarah, served in ministry assignments in Oklahoma and Texas after graduating from Southern Nazarene University. Together, they are raising four boys.

Rev. Jeren Rowell, Ed.D., District Superintendent, Kansas City District Church of the Nazarene
: Jeren Rowell served as pastor for twenty-six years in local congregations and for the past eight years in the ministry of superintendency. He is also adjunct faculty for Nazarene Theological Seminary in Kansas City.

Rev. Eric Severson, Ph.D., Adjunct Professor, Eastern Nazarene College, and Affiliate Professor of Philosophy, Nazarene Theological Seminary
: Eric Severson teaches for both Eastern Nazarene College and Nazarene Theological Seminary. He is also the executive director of the Center for Responsibility and Justice and has served as pastor at Grandview Church of the Nazarene in Missouri. He received his Ph.D. from Boston University and has written and edited several books, including *Levinas's Philosophy of Time* (Duquesne University Press, 2013), *Scandalous Obligation* (Beacon Hill Press of Kansas City, 2011), and *I More than Others: Responses to Evil and Suffering* (Cambridge Scholars Publishing, 2010).

Rev. Henry W. Spaulding II, Ph.D., President, Mount Vernon Nazarene University, Mount Vernon, Ohio
   Henry Spaulding II currently serves as the president of Mount Vernon Nazarene University. He has been on faculty and served in administrative assignments at Eastern Nazarene College, Trevecca Nazarene University, and Nazarene Theological Seminary. He also served two congregations of the Church of the Nazarene as senior pastor. He has an earned doctorate from Florida State University.

Henry W. Spaulding III, Ph.D. Student, Garrett Evangelical Theological Seminary, Chicago, Illinois
   Henry Spaulding III is currently a full-time doctoral student in Christian ethics at Garrett Evangelical Theological Seminary. He did his undergraduate degree at Trevecca Nazarene University and holds an MTS from Duke Divinity School.

Rev. Richard P. Thompson, Ph.D., Professor of New Testament, Chair, Department of Religion, Northwest Nazarene University, Nampa, Idaho
   Richard Thompson has taught for twenty years in Christian universities in Illinois, Michigan, and Idaho. He has also served in pastoral ministry in New York, Maryland, and Texas. He received his doctoral degree from Southern Methodist University in Dallas, Texas, and is the author of the Acts volume of the New Beacon Bible Commentary series.

one
INTRODUCTION
WESLEYAN ECCLESIOLOGY

Diane Leclerc and Mark A. Maddix

At a recent meeting of pastors and professors, it quickly became apparent that a shared concern of the gathered group was the lack of an adequate ecclesiology in the Church of the Nazarene. This concern is not a new one. An Article of Faith on the church was added to our doctrinal statements relatively recently in our history that sought to address this vacuum. While the addition was a step in the right direction, because of its brevity and its more functional tone (vs. theological), it should certainly not be considered a "final word." The purpose of the recent meeting in Colorado was to continue a conversation that had started years ago regarding clergy preparation in the denomination, but that had been discontinued after some goals were accomplished. In the first of a series of meetings to renew the conversation, it seemed like this pronounced lack of ecclesiology blocked some of the work because ecclesiology is an obvious prerequisite for understanding the purpose, function, and educational preparation of clergy.

Having experienced the meeting firsthand, we wondered if a book on the subject could take us a step closer in our process of developing an ecclesiology denominationally. In the same spirit and structure of the two previous books we coedited—*Spiritual Formation: A Wesleyan Paradigm* and *Pastoral Practices: A Wesleyan Paradigm*—we proposed a third in the series, *Essential Church: A Wesleyan Paradigm*. As in the other books, a major theme here is the articulation of why and how particularly Wesleyan theology adds to a theology of the church. The book will contain three major sections. The first seeks to answer the question of exactly what the church is—its nature and purpose, particularly in relation to the triune God. The second section focuses more on what the church does—its primary functions internally and externally (in the church and outside in the world). The third section seeks to address how the church is organized—the theology behind the church's structure, regarding clergy, superintendency, and laity.

It is important to us that the audience sees this book not as some definitive word, nor as a singular voice that will put an end to the discussion, but that it is simply trying to take the conversation forward. In light of this, we include writers from many of our colleges/seminaries. We have also purposely included persons from different disciplines, including biblical scholars, systematic theologians, practical theologians, historians, philosophers, and pastors. At this point, we see this book as a "theology book" used in educational settings, but it is also addressed to anyone, pastor or laity, who wants to understand better the function, meaning, and purpose of the church.

* * *

"A more ambiguous word than this, the *Church,* is scarce to be found in the English language,"[1] said John Wesley. We agree with him. Although every doctrine has its complexities, ecclesiology seems more nebulous in ways. Perhaps this is because there is no one orthodox claim, as there is with, say, Christology. Or, perhaps this is because the church has split so many times that the actual number of denominations and ecclesial options is staggering.[2] This leads to the question of *which* church? Which church demonstrates the correct meaning, purpose, functions, and politic of the true church? Certainly those of us who follow a Wesleyan paradigm have a guideline to follow when constructing our theological, practical, and functional ecclesiologies? Yes, and no. There *is* a determinable Wesleyan "ethos" that can act as a compass. On the other hand, specific elements of Wesley's thought can be used to support various ecclesiologies. While Wesley himself says "church" is an ambiguous term, we can say further that his own ecclesiology is also somewhat ambiguous. At least in the way it is utilized. According to Gwang Seok Oh:

> Many interpretative works have attempted to rediscover Wesley's ecclesiology and apply his principles and forms to modern expressions of the church. However, the multifaceted Wesley and the complexity of the situation surrounding the origins of Methodism provide warrant for

any number of divergent perspectives on the church. Those who see the life of the church in spiritual dynamic of small groups may point to the class meeting and the loose organization of Wesley's Methodist societies for their model of the church. Those who have more institutional and ecumenical concerns may stress Wesley's life-long allegiance to the Church of England and view him as the champion of conciliation and reform *within* the ecclesiastical structures. Some may point to Wesley's conservative policies regarding the administration of the sacraments and use of liturgical forms in their criticism of the free style of worship in many contemporary churches. Others may stress Wesley's willingness to discard the practices of the established church for the flexibility of field preaching and extemporaneous prayers . . . It would appear that the eclectic nature of Wesley's thought and actions creates the same problem for ecclesiology that also annoys those who endeavor to find some hermeneutical key for his systematic theology.[3]

So what, then, can be said of Wesley's ecclesiology? Are there any facets that are characteristic of his theology as a whole? We would propose three major themes that can be considered characteristic of a Wesleyan paradigm in regard to the church. This is not to say that these three elements aren't found in other theological traditions. But we are affirming that these aspects of the church rise to the surface of Wesley's thought and characterize the scheme of theology that takes his name. They are found in Wesley's sermon "Of the Church."

First, the church is where God is appropriately worshipped, the Word is rightly preached, and the sacraments are properly practiced. Wesley says this specifically in his sermon on the church. "The definition of a Church [is the place] in which the pure word of God is preached, and the sacraments duly administered."[4] There is no doubt that Wesley highly esteemed rather high forms of worship. He even claimed that "according to this definition, those congregations in which the pure Word of God (a strong expression) is not preached are no parts either of the Church of England, or the Church catholic; as neither are those in which the sacraments are not duly administered."[5] This is Wesley's ideal, following the Church of England article statement.

He goes on to say that there may be legitimate congregations who do not practice the sacraments. But he attributes this to wrong theology and never implies that the sacraments are optional. In the same way, "I dare not exclude from the Church catholic all those congregations in which any unscriptural doctrines, which cannot be affirmed to be 'the pure word of God,' are sometimes, yea, frequently preached."[6] What he does to manage this is to point to an even higher standard of a true church: "Whoever they are that have 'one Spirit, one hope, one Lord, one faith, one God and Father of all,' I can easily bear with their holding wrong opinions."[7] In other words, this early form of a confession or creed binds persons to the church catholic, even when the ideal is not met.

The real question is whether God is receiving the church's full worship. It is implied that being of "one Spirit, one hope, one Lord, one faith, and one God" is to ascribe to God that God is indeed worthy of praise. One of the worst sins for Wesley is the sin of idolatry. To put anything in the place of God affects not only our ability to worship but also our ability to be fully human.[8] A Wesleyan ecclesiology must include worship, preaching, the sacraments, and creedal confession if it is to reach the ideal. The Holy Spirit takes these practices and binds congregants together in perfect unity.

Second, the church is a gathering where its people are intentionally present to each other. The church is a healing community, a place of deep acceptance, a place of compassion, kindness, humility, gentleness, patience, forbearance, forgiveness, and love.[9] It is a community of the Spirit that shows the fruit of the Spirit, even as the Spirit enables each to display their gifts to the body. Each part is equally valuable. The parts are interdependent on the others. And the parts display empathy as an expression of mutual love. According to Wesley, the church is called together to "walk worthy of the vocation wherewith we are called."[10] This walking together is "with all lowliness" as we are clothed with humility, and as we experience God's cleansing and God's empowerment.[11] It is also a walk of "longsuffering" and "forbearing one another in love." This

> seems to mean, not only the not resenting anything, and the not avenging yourselves; not only the not injuring, hurting, or grieving each other, either by word or deed; but also the bearing one another's burdens; yea, and lessening them by every means in our power. It implies the sympathizing with them in their sorrows, afflictions, and infirmities; the bearing them up when, without our help, they would be liable to sink under their burdens; the endeavoring to lift their sinking heads, and to strengthen their feeble knees . . . the true members of the Church of

Christ "endeavour" with all possible diligence . . . to "keep the unity of the Spirit in the bond of peace."[12]

Wesley, of course, had means and mechanisms for how this type of mutual life is to be lived. His classes and bands still serve today as models for life together. There persons not only held each other up but also challenged each other and held each other accountable. Put most simply, they were confessional communities. And where there is confession there is healing.[13] This is a place where we would do well to revitalize mutual confession for our shared benefit. Worship is a key element of the church. Shared life is a key element of the church. But the church was never intended to keep to itself, even as its internal functions are indeed good. The people of the church are to go out to the world. There is a rhythm to the Christian life—we are gathered in in order to be breathed out.

Third, the church is missionally engaged with the world, offering hospitality, justice, liberation, and the proclamation of the kingdom of God. Life together provides what we need, individually and corporately, to live in the world as beacons of Light. We are strengthened by each other through the Spirit, in order that we may encounter the world as Christ's representatives. And what do we represent? God's love, salvation through Christ, life in the Spirit. But we are also to be agents of change, to welcome the stranger, bring justice to the helpless, to offer liberation for the oppressed, and live as citizens of God's kingdom.

In the following chapters, the reader will find various expressions of the church's call to worship, live life together, and change the world.

Part 1: The Church at Its Core

The first section of the book seeks to answer the question of the nature and purpose of the church, particularly in relationship to the triune God. Dr. Eric Severson's chapter proposes that the kingdom of God is an *event*, rather than an institution. He argues that the goal of ecclesiology should be to attend to the kind of events that bear the markings of this elusive kingdom. The event of church is something that happens beyond, outside of, and sometimes even *despite* our organizational efforts. So the doctrine of the church is not so much about a special set of ideas as about positioning our lives together in such a way that we might participate in *something* of God *happening*. Severson claims that the event of the church is the scandalously particular appearance of the life of Jesus Christ in the face-to-face relations between human lives. Church happens not when some script is followed to the last detail, but when the story of the cruciform love of Jesus of Nazareth is carried on in the midst of a community.

Henry Spaulding II and III, a father and son duo, provide a Trinitarian ecclesiology rooted in the history of the church. They illustrate that the church is an expression of the triune life of the Godhead. This is both an affirmation and an invitation for all of humanity to join in the harmonic unity of the triune life. The church exists at the intersection of the divine and human order. Thus, the church arises from God toward humanity as the triune identity receives the echo of praise from those who have been redeemed. The church is formed by God alone and as such is identified in time through the triune life of God. It also does not separate mission from its agenda, for mission is what God calls the church to be in the world.

Mark Mann's chapter builds on this Trinitarian ecclesiology by focusing on the central role that Christology plays in the church. He is quick to affirm Trinitarian theology that is not Christocentric, but that the doctrine of the Trinity by definition requires that Christology be at the center of our understanding of who God is and what God is doing, and therefore is foundational for all dimensions of theological reflection. He also shows that Christology is tied closely with the work of the Holy Spirit since the Holy Spirit is God's enlivening presence in the world, giving life, purpose, and mission to the church.

Building on Mark Mann's chapter on Christology and the work of the Holy Spirit, Diane Leclerc's chapter on the pneumatology, the work of the Holy Spirit, provides a theological foundation for how the church is initiated, sustained, and a conduit of God's mission in the world, *missio Dei*. The church is dependent on the work of the Holy Spirit, and without it, God would not be about to bring about divine and eternal purposes. God has called the church to act with the Spirit synergistically to convey God's purposes. She develops a Wesleyan phenomenology by showing that the Spirit is active to awaken persons of their sin, to provide forgiveness and healing and sanctification to believers.

Tim Crutcher shows how the church was formed and depicted by Luke in the Luke-Acts narrative. These early followers of Jesus began to figure out who they were, and during the next few centuries various Christian writers and thinkers reflected on the nature of the church. Through their struggles, both internally and externally, a consistent theme emerged and crystalized into four attributes of the church in the Nicene Creed, "We believe in One, Holy, Catholic, and Apostolic Church." Crutcher expounds the significance of each aspect of the creed and reminds us that when we recite the creed we affirm the work of the Holy Spirit that historically links us back to Jesus' original followers as we continue the mission of those followers in the world.

The last chapter in the core essentials section is written by Deirdre Brower Latz. Deirdre develops a Wesleyan understanding of the relationship of the church to culture and provides emphasis on postmodern marks of the church. A Wesleyan stance toward culture is not rejecting it, nor assimilation within it, but is profoundly hopeful toward it as a type of via media. With Wesleyan theology as the starting point, she claims that the cultural correlation that Wesleyans undertake is one of engaging with culture. She asserts that the church in the Wesleyan tradition must engage with postmodern elements, which will result in enrichment and revitalization as able participants and agents of change for the sake of Christ in the twenty-first century.

Part 2: The Church's Essential Functions

The second section of the book focuses on the primary internal (in the church) and external (outside in the world) functions of the church. Jeffrey Barker begins the discussion by focusing on worship as a primary function of the church that shapes our understanding of ecclesiology. He asserts that in worship God's people gather to remember the cosmic scope of God's salvation and their personal reception of this gracious gift. Each week in worship, the ecclesia participates anew and bears witness again to God's cosmic-shaped salvation. Christian worship proclaims God's salvation through the person and work of Jesus the Christ witnessed to by the Spirit. Barker articulates a Wesleyan approach to worship that honors God, transforms the worshipper, and compels him or her to acts of love and service in the world. For Wesleyans, the telos of worship is God's honor and the church's edification.

A central aspect of a Wesleyan approach to worship includes the sacraments. Brent Peterson's chapter illustrates the close interaction of John and Charles Wesley between the church (ecclesiology) and the soteriological healing found in the sacraments of baptism and the Lord's Supper. Peterson develops more fully the role of the sacraments of baptism and the Lord's Supper as the primary occasions where God grows (baptism) and sustains (the Lord's Supper) the church, even as its healing and sanctification precipitates the further redemption of the world. Peterson views the sacraments as a "means of grace" whereby God offers healing to persons as persons respond to God's invitation of healing.

A Wesleyan view of ecclesiology includes the people of God gathered around Word and Table. Coupled with Peterson's focus on the Eucharist, James Fitzgerald's chapter includes the proclamation of Scripture. Fitzgerald's chapter illustrates the importance of preaching and the kerygmatic function the church plays in proclaiming the good news of the gospel to all the world. He articulates that while Wesley emphasized the role of preaching, both for clergy and field preaching, he was not willing to separate that from the broader scope of the life and work of the church. He always held to the importance of *both* properties of the church—the preaching of the Word and the administration of the sacraments.

Mark Maddix's chapter provides a holistic Wesleyan approach to Christian education through catechesis. Central to this catechetical process is Wesley's view of the "means of grace." By viewing Wesley's categories of the instituted and prudential means of grace, along with the acts of mercy, a suggestive way of ordering educational practices into three complementary approaches to Christian education includes *formation, discernment,* and *transformation*. Maddix develops each of these educational practices as avenues that help persons grow in holiness of heart and life.

The success of Methodism can be attributed to the development of formative communities that nurtured growth and development among believers. Dean Blevins develops Wesley's approach to community through his small group system. These groups provided a habitus for deeper, spiritual healing and empowerment. Blevins articulates that for Wesley, Christian community provided the context and the means for spiritual formation through an accountable discipleship anchored in shared story, shared practices, and relational bonds. Wesleyan formation occurs primarily through community, whether in the worshipping community or through smaller fellowships of disciplined discipleship; fellowships where people covenant together in a common Christian story to practice differing means of grace and lovingly hold one another accountable through transparent but disciplined relationships.

Kristina LaCelle-Peterson's chapter on the church as liberator provides a Wesleyan approach to egalitarian liberation of all social classes, with particular focus on the liberation of women. Since all persons are deemed equally worthy recipients of God's grace, from God, then it follows that all are welcomed to participate in the redeemed community. Radical egalitarianism was a feature of the ministry of John and Charles Wesley's small groups and revivalism during the eighteenth century and was predominant in early American Methodism. A Wesleyan ecclesiology today includes an egalitarian view of leadership, including all social classes of society.

Stephen Riley's chapter on the church includes acts of compassion and justice that illustrate the central mission of the church as the proclamation of the good news and redeeming of all creation. When the church is faithful to its central mission, lives are transformed and right relationship with God is restored. Riley, an Old Testament professor, argues that the concept of *shalom* encompasses the good news of wholeness, justice, compassion, and righteousness. He shows that within Israel's life with God, the clearest example of what it means to live in *shalom* is found in the life, death, and resurrection of Jesus Christ. This takes place through acts of justice and compassion.

The final chapter in section two is the church as a witnessing community. David Busic develops this idea from Acts 2 and the coming of the Holy Spirit. He says that the church was born to bear the good news of Jesus, to be witnesses, and we are empowered by the Holy Spirit to be God's witnesses in the world. He also gives focus to the role of the *heralder*, who is called to proclaim the good news through preaching.

Part 3: The Church as Organized Organism

The third section addresses the theology of how the church is organized, which includes the church's structure, clergy, superintendency, and laity. Richard Thompson provides a Wesleyan approach to the church by giving focus to the biblical metaphor of the body of Christ. He develops the metaphor of the body of Christ from Paul's letter to the church of Corinth that includes God's sanctifying work in setting apart the church as God's holy people and the role of Christians in loving one another, which results in the church functioning to live out that divine work as the holy people of God. Since the heart of Wesleyan theology is love, then Christians are to express that love in loving relationships. As divine grace shapes us, it enables the church as God's people to be a missional people.

One of the overarching tensions in developing an ecclesiology is the relationship between the ordained clergy and the laity. Rebecca Laird engages in this discussion by giving focus to theology of the laity built on the Reformation theme of the priesthood of believers. She shows that this false dichotomy of clergy and laity is not consistent with the scriptural witness of the *laos* (laity), referring to all who seek to be disciples of Jesus Christ. She shows how John Wesley empowered laity to serve in ministry through witnessing, caring for the poor, and leading small groups. It was Wesley's leadership that opened the door for others to engage in preaching, teaching, and administration that reviled the Oxford-qualified ordained.

Continuing this conversation about clergy and laity, Brent Peterson provides a Wesleyan approach to ecclesiology that includes a robust theology of ordination. Peterson explores the relationship of the clergy to the church and to the laity, as well as the clergy's responsibility to preach, administer the sacraments, and order the church. He also offers insights into what pastors are *not* called to do. Pastor Jeff Crosno's chapter moves beyond the traditional role of the clergy, such as preaching and the sacraments, and raises concerns about having an adequate ecclesiology that is adaptive rather than functional to sustain a pastor's life. He develops the metaphor of the "designated reader" from the Old Testament idea of what a king should be like. Crosno argues that the king is someone who embodies absolute dependence upon God by refusing to be self-deceived by human power. Serving as the "designated reader," the king becomes a public and visible reminder of the trust and piety to which his subjects are called. Crosno asserts that the church could use this image to affirm priorities that value the formation of holy character above mere competency in pastoral technique or methods.

The final chapter, written by Jeren Rowell, gives a functional theology of the role of the superintendent—the pastor of pastors. He develops the role of overseer or superintendent from New Testament texts, with focus on the Greek word *episkopes*, often translated "bishop." These texts suggest that the *episkopes* is *going*, *visiting*, and *seeing* and can be viewed not only in terms of the practices of oversight and accountability but especially in terms of an oversight that is informed by God's initiating movement toward us in love. Rowell shows that as God moves toward us in love, so those called to and charged with oversight in God's church should move toward the people of God in love rather than employing models of leadership that become hierarchical and deferential. He concludes the chapter by giving some practical examples for those who serve as superintendents.

Conclusion

As you read these chapters we invite you to enter into the continual conversation about Wesleyan ecclesiology and how it can be lived out and practiced in our local congregations today. We realize this book doesn't always provide definite answers but does raise important questions for those in the Wesleyan tradition as we grapple with an adequate ecclesiology that empowers and shapes us to love God more fully and to live out God's redemptive mission in the world. May God be glorified through the church!

PART 1
The Church at Its Core

two
THE CHURCH
THE EVENT OF THE KINGDOM OF GOD

Eric Severson

Archaeologists often point out that humans have, for all of human history, been social creatures. Building on this, philosophers, anthropologists, historians, and others have guessed at what glues a human community together. Such a matter is far from trivial in any journey to understand the meaning and purpose of Christian community. To ask "what does it mean to be the church?" is to find oneself already immersed in questions about the threads that bind humans together in groups of all sorts. This would include teams, families, gangs, mobs, clubs, and villages. There is surely no singular answer to the question; communities are radically different from one another. But the burning question that drives this chapter can be stated simply: is the church of the same genre of other communities or is it another kind of gathering entirely?

Philosopher Thomas Hobbes imagined that human history begins with violence and contention. In the anarchy that precedes community, people fought for every scrap of security, resources, and food, and for their very survival. Without help from a community, Hobbes proposed that life was "nasty, brutish and short."[1] He calls to mind a scattered race of cave-dwelling individuals with bloodshot eyes, guarding the few treasures of food and warmth from the chaos of the wild world. The cohesion of community, Hobbes suggests, arises out of the great benefits to be found when people join forces against the wild instead of treating one another as part of the wilderness. Community means that individuals can rest with less worry that they will lose their belongings or even their lives as they slumber. When humans band together they create unwritten "contracts" that take on moral importance. To fail to keep up your end of the bargain is to be ostracized, to be unethical. For Hobbes, this is the source of all morality. We deem actions to be ethical when they benefit the society, and unethical when they do not.

We have good reason to doubt Hobbes historically and anthropologically; it is unlikely that his thoughts on early human history are accurate. However, his theory still gets mileage when we stop to think about what drives communities and forms their understanding of how members should live. We do, as Hobbes suggests, tend to gather our sense of morality from the communities that we inhabit. We also, following Hobbes, tend as a species to gather into groups to confront the chaotic challenges of living on planet Earth. We form "alliances" in business, on playgrounds, and on reality television shows. We create partnerships, in business and in play, and we sustain these partnerships as long as they are profitable.

The logic of community, as presented by philosophers such as Hobbes, remains based on self-interest. Human beings pull together when it helps us succeed, and then we turn against one another when the profits and benefits dwindle. Marital communities are all too often formed in this way. And, as I will soon argue, churches are often controlled by this *Survivor* mentality as well. The proliferation of denominations in Christianity testifies to this logic; we band together until disagreements make things uncomfortable or unprofitable. Then we seek a better alliance with more like-minded people, only to discover that the cycle again repeats itself. Hobbes got at least this much right: human communities tend to form as a function of the self-interest of individuals. This leaves us with a rather uncomfortable situation. Without reflection and consideration, our "ecclesiology" will conform by default to the dynamics of nature, of "the wild." Without some careful attention to the alternative dynamics of the kingdom of God, ecclesiology will be subtly constructed on the shifting sand of self-interest. This book, among other goals, seeks to illuminate the difference between other kingdoms and the kingdom of God. For my part, I wish to argue that communities of Christians should gather as communities that are categorically different from other groups.

Ecclesiology's Elusive Goal

Under oath, and beneath the scrutiny of learned inquisitors, Joan of Arc was asked to describe the relationship between Jesus Christ and the church. Her answer was simple and profound enough to find itself recorded in the Roman Catholic Catechism: "About Jesus Christ and the Church, I simply know they're just one thing, and we shouldn't complicate the matter."[2] Her famous response has not always sat well with Protestants, who have from the outset been reluctant to bestow such lofty ideals on the tattered and fallible collections of human beings that call their gatherings "church." Ecclesiology has in Protestant circles often spun its wheels; Luther left out *sola ecclesia* for a reason. There are certainly high-ecclesiology Protestants, just as there are Low-Church Catholics. Yet on the whole, Protestant congregations and denominations, including Wesleyan ones, have treaded softly when it comes to declarations about the importance of the church in theological matters. It is far from settled whether holiness requires the church, whether salvation requires the church, or even whether the church is to be considered anything more than a site for the gathering of like-minded people.

Joan of Arc wished to keep the matter simple, and her one-for-one equation of the church with the "body of Christ" allows for an undeniably streamlined simplicity. There are obvious reasons to question Joan's enthusiastic endorsement of the one-for-one correlation between the church and the body of Christ. Yet as the Protestant churches rebelled against such an endorsement of ecclesial leadership, another equally simplistic alternative arose.

The history of Christian leadership, on both sides of the Protestant Reformation, is rife with stories of corruption and abuse. As a result, there is a powerful temptation to dismiss the idea that the "church" plays anything but a trivial or peripheral role in Christian life. To cave to this temptation, however, is to fall into a vortex of individualism that threatens the very heart of the gospel. Furthermore, to dismiss ecclesiology is to default to the models of human community described by folks such as Thomas Hobbes. Without a robust ecclesiology we are bound only by common tastes, doctrinal agreements, and mutual interest. We pull together only because cooperation is a better strategy for success. Unsurprisingly, such an ecclesiology (or lack thereof) leads to splintering and division. And we are left with a substantial movement in Christianity today that "likes Jesus but not the Church."[3]

A third alternative moves between these two oversimplifications of the concept of the church. We must avoid the hazardous allure of the unquestioned assumption that ecclesial bodies are necessarily the "body of Christ," as well as the perilous trivialization of ecclesiology. Joan was right about one thing for sure: serious attempts at ecclesiology will "complicate the matter." Ecclesiology has often been marginalized because it is hard work. Yet despite their difficulty, the labors of discerning and exploring the nature of the kingdom of God are absolutely necessary for Christians to avoid critical distortions of the gospel of Jesus Christ.

The Church as Event

Moving quickly to the heart of my thesis, I wish to propose that the "kingdom of God" is an *event* rather than an institution. The goal of ecclesiology should be to attend to the kind of events that bear the markings of this elusive kingdom. As such, the church is the "body of Christ" not by birthright but because it is the site of such events. The labors of the church are principally preparation and vigilance for the way the holiness of God interrupts the often secular banality of our everyday lives. What is needed, therefore, is a theology of the *event* of the church. And I think we have reason to believe that such events are not just instances of effective cooperation or team building. The event of church is something that happens beyond, outside of, and sometimes even *despite* our organizational efforts. So the doctrine of the church is not so much about a special set of ideas as about positioning our lives together in such a way that we might participate in *something* of God *happening*.

This helps explain the obvious dissonance between the teaching of Jesus and the practices that help teams and corporations succeed. In the story of the Good Samaritan, Jesus appears to advocate the dangerous and costly practice of mending the bodies of outsiders and strangers.[4] It is the nearly worthless widows-mite offering that he prizes as the greatest gift.[5] In the Sermon on the Mount, we are taught to turn cheeks, walk extra miles, part with our coat when asked for a shirt, and all kinds of other unproductive activities.[6] People who win in business and on *Survivor* get good at creating communities, but not the kinds of communities we read about in the New Testament. Blessed are the meek? Hardly the stuff that wins Super Bowls or Nobel prizes.

None of this is to say that we should not do business, build teams, win prizes, or seek cooperation. Yet it may be time to take seriously the possible distance between these events and the "kingdom of God." We throw ticker-tape parades for victories in sports and in war, and these triumphs are punctuated with grateful words about God's blessings and endorsements. It is for this reason that Karl Barth insisted that the order of the Christian church must be Christ, and that this means the logic of the church will be "clearly and sharply differentiated from every other kind of 'law.'"[7] Barth calls this a "living law," and as something living it remains categorically different from the hard and ossified order of "other human societies."[8] Luther's way of saying this was to insist that the true nature of the church is "hidden," evading boundaries and articulation.[9]

So we must busy ourselves theologically with the mysterious events that seem to abound in Jesus' teachings, in the life of the church in the New Testament, and in the history of Christianity. Along the way, we must expect that the way of Jesus and the way of the church may sometimes look similar but remain categorically distinct. The core narrative of Christianity is a peculiar one when aligned with the battle-victory logic that we use to rally support in our everyday endeavors. Jesus seems to repeatedly make this point by refusing to "call down angels," denouncing Peter's sword-flashing defense, and praying forgiveness for those who thrash and mutilate his body. Christians misunderstand the resurrection if it is thought of as another comeback story, as a Hail Mary pass that miraculously delivers victory against the longest of odds. Rather, the resurrection of Jesus is an affirmation of the cross and its suffering love; it is confirmation that the way of the world and the way of Jesus are categorically different.

With perilous ease, we confuse and conflate these distinct ways of being in the world. As long as the concept of church is principally considered another kind of "team," "corporation," or "club," we are sure to privilege the way of this world over the way of the kingdom of God. What happens in the church is categorically different from what happens on teams and in corporations. Such a claim does not discount the fact the "event" that I am calling "church" can happen in the midst of any context. The doctrine of the incarnation underscores the impossible possibility that the holy might interrupt the banal even where it is least expected. The role of ecclesiology is therefore the honing of the discipline of vigilance; by figuring out how to be church we best position our life together to give way to the *event* that is the "body of Christ."

The work of Dietrich Bonhoeffer is helpful in this regard. Bonhoeffer expressed concern about the way theology has come to think of truth in a decidedly nontheological manner. Truth, across philosophical and juridical history, has hinged on the discovering of ideas and facts that any given person can "know" and therefore "understand." The concepts of knowledge and understanding have been inflected in vastly different ways, but seldom has "truth" indicated something like a happening or an event. Yet for Bonhoeffer, "Truth is not something static in and for itself, but an event between two persons. Truth happens only in community."[10] Theological truth, then, is perhaps categorically different from the truth puzzles that occupy scientists, mathematicians, archaeologists, and so forth. The truth Bonhoeffer has in mind is the kind of ephemeral event that cannot be reproduced in the vacuum of privatized understanding. The "body of Christ" is therefore not some kind of concept, or set of concepts, that can be collected to constitute ecclesiology. Rather, the "body of Christ" is an event in the world. The role of ecclesiology is nothing more than the making ready of tattered and fallen human communities to participate in such events.

And here we find an alarming opposition between ecclesiology and the successful team-building models of Hobbes, the NFL, and Wall Street. Both models for community cannot help but hope for success, for cohesion, for camaraderie, for sacrificial acts that reinforce group goals. And because of these similarities we are doomed to be constantly bombarded by church growth models that utilize successful strategies from the school of Thomas Hobbes and his competitive friends. But resistance is not futile.

Sacraments as Vigilance

The way of the church, and the burden of ecclesiology, must attend to the dynamics of the *event* of the kingdom of God. Yet the "happening" of church is not elusive in the needle in a haystack fashion, nor is "being the church" a kind of aspirational goal that might be achieved by way of checklists and strategies. The event of the church is the scandalously particular appearance of the life of Jesus Christ in the face-to-face relations between human lives. Church happens not when some script is followed to the last detail but when the story of the cruciform love of Jesus of Nazareth is carried on in the midst of a community. And this is elusive only because it is never a possession, never something "at hand" as an object or accessory. As the beloved Shulamite bride in the Song of Songs, we must be repeatedly reminded that love is not something one grabs or even seeks, but that for which we must intentionally make room. "Do not stir up or awaken love until it is ready," the lovers are repeatedly warned (Song of Songs 2:7; 3:5).

We would find it preferable if there were some more handy and formulaic manner of invoking and sustaining the event that is the kingdom of God. We are surely tempted to turn any line from the Bible that seems amenable to this interpretation into such a formula. When Jesus promised that "where two or three are gathered in my name, I am there among them" (Matt. 18:20), he was after something much more important than the polity of Christian gatherings. To attend to the needs of people we deem to be the "least of these" is in no way some guarantee that we have fed, welcomed, healed, nourished, and visited the Son of Man himself.[11]

These movements are potent, but also potentially vacant and hollow without the *something* that appears in the midst of our labors. These acts of gathering, hospitality, sacrifice, and service are nothing in themselves. Indeed, these activities can often be unhelpful, destructive, and unloving. The event that is church is that which arises and arrives as a *gift* in the midst of our labors. To participate in the kingdom of God is to practice hospitality with the unreasonable hope that the other will be full of a grace that is not ours to contribute. The word *liturgy*, from its Latin roots, means literally "the work of the people." Acts of hospitality and justice are like worship, like liturgy; they are clay vessels unless their labors are lifted by grace. And this means that, ironically, feeding the homeless is never, for the church, the achievement of anything. Apart from the grace of Jesus Christ, it might be precisely the reverse. These movements are instead acts of waiting, of hoping, of expectation, and of vigilance.

The road to team and corporate success by the standards of the world moves through models of efficiency, leadership habits, and effective strategies. Churches surely need to keep the lights on and the pastor paid, and this requires no small amount of efficiency and acumen in many contexts. But ecclesiology cannot be derived from the logic that makes businesses and teams successful. The theo-logic of the ecclesiology must be otherwise derived. My suggestion is that the posture and passivity of the sacraments provide the basis for ecclesiology. In the sacraments of baptism and the Lord's Supper, the labors of the people—the liturgy—are not the achievement of some goal but the posture of openness and receptivity. The sacraments are woefully distorted and misunderstood when they are taken to be about spiritual achievement or are treated as spiritual talismans. Rather, the community breaks bread and *waits*. The identity of the church is found in the waiting, like the hiatus when the human body is submerged in the baptismal waters.

Ecclesiology stands vulnerable between orthodoxy ("right belief") and idolatry. The stuff that makes for balanced budgets and church growth is not *evil* until we forget that it comes with its own inherent logic, the sinister and competitive logic of Thomas Hobbes. The church may often *look* like another storefront business alongside others in the world, like another horse in the race to success, security, and victory. In these moments the church will be at its most vulnerable; it will shudder at the idea of leaving the ninety-nine to find the one.[12] The "highly successful" church will be inclined to make decisions that protect to the bottom line, that secure a long future, and that see the big picture. The theo-logic of the gospel seems to run in another direction, moving toward the cross of worldly defeat, leaving its future in the hands of the triune God.

Questions for Discussion

1. What type of human community seems to occur naturally in the world?
2. What might be different about the form of community that constitutes the Christian church?
3. What is the difference between thinking of the church as an *event* rather than as an *entity*?
4. What might be the cost of seeking an ecclesiology modeled after the ideas suggested in this chapter?

Suggestions for Further Reading

Hauerwas, Stanley, and William Willimon. *Resident Aliens*. Nashville: Abingdon, 1989.
Moltmann, Jürgen. *The Crucified God*. New York: Fortress Press, 1993.
Yoder, John Howard. *The Politics of Jesus*. Grand Rapids: Eerdmans, 1994.

three
TRINITARIAN IDENTITY
THE CHURCH'S TRUE FOUNDATION

Henry W. Spaulding II and Henry W. Spaulding III

Paul refers to the church as "all the members of God's family" (Gal. 1:2), "the church of God that is in Corinth" (1 Cor. 1:2), "God's beloved in Rome" (Rom. 1:7), and "all the saints in Christ Jesus who are in Philippi" (Phil. 1:1). The apostolic church had a clear understanding that it belonged to God. Even more than that, the early church believed it was the presence of God in the world. Article XI of the Church of the Nazarene affirms that the church is "the community that confesses Jesus Christ as Lord, the covenant people of God made new in Christ, the Body of Christ called together by the Holy Spirit through the Word."[1] This statement very concisely frames the triune identity of the church. The Catechism of the Catholic Church affirms, "The Church is one because of her source: 'the highest exemplar and source of this mystery is the unity, in the Trinity of Persons, of one God, the Father and the Son in the Holy Spirit.'"[2] From the beginning and until now the church is an expression of the triune life of the Godhead. This is both an affirmation and an invitation for all of humanity to join in the harmonic unity of the triune life.

Because God calls all humanity to be baptized in the name of the Father, the Son, and the Holy Spirit and to be taught to obey the commands of God, the church must also be understood to involve human persons. Dietrich Bonhoeffer writes, "What the Church 'is' can only be answered if we say both what it is from the viewpoint of human beings and what it is from the standpoint of God. Both belong inseparably together. It is in this dual nature that it (the Church) exists."³ The church exists at the intersection of the divine and human order. Thus, the church arises from God toward humanity as the triune identity receives the echo of praise from those who have been redeemed. The church is formed by God alone and as such is identified in time through the triune life of God. Robert Jenson affirms, "As the Church shares in the life of the triune identities, she shares in the relation of the Son and the Spirit to the Father . . . The great goal of our *koinonia*, for which the Son works and to which the Spirit draws us, is the Father's Kingdom."⁴

This chapter will argue that the church is shaped by the triune identity of God and as such exists as an institution for humanity. We will show this by pointing toward the freedom of God to be for others. Next, we will explore Bonhoeffer's analysis of the *analogia relationis* (analogy of relations) as the way the church is shaped by the triune life. Finally, we will look at the freedom of the church to be the church due to the eschatological drawing of creation by the Trinity.

The Being of the Triune Life

The being of God subsists in relationality and freedom to act. Namely, the very heart and existence of God is an existence of relationship and freedom for the created order. We will treat each of these two aspects of God as a coherent whole, because only if God's being is inherently relational and free does the triune life shape the church to be for the world as the way the Trinity itself is for the world.

David Bentley Hart writes, "The Christian understanding of God [is] a *perichoresis* of love, a dynamic coinherence of the three divine persons, whose life is eternally one of shared regard, delight, fellowship, feasting, and joy."⁵ The word *perichoresis* suggests how the divine life is relational. The word amounts to what the tradition of the church has referred to as a dance—namely, the Trinity consists in the triune persons dancing on the path of peaceful flight. Furthermore, the word is also meant to denote that the persons interpenetrate each other—they are one. There is an aspect, then, that the persons mutually dwell within one another. God is a Being-in-Communion. And just as God is a Being-in-Communion, so the church exists as communion, thus sharing the divine life as fellowship.

Communion is crucial for the orthodox understanding of the Trinity and for our discussion of how the Trinity intends to shape the world. Thus, for Hart, the very inner dynamic of the triune life consists in "shared regard, delight, fellowship, feasting, and joy."[6] This presents the invitation of God to us to be the church. Therefore, the church as it receives its being from God mirrors the identity of the triune life. While the church may exist imperfectly at times, it is guided "to express its life in the unity and fellowship of the Spirit."[7] By grace, the church bears witness to the kingdom of God, a place where "there is no longer Jew or Greek . . . slave or free . . . male and female" (Gal. 3:28). The church becomes a place where difference does not need to be dissonance.

God's life is unique in that it is free to act. Karl Barth writes, "By the revelation of God, in which God meets us as the Lord of [persons], we are forbidden and restrained from confusing and comparing the being of God with this working of [people]. God is not the being moved in and by us, which we know or think we know as our movement of nature and spirit."[8] If anything, we are moved by God. This movement in Barth is vital. If God were to be equated with our human musings, then it would not be a Trinitarian-formed church. The being of God is utterly free and equated with what God has shown the world in revelation. God acts and then the identity of the divine life can be detected in the world. Barth attempts through this to take God out of the abstract category of Spirit and place God in the concrete arena of human workings.[9] Such abstraction inadequately frames the work of the Spirit and makes the church a mere human construction.[10] Rather, we are conditioned and determined by God's being. God is free to act according to God's will. The church is not a human idea; it is a response to the call of the Word of God through the Spirit.

The Being of the Church in the Form of the Being of God

The being of the church directly relates to the being of God. It is of vital importance, however, to determine just how the church relates to the being of God. In the above section, we have discussed the relational character of the God who freely invites humanity into the triune life. In fact, the church is constituted by the free offer of God making room (Jenson). God is relational both in and out of God's very own nature, which means that the church depends upon God for its life. According to Jenson, "As it is, God's story is committed as a story with creatures. And so he too, as it is, can have no identity except as he meets the temporal end toward which creatures live."[11] The triune life pours out into the world and takes shape in the communion of the saints as a free offer of God.

Dietrich Bonhoeffer sheds light on the nature of the church as an *analogia relationis* (analogy of relations). This analogy of relations is contrasted with the *analogia entis*[12] (analogy of being). To put it simply, the analogy of relations states that the church is analogous to God. One might go so far as to say that the church exists as an incarnation. The words of 1 Peter offer us insight, "Come to him, a living stone, though rejected by mortals yet chosen and precious in God's sight, and like living stones, let yourselves be built into a spiritual house, to be a holy priesthood" (2:4-5). Later we read, "You are a chosen race, a royal priesthood, a holy nation, God's own people, in order that you may proclaim the mighty acts of him who called you out of darkness into his marvelous light" (v. 9). The church finds its identity in the God who invites broken humanity from the darkness into the light. Therefore, the God who is Being-in-Communion proclaims "how you are God's people" (v. 10). The analogy of relations as the way the church is in the form of God, then, is a helpful insight to move the church into an understanding of itself as for others.

The analogy of relations serves as an appropriate model for understanding the relationship between the church and God precisely because it dispels any notion of the church not being for the world by its very nature. The pattern might be stated as such: from God and for the world. As Dietrich Bonhoeffer writes,

> The "image that is like God" is therefore no analogia entis in which human beings, in their existence in-and-of-themselves, in their being, could be said to be like God's being . . . The likeness, the analogia, of humankind to God is not analogia entis but *analogia relationis*. What this means, however, is, firstly, that the relatio too is not a human potential or possibility or a structure of human existence; instead it is a given relation, a relation in which human beings are set, a justitia passiva![13]

Thus, in Bonhoeffer's analysis, the church, being related to the nature of God's relationships, requires that the church be for others. In other words, the church is only good because it is in the world. The world is good because God creates it. The church's mission, however, in the world is to be in appropriate relationship to one another and thus model that for the rest of the world. The church is the place where others are loved and related to correctly. As Bonhoeffer again writes,

> Only where God and the brother, the sister, come to them [the church] can human beings find their way back to the earth. Human freedom for God and the other person and human freedom from the creature in dominion over it constitute the first human beings' likeness to God.[14]

The church cannot understand itself in isolation from the world but is always being sent into the world as God has done in the Trinitarian procession. Furthermore, as God seeks the redemption and sanctification of the world through the sending of the Son and the Spirit, the church is sent into the world as an analogy for God to help the world by inviting the world into communion with God. The church is essentially for humanity because the triune God is essentially for humanity. Thus, the church represents the reality where the potential to become fully human, or rather a place to be trained in holiness, is represented.

Missio Dei, Church, and Trinity

Helping humanity realize its potential in God, or to become holy requires that the church take seriously the content of the *missio Dei* (i.e., the mission of God). "What is the mission of God?" In the modern church, one sees how the mission can function as an ideal or concept or strategy. The task of this chapter is to show how the mission of God possesses content as action, or a habitus. Habitus is as sociologist Pierre Bourdieu writes, "The system of structured, structuring dispositions . . . which is constituted in practice and is always oriented towards practical aims."[15] This denotes the fact that the mission of God for the church *is* an action taken upon every individual as well as the church universal. Furthermore, the mission of God for the church understood as habitus constructs the way the church acts publically. The reason the use of habitus is fruitful for our discussion of the church is that the mission of God for the church is modeled in the triune life. Namely, the way God chooses to be public in the created order is mirrored in the church in her public life. The mission of God (as an action) is of the being of God. The Trinity is the mission of God; it is the compressed telling of the entire Christian story.

The mission of God for the church as habitus denotes a public "performance." As Roger D. Haight writes,

> The church consists in a certain number of basic activities by which it posits itself in history. It is thus constituted by human freedom. At the same time this freedom is both received as a gift and channeled in a direction by the social habits it has learned from Jesus of Nazareth and the history of its life in the Spirit.[16]

Following Haight, the habitus of the church in public life means its central function is to be a place of public and social action, namely, of relation,

> The church exists in a manner analogous to a living social organism. It is constituted by and consists in a set of actions that bind people together in relationships. This way of viewing the church appears most clearly in its genesis, but the principle also applies at any given time.[17]

Furthermore, the church's mission as habitus means not that it is public for no other reason than its mission. It is public insofar as it is in correct relation to the world. Thus, to be a social creature ecclesiastically consists of being for the other in a loving manner. It cannot be public for itself alone because it would lose the center that enables it to be with others, to be relational. If it cared only for itself, and its mission consisted of self-maintenance, it would be an institution of selfishness and thus abuse others. Therefore, the center of habitus as the mission of God must possess the content of Christ, because Christ is the means by which we can be for others.

Thus, habitus is a christological act, because Christ was the way the triune Godhead chose to be public. The Spirit is the means by which this public life continues. This reality must be central for the mission of God to be in the church, namely, for it to be habitus, because as per our discussion, the church is *analogia relationis*. For the church to be mission, to have mission, or to even be in relation, the habitus must first exist in God. The church has as a part of its history a rich tradition of the *missio Dei* as inherent to the understanding of the Trinitarian life. Augustine writes in *De Trinitate* (*On the Trinity*) on the missionary aspect of the triune life,

> So the Word of God is sent by him whose Word he is; sent by him he is born of. The begetter sends, what is begotten is sent. And he is precisely sent to anyone when he is known and perceived by him, as far as he can be perceived and known according to the capacity of a rational soul either making progress toward God or already made perfect in God.[18]

Thus, God's sending of the Word in the Son begotten of the Father makes God available to be completely for the human. This is the original act by which God gathers the world unto himself in triune relation. Augustine continues,

> But just as the begetter and the begotten are one, so are the sender and the sent, because the Father and the Son are one; so too the Holy Spirit is one with them, because *these three are one* (1 Jn 5:7). And just as being born means for the Son his being from the Father, so his being sent means his being known from him. And just as for the Holy Spirit his being the gift of God means his proceeding from the Father, so his being sent means his being known to proceed from him.[19]

Thus, the missionary act continues in the Spirit's procession to the world bringing creation into the being of God. This rhythm, which the triune life enjoys, falls to the church as a way of being sent from the fellowship with triune life to the world in a manner that the world may know it is from God. If the church is shaped by the triune life, then Augustine enlightens us into the way we are to understand our vocation.

A practical example of this habitus, as mirroring the "sent quality" of the triune life, is the practice of friendship making toward the margins. We must be clear, however, as to the mode by which we seek out friendships. The church cannot seek to colonize the corners or margins of society for the sake of conforming the marginalized to our image. Rather, as indicated earlier of the being of God as a free act, God's being is not equated with any particular human being's existence. Rather, God is God alone and is free to be for us. One could read this move of God toward us as a mode of genuine encounter for friendship, or relationally.[20] Thus, our move toward the margins is one of genuine encounter and friendship as a practice that embodies and is shaped by the triune life. This particular practice of habitus changes the church's emphasis on success. And Chris Heuertz and Christine Pohl write,

> Our love for Christ and our experience of Christ's love for us motivated and compelled us to make the cross cultural moves that we did. Enthralled by Jesus' goodness and beauty, we wanted everyone to know him. But we didn't want to compromise the integrity of Jesus' goodness or our friendships by using them strategically . . . In relationships and friendships with those who are poor, we were learning to follow our friends to God's heart. Along the way, we redefined success in terms of faithfulness.[21]

Thus, the argument of this chapter finds its tangible expression in the practice of friendship-making at the margins.

Eschatological Consummation and the Apocalyptic Present

Robert W. Jenson writes concerning the eschatological consummation of the church,

> We will at the end be taken into God. But according to the teaching here proposed, God creates by accommodation in himself, and the church consists now in communion with God. We already live, move, and have our being in God even as rebellious creatures, and in the church with willing personal participation.[22]

Herein lies the paradoxical present. The church is, as stated above, a place linked to the reality of God, as agents of missionary freedom. It is essentially for people as God is for people. This is our present and what it means to live, to move, and to have our being. Our future, however, consists of being taken into the good future of God. The church as eschatological is a promise.

Being taken into the good future of God shows that it isn't the church's responsibility to save the world. According to Jenson, "The church has a mission: to see to the speaking of the gospel, whether to the world as message of salvation or to God as appeal and praise."[23] Rather, God is the one who ultimately brings the world to God's future of goodness. This future of goodness is constituted by promise. The triune God is bound to all creation to bring it to its good end. The church, as the mission of God, helps the world live into that good future. The church is able to help in this way because it is uniquely marked by the revelation of this promise.

Since the community is marked by this promise, it can see the world apocalyptically. This understanding becomes a Christian hermeneutic for comprehending the mission of God to the world. Theology understood apocalyptically means, in the Greek sense of the word *apokalupsis*, revelation. The triune life of God reveals God to the world. When the church is founded upon revelation, namely, revelation of the eschaton, it means that the vision provided constitutes a way of seeing the world. When the church sees the world, it sees it within the context of the good future of the triune Lord. Therefore, the church's mission, ministry, and existence fully finds itself in

Trinitarian expression when it sees the world through this revelation, that is, apocalyptically.

When the church finds its rest in God, and relieves its anxiety of saving the world, it truly finds a mission. Its mission is to find ways of neighbor love and friendship as an expression of the triune life. The fallenness of the world complicates this mission, but only as the church receives its identity in God and reflects that identity to the world, is it truly the church. The kingdom of God has come in Jesus Christ. The kingdom of God is present in the triune identity of the church as mission. The eschatological consummation of the church in the triune life finds the relief for the church from the anguishes and difficulties of the mission in such a context. As Christopher Morse writes,

> The news [namely of the promise of the eschaton], whether we may view it as credible or not, becomes that our help is in the name of the One who does not make *any* situation we face on earth, however threatening or devastating, to be without the overarching forthcoming of an unimpeded dominion of love and freedom.[24]

The wealth of goodness in the triune shaping of the church finds its ultimate meaning in the fact that we are promised a good future. Our mission is to remind the world of this good forthcoming future. Furthermore, if the world rejects the church and reacts violently against the promise of heaven, God's good future is the context in which we continue to perseverance. Were it not for this triune shaping of the church, such events would not be possible. Jenson writes,

> Thus the church's present reality anticipates, in all brokenness and fallibility, the end of all things, exactly as the end is the Trinity's embrace of "all in all." We may say: the communion that is now the church is itself constituted by an event of communion or anticipation, with the communion that is the Trinity. It is this last twist that locates the church at the gate of heaven.[25]

The church, as constituted by the triune life, is the foretaste of the world to come.

John Milbank writes in *Theology and Social Theory*,

The association of the Church with the response of the Spirit which arises "after the Son," and yet is fully divine, shows that the new belongs from the beginning within the new narrative manifestation of God. Hence the metanarrative is not just the story of Jesus, it is the continuing story of the Church, already realized in a finally exemplary way by Christ, yet still to be realized universally, in harmony with Christ, and yet differently, by all generations of Christians.[26]

This chapter has attempted to capture what it means to say that the church should be identified through its triune identity. Toward this end we have argued that the Trinity offers important clues for understanding the origin and embodiment of the church. The economy of God's presence in the church points toward the communion of God. We are a temple and a body constituted by the free gift of God. We have also sought to show that the God who is for us, who makes room for us, calls the church to be for others. Understanding the church as a habitus makes it plain its mission is of the very being of God. The mission is not an isolated agenda or action, rather it is what God calls the church to be in the world. We called attention to the church as promise. The church becomes a new way to see the world or, as Milbank indicates, a metanarrative. This is the promise of what God is doing in the world through the church as we anticipate "the consummation at the coming of our Lord Jesus Christ."[27]

Questions for Discussion

1. How might the construal of the self through the lens of the church change the modern self?

2. How does the way the church is depicted in the Pauline epistles inform our understanding of the church?

3. What specific practices in the church might help illuminate the triune life of God?

4. How does the understanding of God as triune change the natural rights discussion in Western culture?

5. How does the Trinity enable a better understanding of mission?

Suggestions for Further Reading

Bonhoeffer, Dietrich. "What Is the Church?" *Berlin: 1932-33*, vol. 12. Edited by Larry I. Rasmussen; translated by Isbel Best and David Higgins. Minneapolis: Fortress Press, 2009.

Bourdieu, Pierre. *The Logic of Practice*. Translated by Richard Nice. Stanford, CA: Stanford University Press, 1980.

Cavanaugh, William T. *Migrations of the Holy: God, State, and the Political Meaning of the Church*. Grand Rapids: Eerdmans, 2011.

Flett, John G. *The Witness of God: The Trinity, Missio Dei, Karl Barth, and the Nature of Christian Community*. Grand Rapids: Eerdmans, 2010.

Gelder, Craig Van, and Dwight J. Zscheile. *The Missional Church in Perspective: Mapping Trends and Shaping the Conversation*. Grand Rapids: Baker Academic, 2011.

Haight, Roger D. *Christian Community in History*. Vol. 3: *Ecclesial Existence*. New York: Continuum, 2008.

Harvey, Barry. *Another City: An Ecclesiological Primer for a Postmodern World*. Harrisburg, PA: Trinity International Press, 1999.

Hauerwas, Stanley. *A Better Hope: Resources for a Church Confronting Capitalism, Democracy, and Postmodernity*. Grand Rapids: Brazos Press, 2000.

Heuertz, Christopher L., and Christine D. Pohl. *Friendship at the Margins: Discovering Mutuality in Service and Mission*. Downers Grove, IL: IVP, 2010.

Jenson, Robert. *Systematic Theology*, 2 vols. New York: Oxford University Press, 1997, 1999.

Kung, Hans. *The Church*. Garden City, NY: Doubleday and Co./Image Books, 1976.

McCormick, K. Steve. "The Church after the Likeness of the Holy Trinity Is the Church after the *Missio Dei*." *Didache Faithful Teaching* 7:1 (June 2007). Available Online (accessed 12/27/11) at http://didache.nazarene.org/pdfs/GTIIE_McCormick.pdf, 12.

Moltmann, Jürgen. *The Church in the Power of the Spirit: A Contribution to Messianic Ecclesiology*. Translated by Margaret Kohl. New York: Harper and Row, 1995.

Schmiechen, Mr. Peter. *Saving Power: Theories of Atonement and Forms of the Church*. Grand Rapids: Eerdmans, 2005.

Wells, Samuel. *God's Companions: Reimagining Christian Ethics*. Malden, MA: Blackwell, 2006.

four
PUTTING CHRIST IN HIS PLACE
ECCLESIOLOGY AND CHRISTOLOGY IN THE NAZARENE TRADITION

Mark H. Mann

> "[The Church] is not an ideal which we must realize; it is rather a reality created by God in Christ in which we may participate."
> —Dietrich Bonhoeffer, *Life Together*

Introduction

A complaint that I often hear from colleagues and friends in the Church of the Nazarene is that our church has no ecclesiology. In many ways it is this very sentiment that has served as the impulse for this collection of essays, all on the topic of ecclesiology by pastors, theologians, and biblical scholars, as well as the general theme for the Nazarene World Theology Conference in Nairobi, Kenya (2014). I believe that this claim is incorrect, or at least only partially correct. That is, throughout our history we have had an ecclesiology, even if it has not always been effectively articulated within official Nazarene teachings. What is also the case is that Nazarenes as a whole have begun to rethink their assumed ecclesiology, and so we do find ourselves at a place as a denomination where there is no clear, universally affirmed view of the church.

My objectives in this chapter are fourfold. First, I will elucidate the traditionally assumed Nazarene ecclesiology, identifying also the historic roots of this view and the important function that this ecclesiology played in the early formation of the Church of the Nazarene. Second, I will identify the practical and theological problems with this ecclesiology that have led to the current malaise within the church. Third, I will argue that the Church of the Nazarene needs to recover an understanding of the church grounded in

Christology. That is, I believe that we need to reorient our understanding of the church most fundamentally in terms of its relationship to God as the body of Christ. Finally, I will conclude by outlining some of the implications of grounding our fundamental ecclesiology in Christology for our understanding and practice of the sacrament of baptism.

Nazarene Ecclesiology in Historical Perspective

Nazarene theologians can be forgiven for believing that their church has been bereft of an ecclesiology, or at least sensing there to be great confusion among Nazarenes. It was not until the 1989 General Assembly that Nazarenes officially affirmed an Article of Faith defining the fundamental nature of the church, and this statement has recently undergone revision.[1] Add to this that the current statement expresses a more communitarian notion of the church in contrast to the more individualistic membership and sacramental practices and other *Manual* statements on the nature of the church, and it is clear that, when it comes to ecclesiology, the Church of the Nazarene is a tradition in some flux.

Historically, however, even though Nazarenes have not been explicit in our ecclesiology, we have affirmed an ecclesiology that emphasizes that the church is an "association of believers," or what is often called a "believers' church." This has been expressed not only in official Nazarene teachings but in various church practices as well. So, for instance, scattered throughout the Nazarene *Manual* through much of Nazarene history we find the Church of the Nazarene spoken of explicitly as a "voluntary association" of believers who have come together in common worship, fellowship, and, especially, mission to bring the gospel of Christian holiness to the world.[2] And this is exactly the implication in calling a church a believers' church—it is most essentially a community of believers, an aggregate of regenerate individuals who have gathered in common belief and purpose. The clear emphasis in the use of such language is that individual faith precedes the church and that the church exists when redeemed persons come together.[3]

As Nazarene historian and archivist Stan Ingersol has aptly pointed out, that the Church of the Nazarene is a believers' church is most prominently expressed in our sacramental practices, especially baptism.[4] Although, throughout our history, Nazarenes have always affirmed the use of infant baptism but have practiced it rarely.⁵ Instead, Nazarenes have emphasized baptism as an act testifying to the saving grace that the believer has already received.⁶ In other words, saving faith precedes membership in the church; individual persons get saved then choose to join the church. Indeed, it is not infrequent for Nazarenes to be baptized many years after they have come to saving faith, even years after they have chosen to become official members of the Church of the Nazarene.⁷ The Church of the Nazarene, then, throughout its history has been quintessentially a believers' church. What is of central importance is the faith and growth in Christ of individual believers who form the church when they come together in Christ's name.

Such an understanding of the church has played an important role in the development of evangelical Christian faith and has its roots in two similar but also different Protestant movements: Anabaptism and Pietism. The Anabaptist movement arose quite early in the Reformation as a response both to Catholicism and the rise of state-sponsored Protestant churches. Early Anabaptists' concern was the general assumption that being "born and baptized into" a national church (German Lutheran, Church of England, Dutch Reformed, etc.) was sufficient for experiencing new life in Christ. They believed that salvation required the kind of personal appropriation of faith simply not possible for infants or children, that only "adult" believers could truly be saved and thus part of the church through its initiatory rite—baptism. Therefore, those that had been baptized as infants decided they needed to be baptized again, thus the moniker they were given: "Ana" (again) baptist.⁸

The Anabaptist emphasis on salvation as essentially a personal and, therefore, largely individual matter began to make its way into the magisterial churches (that is, official "state" churches, such as the Reformed, Lutheran, and Anglican) in the seventeenth and eighteenth centuries through the Pietist movement. While accepting the fundamental alliance between official civil and ecclesial authority and the practice of infant baptism, Pietists also strongly emphasized the importance of personal faith, affirming the necessity of the personal experience of faith in and devotion to Christ. Pietists would come to see themselves as an *ecclesiola in ecclesia*—a kind of "little church" within the "larger church." That is, while refusing to separate officially from the national church, they understood themselves to form a community of true devotion to Christ within it.⁹

Pietism has exerted a significant influence on the Wesleyan movement and the Church of the Nazarene. John and Charles Wesley experienced their evangelical conversions under the influence of the Moravians, a German Lutheran pietistic group. In fact, it was while in attendance at a Moravian society meeting that John had his famous Aldersgate experience and felt his "heart strangely warmed." And, although the Wesleys would in subsequent years come to distance themselves from the Moravians, the Evangelical Revival and early Methodist movement were in many ways an Anglicized Pietism. At the heart of the revival was a call to a deeply personal faith—repentance, conversion, sanctification—and Methodists clearly understood themselves as a kind of *ecclesiola in ecclesia*—a movement within the Church of England called to reform the larger church.[10] And, a significant part of that reforming was to be the revival of true, heart religion—that is, personal piety.

The *ecclesiola* would become *ecclesia* when Methodism—especially in America—would make the formal break from the Church of England in the late 1700s, though Methodism as a distinct ecclesial movement would maintain certain vestiges of Anglican ecclesiology, such as infant baptism. Nevertheless, as Methodism would move into the American frontier and take on the practices and ethos of revivalism, the stage had been fully set for the emergence of a Wesleyan denomination that would generally understand itself as a believers' church—an association of believers gathering together in common mission.

In fact, the idea of the church as an association of believers would play an important role in the formation of the early denomination. The three main parent bodies (Church of the Nazarene, Association of Pentecostal Churches of America, and Holiness Church of Christ) had slightly different ecclesiological teachings and practices. For instance, some were more episcopal in polity, others more congregational; some were more sacramental than others, and different groups advocated different baptismal practice.[11] But what they all held in common was an emphasis on the Wesleyan doctrine and experience of Christian holiness and a sense that God had called them together for the promotion of Christian holiness. Considering that the story of the church in America up to this point had largely been one of perpetual conflict and division, that three rather different denominational bodies would be forging a union—especially across North-South lines—was an unprecedented move. They were in fact an association of believers joining together from a wide variety of denominational backgrounds, and to think of themselves as such no doubt helped quell the fears of some concerned about what might be sacrificed or compromised in the formation of unity.

Importantly, early Nazarenes did affirm themselves to be a part of the "one, holy, catholic, and apostolic" church, embracing a denominationalism that acknowledged all believers as true brothers and sisters in Christ no matter their ecclesial affiliation.¹² In this sense, early Nazarenes understood themselves as a kind of *ecclesiola in ecclesia*: they were, like the early Methodists, a special order of believers within the larger "church of God" called to lives of holy devotion to Christ and given the special mission to bear witness to the entire church the experience and truth of Christian holiness.¹³ In this sense, they truly were a believers' church—an association of believers whose common faith had brought them together in common mission and ministry.

Problems with a Nazarene Believers' Church Ecclesiology

An ecclesiology that envisions the church as fundamentally an association of believers provides a helpful corrective to the view that being Christian is a kind of birthright, not requiring a vital, personal relationship with God. Indeed, there are many things to laud about the believers' church model, including the fact that Scripture sometimes does speak of the church in just this way. In fact, the term used in the New Testament for church is *ekklesia*, which literally means "gathered." In a profound and true sense, the church *is* the gathering of believers in Christ's name, choosing to associate together for common purpose and fellowship. But there are also profound problems with such an understanding of the church, especially when set loose from its christological moorings. We will first look at some of the practical problems with this ecclesiology, then identify the scriptural and theological shortcomings.

The main practical problem of a believers' church ecclesiology is its inherent individualism. The assumption that underlies such a view of the church is that the faith of individual believers comes prior to the church, that Christian faith is first and foremost a matter between the individual person and God. This is a notion that has been very appealing to Westerners, and especially Americans, who prize their individual freedom, autonomy, and embrace ideals of rugged individualism. And it is therefore no surprise that such an understanding of the church would especially take root in the frontier revivalism so important to the spread of Methodism and the rise of the Holiness movement in America. Ironically, this was the central insight of and provided much of the power for the early Anabaptist and Pietist movements: Christian faith is not merely a birthright, nationality, or corporate experience, but also requires personal commitment and devotion. God does call individuals to lives of personal faith and service.[14]

But there is a dark underside to emphasizing the individual aspects of faith, which has become all too apparent in the age of the "spiritual but not religious" and the "nones"—the term sociologists often use to define the increasing numbers of people claiming no religious affiliation. The sad irony is that a large percentage of the nones have a Christian upbringing and therefore great affinity for Christian belief and high regard for Jesus; it's the church they are happy to do without.[15] Indeed, such persons have fully bought into the notion that Christian faith is essentially an individual, personal matter, that what really matters is that one has a personal relationship with God.

Those who would defend a believers' church ecclesiology would, of course, not advocate such individualism, and they could easily point to an inherent irrationality in the belief, for instance, that one can actually succeed in the Christian life without the church. Yes, they might point out, one may in theory come to Christ on a desert island by some immediate act of God through the Holy Spirit, but "iron sharpens iron" and individual believers need the fellowship of other Christians in order to grow in faith and holiness. Moreover, those who have come to knowledge of Christ have only done so under the influence of the church—that is, Christian parents, pastors, and friends. Indeed, even the Bible itself is in some sense a product of the church. It was the early church that wrote down and put together Scripture and the church through the ages that has translated and continues to publish and distribute Holy Writ. The problem, then, is not the believers' church ecclesiology but the failure to realize the vital importance of Christian community for growth in Christ and the fulfillment of Christian mission. In other words, to steal a phrase from Reuben Welch, "we really do need each other" to thrive and succeed as Christians.[16]

There is, of course, some truth in all of this. Certainly God intends the church as a means for the growth of believers. But it also belies a deeper biblical and theological problem with such an ecclesiology, for it still posits the chief purpose of the church in terms of its instrumentality. That is, the main function of the church is to be a means for individual spiritual growth. In this sense, the primary function of the church is anthropocentric: God created the church to serve individual human needs. While this is no doubt part of the picture, it is only part, and certainly not the most important part. Indeed, this is the core problem with a believers' church, at least as expressed in traditional Nazarene ecclesiology: it ultimately envisions the church as a *human* community forged through the mutual agreement of individual *believers*. In other words, it gives priority to human decision and behavior when defining the church and makes secondary the divine nature of the church and the deep sense in which the church (and individual believers) truly belongs to God. This is the importance of rooting ecclesiology in Christology: it is to recognize that the church ultimately is not ours or even us but God's and God in Christ working in and through us. In other words, to reenvision ecclesiology in terms of Christology—that is, the church first and foremost *is* the body of Christ—is to ground our understanding of the church in who Christ is and what Christ is doing, not in who we are or what we are doing.

Christology and Ecclesiology

In a certain sense, Christology is, or at least should be, the foundation of all Christian theology. Theology is by definition disciplined reflection on the nature and work of God. But, for Christians, all that we understand about God has to do with the early church's experience of Jesus Christ as Lord and Savior, and their recognition through their experience of the death and resurrection of Jesus that, in Jesus' life and teachings they had not merely encountered a good man or prophet through whom God spoke, but the Messiah, the Savior, the very Son of God. In the wake of their experience of the risen Christ, they came not only to see Christ as one who had died for their sins to reconcile them to God but also to see Christ as the Lord of all creation, the Master of heaven and earth, the Lord of life! In other words, everything that they understood about God—the nature and character of God, God's plan for creation and humanity, God's plan for salvation, God's designs for morality and the good life, how God intends that we should live in relationship to others, and so forth—was born from their experience and understanding of *who Christ is*. This is why nearly all of the great theological controversies of the early church were christological in focus and nature, why the heresies of the first four centuries (Ebionism, Docetism, Monarchianism, modalism, adoptionism, Sabellianism, Arianism, Apollinarianism, Eutychianism, Nestorianism) were all christological heresies and thus why the early creeds of the church are so very important. Early Christians understood well that all of Christian faith hung in the balance when it came to understanding who Christ is. If we misunderstand who Christ is, we misunderstand who God is; if we misunderstand who Christ is, salvation itself is jeopardized; if we misunderstand who Christ is, all of Christian faith comes crashing down.[17] This is what we mean when we speak of Christology as the foundation of theology: all of Christian theology begins with and points to our understanding of God's self-revelation in Jesus Christ.

One could argue that the Christian understanding of God is essentially Trinitarian, that theology should be theocentric in a Trinitarian sense, rather than Christocentric. This is a valid point, and I do not mean to say that we should think of God as anything but in an orthodox Trinitarian way. Nor do I wish to discount the important role of the Holy Spirit in Christian life and faith or pneumatology as an important aspect of Christian theology, much less in our reflection on the fundamental nature of the church. Indeed, Scripture is adamant that the Holy Spirit is God's enlivening presence in the world, giving life, purpose, and mission to the church. For this reason we typically think of Pentecost as the birthday of the church. But Scripture and Christian tradition are also adamant that the person and life of the Holy Spirit are deeply tied to Christology. The Spirit is properly the Spirit of Christ (Phil. 1:19). The Spirit reveals and glorifies Christ to the church (John 15:26 and 16:14-15; 1 John 3:24; 4:13). The Spirit unites us to God, in Christ, and transforms us corporately into the body of Christ (1 Cor. 12:13; Eph. 2:14-18, 22; 4:3). Indeed, in focusing on the powerful events of Pentecost, we forget that the Holy Spirit was initially given to the disciples when the resurrected Christ appeared to them and breathed the Holy Spirit upon them (John 20:22). The point here is that the work and life of the Spirit is intimately tied to Christology. Indeed, this is central to what the doctrine of the Trinity (especially in its Western interpretation) is about: the life and work of the Father, Son, and Holy Spirit are always interwoven.[18] The doctrine of the Trinity by definition requires that Christology be at the center of our understanding of who God is and what God is doing and is therefore foundational for all dimensions of theological reflection.

If Christology is in some sense the true foundation of all Christian faith and theology, so also should Christology be the foundation for ecclesiology. Indeed, this is exactly what we find in Scripture, which is perfectly clear in giving priority to Christology in defining the fundamental nature of the church. Take Matthew 16:18, for instance. Unfortunately, when this passage is most often referenced, it is in a debate regarding whether the pope, as bishop of Rome and ecclesiastical successor to Peter, should be considered the supreme vicar of Christ and leader of the universal church. But what is often missed here is Jesus' declaration that the church is *Christ's* and that *Christ* is building the church. In a similar fashion, both 1 Corinthians 3:10-11 and Ephesians 2:20-22 speak of Jesus Christ as the foundation (or cornerstone of the foundation) upon which the entire church is built. Ephesians 2:21-22 is especially clear: "In him the whole structure is joined together and grows into a holy temple in the Lord; in whom you also are built together spiritually into a dwelling place for God." It is not we who form the church through believing and choosing to associate together in common mission. It is ultimately God, in Christ, to whom the church belongs and who is building *us* to be the church.

This same point is driven home again and again in Pauline writings through the metaphor of the church as the body of Christ. In these passages (Rom. 12:4-5; 1 Cor. 12:12-26; Eph. 1:18-23; 5:25-32; Col. 1:17-20; 3:14-16) we find the church defined not in human but divine terms. The church is the living, breathing body of Christ. Individually, believers are merely "members" of this body. The implication is that, from a Pauline perspective, there is *no such thing* as a solo Christian or an individual believer apart from the church. Such a person is like a "dismembered" limb, and like a hand or arm that has been cut off from a human body, it can only rot and die.[19] This is to say: not only do we need the church to grow in Christian faith, but also without the church there is truly *no such thing* as Christian faith. As the head of the body, Christ comes first, then comes the body, then comes the individual member. In other words, one is a Christian not primarily by virtue of one's individual, personal faith in Christ, but because one is a member of the body of Christ, the church. It is the church that ultimately defines the faith of an individual, not the other way around, because life in Christ is found by being a member of the body of Christ.

To help clarify the point that I am making here, let us imagine for a moment that we might think about salvation as if it could be loosened from its christological moorings—that is, defined primarily from a human perspective, instead of the divine. What we are left with is an understanding of salvation that focuses on human sin, human faith, human decision, human repentance, and human effort. We would, of course, especially as Wesleyans, affirm that all of these are important aspects of salvation. God will not save us without our repentance and faith, and our growth in sanctification requires considerable effort and discipline. But we know perfectly well that this is only part of the story, and by far the least significant part.[20] Far more important for our understanding of salvation is what we affirm God in Christ to have done for us. We are lost in sin without the atoning sacrifice of Christ. We are incapable of being convicted of our sin, much less of being moved to repentance, apart from the divine initiatives of prevenient grace. Our decision for Christ and our efforts to grow in Christlikeness not only have Christ as their proper end but are fully empowered by the gracious mercy and sanctifying presence of Christ by the power of the Holy Spirit. The point here is that any soteriology not rooted in Christology—in who Christ is and what God in Christ has done and is doing—is not a true Christian soteriology but a humanistic philosophy of human self-development cloaked in Christian trappings.

This is exactly the problem with in ecclesiology that focuses on the church as an aggregate or association of individuals. It has the wrong starting point. Yes, the church is a community of believers, but not primarily. First and foremost, the church is the body of Christ. It is formed primarily not by human decisions to believe and then associate together in common mission and worship, but by what God in Christ has done on the cross and through the resurrection. Its life is not primarily the faith of individuals and their commitment to God and one another, but by the grace and mercy of God in Christ through the body of Christ, the church. We are in truth reconciled to God not as individuals but only as members of the body of Christ. Our destiny is not to find salvation as individuals but to become members of the body of Christ and in this way to be saved.[21] The church is ultimately not about you and me and what we have done or are doing. The church is ultimately about Christ, who Christ is, what *Christ is doing* in and through *us* to reconcile the world to God (2 Cor. 5:16-19).

Again, I am not saying that individual faith is unimportant or that the salvation and sanctification of individual Christians is somehow contrary to God's purposes for the church. On the contrary, just as one of the purposes of the incarnation, the cross, and the resurrection is the salvation of individuals, so also does God intend the church to be a means of grace for individuals. Instead, what I am arguing is that, from a biblical perspective that appropriately views the church from a christological perspective, the church is neither primarily a community of individual believers in association together nor an instrumental means of grace for individuals, but only these things secondarily and by virtue of its *first* being the living, breathing body of Christ.[22] This is, to put it simply, what it means to ground ecclesiology in Christology: it is to recognize the church to be essentially and primarily the body of Christ and only derivatively an association of believers coming together in common mission.

Implications for the Church of the Nazarene: Sacramental Renewal

As noted previously, changes to Nazarene doctrine began first with the addition of and then subsequent changes to the Article of Faith on the church and have initiated a shift away from the overly individualistic believers' church ecclesiology assumed for most of Nazarene history. The article, for instance, does affirm that the church is the body of Christ as one metaphor, even not the driving metaphor, for understanding the church. This statement also importantly frames the life and mission of the church primarily in terms of God's call, "the unity and fellowship of the [Holy] Spirit," and "the redemptive and reconciling ministry of Christ in the power of the Spirit" (34-35). This is a significant step forward in terms of recovering a Christocentric, rather than an anthropocentric, ecclesiology for the Church of the Nazarene, but it is only a step.

Indeed, more work needs to be done, and perhaps the most important place this needs to happen regards Nazarene doctrine on the sacrament of baptism. As noted previously, in keeping with our believers' church ecclesiology, Nazarenes have tended almost solely to practice believers' baptism, and even then to emphasize baptism as primarily a testimony to grace already received. Baptism, again, is to be "administered to believers," is "declarative of their faith," and is a "sacrament signifying acceptance of the benefits of the atonement" (35). In other words, faith and salvation are primarily individual, personal matters, and we are to be baptized to testify to this. But this is not the way that most of the church, through its history, has understood baptism.[23] Instead, the church has primarily understood baptism as a means of grace, a salvific event, through which persons are incorporated into—that is, become members of—*the body of Christ*. Indeed, even Anabaptists have historically affirmed the *necessity* of baptism for church membership and reception of the full benefits of new life in Christ. Another significant step forward, then, toward the practical recovery of a Christocentric ecclesiology would be to require baptism for membership in the Church of the Nazarene.

Ironically, Nazarenes maintain vestiges of a Christocentric ecclesiology in their acceptance of the practice of infant baptism. It is important to note that, in the *Manual*'s defense of the practice, it notes that baptism is a "symbol of the new covenant" (35). What exactly is meant here by the word "symbol" is unclear, but what is clear is that this is dichotomous with the rest of the article in its emphasis on baptism as signifying "acceptance of the benefits of the atonement" and as "declarative of the faith" of believers. Infants are not capable of "belief" or "acceptance" of the benefits of the covenant. This article is, therefore, fundamentally incoherent in both affirming infant baptism and stating that baptism primarily has to do with believers' acceptance and faith. It would be far better to reframe the statement Christocentrically and speak of baptism first and foremost as an act of the church as the body of Christ through which persons are accepted by God into the benefits of the atonement.[24] Indeed, this is the logic inherent in the practice of infant baptism and of the Wesleyan understanding of salvation formally embraced by the Church of the Nazarene as a Wesleyan denomination. That is, it is God's grace and acceptance that saves us, *not* our decision to accept it.[25] Indeed, this would bring Nazarene ecclesiology and sacramentology into far greater agreement with our doctrinal statements on atonement, prevenient grace, repentance, and justification, regeneration, and adoption, as all give priority in salvation to divine initiative *over* human responsiveness. This is not to suggest that saving grace is ever completed in the baptism of a child, any more than it is completed in the baptism of an adult. Indeed, this is why those churches practicing infant baptism have typically required those baptized as infants to go through confirmation—it is of vital importance that they develop and grow into an adult, believer's appropriation of the grace given to them through and the faith embodied for them by their church, as the living body of Christ.

There is much more to be said, especially regarding the sacrament of the Eucharist, but I leave this to other contributors to this volume who make this the focus of their chapters.[26] What I hope is clear is that we should continue the reformulation of Nazarene ecclesiology begun in the work of the 1989 General Assembly by grounding our core understanding of the church more solidly in Christology. This is to affirm more clearly that the church is most essentially the body of Christ, thereby aligning our ecclesiology more closely to the biblical understanding of the church and, hopefully, helping the church avoid the deep theological and practical problems inherent in the type of believers' church ecclesiology embraced through most of our history.

Questions for Discussion

1. What was your baptismal experience? What role has your baptism played in the development of your faith and your relationship to the church? Should persons baptized as infants be considered true Christians? Why or why not?

2. The author argues that one of the chief problems facing the church today is rampant individualism. What are some of the other challenges facing the church? How might thinking of the church primarily as the body of Christ help address some of those challenges?

3. Why do you think most Americans find it much easier to think of Christian faith on individual, rather than corporate, terms?

4. The author focuses in this chapter on his own denominational tradition, the Church of the Nazarene, but much that he says here about this tradition could be said of many evangelical churches today. In what ways is the ecclesiology of your church similar to or different from that of the Church of the Nazarene? In what ways might the author's claims cause you to rethink your own church's ecclesiology?

Suggestions for Further Reading

Bonhoeffer, Dietrich. *Life Together*. Translated by John W. Doberstein. San Francisco: Harper and Row, 1954.

Harper, Brad, and Paul Louis Metzger. *Exploring Ecclesiology: An Evangelical and Ecumenical Introduction*. Grand Rapids: Brazos Press, 2009.

Ingersol, Stan. "Christian Baptism and the Early Nazarenes: The Sources that Shaped a Pluralistic Baptismal Tradition," in *Past and Prospect: The Promise of Nazarene History*. San Diego: Point Loma Press/Wipf and Stock, 2013.

Robinson, John A. T. *The Body: A Study in Pauline Theology.* Philadelphia: Westminster John Knox Press, 1977.

Staples, Rob L. *Outward Sign and Inward Grace: The Place of the Sacraments in Wesleyan Spirituality.* Kansas City: Beacon Hill Press of Kansas City, 1991.

Welch, Reuben. *We Really Do Need Each Other: A Call to Community.* Grand Rapids: Zondervan, 1981.

five
MISSION POSSIBLE
THE IMPORTANCE OF THE SPIRIT IN WESLEYAN ECCLESIOLOGY

Diane Leclerc

The relationship between the Holy Spirit and the church should be unambiguous. The Holy Spirit initiates the church, sustains the church, and uses the church as the primary conduit of the *missio Dei*. Without the Spirit, the church is impotent, stagnant, and irrelevant. The church would disintegrate into nothingness, or worse, into purely human miscellany without the continuous work of the Holy Spirit. Without the church, God would, of course, be able to bring about divine and eternal purposes. But God chooses not to work alone; God has called the church to act with the Spirit synergistically on this earth. Thus church and Spirit cannot be separated in accomplishing God's purposes. We often, however, make the relationship between Spirit and church hazy and vague.

The premise of this book is that we stand in desperate need of strong innovative work on ecclesiology. But I would posit that the hazy relationship between church and Spirit is not only because we lack a strong ecclesiology but also because the church is often plagued with an incomplete or inadequate pneumatology.[1] This chapter seeks to connect ecclesiology to pneumatology, but it also seeks to set forth a robust understanding of the Spirit from a Wesleyan perspective. Wesley and Wesleyan theology have very keen insights into the life and work of the Spirit; besides having "sanctification" to offer the church universal (the reason God "raised up" Methodists, according to Wesley), the Wesleyan perspective on the Spirit should also be communicated more generally, especially in a Western context where pneumatology can be quite anemic.

While the church is, of course, intimately connected to the triune God, the Creator of all things and the Christ of full redemption, biblical language around the meaning, purpose, and function of the church is surprisingly pneumatological. The Bible is clear: it is in and through the Spirit that the church exists. But rather than using such biblical models for our discussion, the dialogical partners used for our purposes here will be the Articles of Faith of the Church of the Nazarene. What is offered in this chapter, then, is a type of exegesis of the pneumatologically relevant articles. I move forward, first, to express a theology of the Holy Spirit from a Wesleyan-Holiness—specifically Nazarene—perspective. In the end, I hope to broaden the way we often perceive the work of the Spirit in the life of the church.

A Theology of the Holy Spirit

1. The Essential Spirit

Article III reads, "We believe in the Holy Spirit, the Third Person of the Triune Godhead, that He is ever present and efficiently active in and with the Church of Christ, convincing the world of sin, regenerating those who repent and believe, sanctifying believers, and guiding into all the truth as it is in Jesus."

Influenced by a Wesleyan paradigm, the Church of the Nazarene emphasizes the full personality of the Holy Spirit, rather than subordinating and depersonalizing the Spirit under language such as "the Spirit of Christ." The Holy Spirit is more than the love between the first two persons of the Trinity and more than the sum of parts or works. The strength of an Eastern-Wesleyan model (vis-à-vis, Western-Reformed) is that it emphasizes the full, "personal" divinity of the Spirit and stresses the essential nature of the triune God. Thus what is stated in Article I is applied also to the Holy Spirit: The Spirit is "creative and administrative, holy in nature, attributes, and purpose." With this firmly in place, the third article of the Church of the Nazarene goes on to discuss the unique economic expression of this unsubordinated Spirit.[2] We will continue our considerations with the five activities listed in Article III, placing them in direct dialogue with the pneumatological references and implications of the other articles.

2. The Spirit Is Active, Convincing the World of Sin

God's prevenient work is synonymous with the Spirit's activity. Technically for Wesley, the way of salvation begins with God's free gift of prevenient grace, given from the moment we are born. Prevenient grace is the presence and work of the Holy Spirit. It is prevenient grace that draws us, awakening our souls to the need for God. This grace, as with all grace, can be resisted. But if it is allowed to do its work, prevenient grace and the presence of the Holy Spirit will bring a person to the place of "awakening." This is the place where we are convicted and convinced of our own sinfulness and helplessness apart from God. But this convincing work of God does not lead us to despair, for we are also convinced of the hope of our redemption. Conviction and hope, then, are not merely human responses to the Spirit's prior work, but rather expressions of the Spirit's imminent work in our hearts as we cooperate with the ever-available grace of God. Our article on repentance (VIII) states that "the Spirit of God gives to all who will repent, the gracious help of penitence of heart and hope of mercy."

3. [The Spirit Is Active] Regenerating Those Who Repent and Believe

Personal awakening is closely connected to repentance in Wesley's scheme; and awakening, if responded to, leads to repentance, faith, and regeneration. Repentance can be equated with "godly sorrow"—"sorrow" in the sense that we are convinced of our condition; it is "godly" in the sense that it does not lead to despair but rather to trust in the sufficiency of God. A second meaning of *repentance* is the actual relinquishing of sin and amending our ways toward God.[3] It is also crucial to invoke the Spirit when we speak of faith itself, for faith is a gift of God and not a human work. Synergistically enacted, Spirit-aided repentance and faith lead to regeneration. (Of note, we have focused great attention in our tradition on the turning *from* sin implied in repentance. It would serve us well to equally emphasize what we are *turning* toward, what we are repenting to; namely, we are turning *toward love*.)

It is the atoning work of Jesus Christ that makes regeneration possible. With regeneration, a person joins "the body of Christ" in a spiritual sense, liturgically celebrated and recognized in adult baptism. From the very earliest liturgies, the Holy Spirit is deeply connected to baptism. But it is also stated directly that the Holy Spirit is active in this regeneration itself. In Article IX we delineate the concomitants of salvation as justification, regeneration, and adoption. And yet we explicitly affirm that it is regeneration in which the Spirit participates. Succinctly put, we are made new creations through the work of the Holy Spirit. Regeneration implies more than justification's forensic meaning (formally wrought by the atonement), and the familial language of adoption as sons and daughters, and co-heirs with Christ. Regeneration not only implies a change in relation to guilt or in our relation to the "family" of God but also affects a change in nature. Regeneration can be correctly linked to "initial sanctification" in the *via salutis*. Holiness is imparted to the regenerated, not just imputed. This work is thus effective through the Spirit's transformative activity, which begins and implies a new birth.

We are also explicit when conveying that it is the Spirit that bears witness to our spirit regarding this transformation in nature and relationship. While Wesley himself adapted the doctrine of assurance through his life (finally suggesting that one could lose the witness without losing his or her salvation), in most instances assurance is the subsequent gift given by the Holy Spirit for the purpose of spiritual confidence before God or before one's own self-doubt. The articles of the Church of the Nazarene suggest that the witness of the Spirit is given again at the moment of entire sanctification. This leads to the fourth activity of the Spirit as found in Article III.

4. [The Spirit Is Active] Sanctifying Believers

Some might argue that this designation glances a necessary christological focus. But if it is understood that the atoning work of Christ is the source of all grace, the statement that the Spirit "sanctifies believers" can be interpreted as the *application* of christological grace through the Spirit's work. It would serve us well here to remind ourselves of our emphasis on the essential Trinity, so as to avoid economic hair-splitting. Sanctification is the work of God in Christ through the Holy Spirit.

Despite the great debate (now "historic") over the problematic aspects and limitations of the metaphor, "baptism of the Holy Spirit" remains a part of our articles. While Article X does list multiple expressions for the experience of entire sanctification, it and Article V state that entire sanctification and heart cleansing are wrought through baptism with the Holy Spirit, thus clearly making it the more dominant metaphor. Is the language of Spirit baptism an essential part of our identity, or could it be that it is more representative of our attempts to hold on to something now anachronistic? Is it still relevant, and is it still communicative? We also claim that through the Spirit "the heart is fully cleansed," which has fairly recently replaced the word *eradication*. Theologically, the word had lost meaning. This could be said also of "baptism with the Holy Spirit." But before we throw the baby out with the bathwater, perhaps meaning might be restored if the denomination restored its sacramental emphasis. If "baptism with the Holy Spirit" draws upon a deep understanding of the meaning of baptism as a metaphorical comparison for the deeper work of God, then perhaps the de-emphasis and "optionalist" tone of the sacraments generally, and baptism specifically in our denomination creates a disconnect that leads to the irrelevancy of baptism as a metaphor.

The Spirit is also mentioned in Article X in its emphases on the indwelling presence of the Holy Spirit, the empowering work of the Holy Spirit for life and service, which includes "spiritual development and improvement in Christlikeness of character and personality." It is crucial that we maintain these statements. Historically, the higher life movement within Calvinism, as expressed by Finney, Mahan, and Keswickianism, required some type of metamorphosis of their Calvinist theology, into a "new Calvinism." How could one maintain the *optimism* implicit in an emphasis on the presence and power of the Holy Spirit and the transformative grace that enables development in Christlikeness, while holding on to a strictly Reformed theology of depravity, sin, and forensic salvation? They simply do not blend. And yet, with generic evangelicalism and persistent fundamentalism vying for the attention of our people, how do we combat this more pessimistic worldview today?

We proclaim our pneumatology, for one. We believe in the immanence of God, through the indwelling presence of the Holy Spirit. We believe that the Holy Spirit, through the same power that raised Jesus from the dead, empowers us for life and godliness, for Christlike character and resolute love. We believe that we can grow in the sanctifying grace of God, being changed from glory to glory, being deepened in our desire and capacity to love God with all our being and our neighbors as ourselves. We do not simply wait for the great escape from this world, but live fully in the here and now as we fulfill the purpose for which we were created, and find ourselves being renewed in the very image of God. Ours is a voice of great hopefulness amid a type of Christianity that preaches fear and despair as it anticipates a dreadful end. The great hope of the church is that the transformative work of the Holy

Spirit in Christians, and in Christian life together, spills out into the world. Wesleyan-Holiness folks were initially postmillennialists for a reason. God has not abandoned us or the world, but particularly through the Spirit God is with us still.

5. [The Spirit Is Active] Guiding into All the Truth as It Is in Jesus

Wesleyan theology is inductive by nature. It is experientially informed. Any declarative statements we might make come from life in God, not from propositional statements to which we then attempt to conform. In other words, we do not state that the Spirit is active, guiding into all truth, period. But rather, that the Spirit is guiding into all the truth as it is in Jesus. The implications of the additional phrase are not accidental, but paramount. Truth is not defined in a "modernist" fashion, objectively attained, analyzed, and asserted. Truth is found in a person, and through experiential "knowledge" of this person. For example, for Wesley it is possible to hold to any or all creedal affirmations and still not be "right-hearted" or related to the Source of truth for such affirmations. Belief is not an intellectual assent to an agreed upon truth but deep, courageous trust in the God who saves. And thus, when the Spirit guides us in truth, we are guided to our soteriological understandings and our experience of grace, as we entrust ourselves to God. Our "spiritual senses" inform our collective theology. For Wesley all truth comes to us in the community of faith, the church.

This brings us to our understanding of the inspiration and purpose of Holy Scripture. We believe that the Holy Spirit inspired the original writers of the canon, and that sufficiently. We believe in the plenary inspiration of Scripture, which entails a rejection of a mechanical or verbal doctrine and absolute inerrancy, and explicitly state that the Bible is perfect in its intention to "reveal God's will concerning us in things necessary to our salvation." No articles are to be written that are not biblically supported. Our position has huge implications for the way in which we interpret Scripture. Soteriology once again guides our interpretive moves.[4]

On matters not pertaining to our salvation, we refuse to force our people to embrace a certain position; in speculative, nonessential doctrines (such as creation and eschatology), we allow, even demand liberty of thinking. Unfortunately, this is not emphasized enough. It falls on pastors, I believe, to teach their congregations methods that are integral to interpretive integrity. All interpretation of Scripture is to be done in the context of community. It is appropriate to enjoin our people to use a Wesleyan-Holiness lens, while always remaining open, as a community, to the guidance of the Holy Spirit in our doctrinal inclinations.

We not only acknowledge that we depend on the Holy Spirit to guide us theologically but also confess our absolute dependence on the Holy Spirit's transformation of Scripture, presently, from words to "food." It is the Holy Spirit that opens our hearts to its words in such a way that it becomes for us a vital means of grace.[5]

The five statements above represent the Spirit's person and work in the life of believers and in the world. It should be forcefully stated that none of the church's work is separated from the Spirit. Conviction, regeneration, sanctification, and revelation are all intricately related to the church of Jesus Christ, only made possible through the Spirit. As the Spirit offers prevenient grace and convicts the world of sin, the church stands as a beacon of light that points to Jesus as the way, the truth, and the life. As the Spirit regenerates persons who believe and repent, the church becomes their home where nurture and care are evident. As persons progress in the transformative work of the Spirit in sanctification, it is the church that has discipled, educated, and encouraged them to places of deep commitment. And yet even these statements do not go far enough, for they still focus on the individual even while acknowledging the church as a community. What if we could say that the pneumatological statements above transcend the individual? What would it mean to say that the church herself is convicted, regenerated, and sanctified through the Spirit? What would it mean to say that the very revelation of God happens in the context of the whole church and not just to individuals? If these "what if" questions were true, we would indeed be able to affirm the article statement that the Spirit "is ever present and efficiently active in and with the Church of Christ" and mean much more "collective." It is important to attend to the suggestion that the Spirit is at work in the church and not just in individuals who participate in church. In other words, the disease of soteriology, particularly in a North American context, is its individualism. A robust pneumatology benefits from ecclesiology in that it guards against this purely individualistic blight. The following four statements represent an extension of the Articles of Faith into an intentionally more collective soteriology *for the church* itself.

Soteriology for the Church

1. The Essential Spirit Creates the Essential Church

While an acknowledgment of the church's imperfection certainly squares with reality, we have still held to the classical marks of the church in their ideal sense. The church is one, holy, universal, and apostolic—in the sense that while yet to be fully and finally realized, the present church *participates* now in these descriptions. Either proleptically, or through some other theological tool, the church has essential qualities with eternal properties. At the very heart of the issue is the affirmation that its essential characteristics find their source in the initiating and sustaining work of the Holy Spirit. And therefore, just as the Trinity—particularly in its Wesleyan interpretation—is characterized as intermingled and without subordination, the church also is to be characterized as an interdependent body with full equality of its parts. In this sense, the church is created in the image of God. It is a mystery of grace how the Spirit can take the great diversity evident in this human gathering and unite it in spirit and in purpose. The language of "body" life is an expression of the interdependence and equality of each participant, called for and enabled by the gracious work of God. Further, the Trinitarian relationship of *perichoresic* love extends to the church, is evident in the church, and then moves through the church to the world, ever drawing others into its unified and holy existence. It is only through the work of the Spirit that this type of love is experienced and made manifest.

2. The Spirit Convicts the Church of Sin

While acknowledging the church's essential and "perfect" quality is an important endeavor, it is important for our purposes here to acknowledge that the church sins and is collectively responsible for that sin. And thus implied, there is a place for denominational confession, such as the confession of the Southern Baptists regarding their position on slavery a hundred and fifty years previously. Sometimes confession needs to be broader than a denomination, but we should at least start there. Dare we ask ourselves for what the Holiness movement, or the Church of the Nazarene, needs to take responsibility?

One example presented itself at a Global Theology Conference in Holland. A theme arose from the African constituency—suggesting that the position of the denomination (one of nonengagement) during the years of apartheid was inadequate and destructive. As I sat there, at first I thought that some representative from our leadership should stand and make a public confession for the collective. No one did. I was angry. It dawned on me weeks later that I, too, was a representative of the whole and that I could have stood and apologized on behalf of the church.

We, unfortunately, do not have the habit of repenting as a collective body. Our repentance is solely focused on our own personal sin. We do not have the vision to see that even the church participates in systemic evil. There are those who are hurt by the church, a denomination, or even a local church. Yes, often these relational sins are committed by individuals. But when such individuals are representatives of the church of Jesus Christ by their association and their faith, others may need to repent on behalf of the whole. One area the Holiness movement bears responsibility for is the religious abuse suffered by countless people under our period of legalism. There is much there that needs corresponding repentance. Ultimately it is the Spirit that brings about the conviction needed that should lead to our Spirit-aided and Spirit-guided repentance.

3. The Spirit Regenerates the Church

The Spirit applies God's redemptive work through Christ to the individual. Individuals who repent and have faith experience new birth; they are new creations, where the old has passed away and the new has come. John Wesley championed the doctrine of regeneration and reminded his people that there was a powerful freedom from sin when persons were made new. He feared a focus on sanctification, entire sanctification in particular, would downplay the fierce work of God done in the heart of a new believer. The church is, of course, synonymous with the regenerate. But we can say more.

The church as a whole is regenerated by God. To generate, to birth, is to bring to life. The church is regenerated in two ways. First, it was the Spirit on the day of Pentecost that enacted the birth of the church. The Spirit was poured out in a way unprecedented in the history of humanity. While the

Spirit has always existed, and has always been working in the world, particularly through prevenient grace, at Pentecost the Spirit was given in a new way. And one of the primary results was the very birth of the church of Jesus Christ. The Spirit came to indwell persons and unite persons into a collective whole. Evidence of this is found in how such persons interacted with each other and with the world. The Spirit gave birth to the church, the same church that exists today.

But we can say more. The Spirit continues to regenerate the church. The Spirit continues to make her new—not just as new individual persons join the church—but as a collective whole, the church is continuously regenerated. This comes as she repents, and as God forgives the whole. The church, across the two thousand year history, has failed God in very significant ways, particularly in her misrepresentation of who God is. But God loves her still. She remains the bride, despite her "spotted" character and her outright sins. God continues to forgive, regenerate, renew, and sustain her. God also continues to sanctify her.

4. The Spirit Sanctifies the Church

The Holy Spirit enables the liberating work of God, which finds fulfillment in sanctification and holy living through perfect love. We believe that we are new creations in Christ, that the old has passed away and the new will come. But further, we believe that the Holy Spirit sanctifies believers, initially, progressively, entirely, and finally. We believe it is more than possible to grow in our ability to express the holy love of God to our neighbors as ourselves, that we grow in our ability to love God with our whole being, and we believe that this infilling of love, through the presence of the Holy Spirit, "excludes sin" (Wesley). This is a liberating work that heals the dis-ease of sin and empowers us for sacrificial living.[6] The Holy Spirit can indeed make our attitudes the same as Christ Jesus, who emptied himself (kenosis) "of all but love." This is a very brief description of God's sanctifying work in the lives of individuals. But what does it mean to say that God, through the Spirit, sanctifies the church?

It certainly means that it is God who makes her holy. The church cannot sanctify herself, but we can speak of a collective purity and power that characterizes her. The Spirit purifies the church from sin. The Spirit can also empower the church to live to its full potential. The Spirit can enable the church to live as Christ lived and to fulfill the two greatest commandments. The holy love of God is meant to be manifest in the life of the church as it cares for each member. It is the work of the Spirit that makes the church one, or unified. The church enjoys the "fellowship" of the Holy Spirit when the church expresses its essence and purpose in worship, preaching, the sacraments, and ministry and in obedience to Christ and mutual accountability. The Holy Spirit is fully immersed in the sanctifying practices and functions of church life. The worship of God is aided by the Spirit, and the Spirit's presence is assured to be in the midst of those gathered in Christ. The whole act of preaching—from text to sermon and delivery—is done by the inspiration, guidance, and presence of the Holy Spirit. Any form of ministry in which the church invests finds fruit only as the Spirit brings it to fruition. Obedience to Christ is possible through the enabling work of the Spirit. Mutual accountability is more than a human endeavor. It is a means of grace. All means of grace are efficacious through the work of the Spirit, particularly the sacraments. The means of grace are sanctifying. The Spirit sanctifies the church as it loves within its walls, so to speak. But sanctification goes further. It also expresses holy love to the world.

A second key aspect of sanctification is that the church is set apart for a particular purpose: the Holy Spirit reminds us of the reality and potentiality of the redemptive work of Christ on earth, through the church; an ethos of embodied empowerment drenched with social optimism should inspire our future. In the words of H. Richard Niebuhr, we as a denomination are called to transform culture, not isolate ourselves from it. The wonder of the Wesleyan Revival and the American Holiness movement was that they were somehow enabled to maintain holiness standards without withdrawing from society; indeed, they were fully engaged in social issues and actually believed they could make a difference as God's agents of compassion, mercy, and justice in the world.[7] More recently, we have done well on the side of evangelism, missionary work, and even compassionate ministries. And yet when it comes to issues of social justice, particularly as North Americans, we have long forgotten our heritage. A spirit of social conservatism has replaced our passion for engaged, embodied, redemptive work, work that used to arise out of our grace-filled optimism. As we have become a mainly white, suburban church in North America, we hardly have contact with those our denomination was created to touch. This is not a new critique. But the question remains, do we believe that as we depend on the Spirit for gracious empowerment there is hope for real societal change? Do we believe the church as a collective whole can change the world? Or do we simply await our escape from a hopeless, "God-forsaken" world? Do we fully understand that God is still omnipresent in the person of the Holy Spirit and will not abandon what has been created? Indeed, God's purposes are to make all things new, including all persons and all of creation. As the church is sanctified she fulfills the grand *missio Dei*. Fulfilling her purpose is made possible always through the Spirit of the living God.

5. The Spirit Reveals God to and through the Church

When it comes to truth "as it is in Jesus," it is important to note that tradition in general, and Wesley in particular, has always emphasized that God reveals truth to the church as a whole. From the earliest writings of Scripture and the creeds, through the seven ecumenical councils and beyond, the Spirit has chosen to reveal Christ's truth through the collective body. Likewise, down through the centuries, even if one person heard the voice of God, it has most often been required that such a revelation must be affirmed by the church. Even a person such as Martin Luther, the primary person who brought about the Protestant Reformation seemingly single-handedly, had his beliefs about *sola fide* confirmed by other groups. If Luther's concerns for the church were not also echoed by others, his single voice would have had little effect.

John Wesley is very clear that revelation comes through the community. Scripture's parts were affirmed as canon by a group. Each ecumenical council was made up of many persons. Their creeds were seen as statements of *"we believe."* Thus Scripture and tradition represent, for Wesley, the truth of the collective whole of the church. Even when Wesley began to affirm the truth that can come from experience, he was quick and strong to point out that the experience to which he referred was the experience of the group, not of a single individual. We may be tempted to listen to individuals' claims that God has spoken directly to them, particularly when our view of Christianity focuses on individual faith. But many scholars today, following Wesley, are stating that we must be extremely cautious about such truth claims. Some have gone so far as to say that an individual should never interpret Scripture in isolation from the church.[8] The Spirit has chosen to reveal God through community most often. This does not mean that prophets aren't raised up at certain times in certain places to challenge a community of faith. God has had to use such corrective measures. But for the most part, the church as a whole is where God has posited truth.

It is the church as a whole that experiences the Spirit's conviction, regeneration, and sanctification as well. It is in the church that the Spirit reveals the God who calls her by name. And it is through the church that God reveals Godself to the world. As Christ is lifted up, the Spirit draws all persons to God. We anticipate a time when all is fulfilled.

Questions for Discussion
1. What does the Holy Spirit do in the lives of individuals?
2. Why is it important to emphasize the full personality of the Holy Spirit?
3. How does a theology of the Holy Spirit help us combat a pessimistic worldview?
4. What is meant by the phrase "the soteriology of the church"?
5. Why is it important to say that the Holy Spirit convicts the church of sin, regenerates the church, and sanctifies the church?

Suggestions for Further Reading
Dayton, Donald. *Discovering an Evangelical Heritage*. New York: Harper and Row, 1976.

Leclerc, Diane. *Discovering Christian Holiness*. Kansas City: Beacon Hill Press of Kansas City, 2010.

Shelton, Larry, and Alex Deasley, eds. *The Spirit and the New Age*. Anderson, IN: Warner Press, 1986.

Stokes, Mark B. *The Holy Spirit in the Wesleyan Heritage*. Nashville: Abingdon Press, 1993.

six
TRADITION AT ITS BEST
THE CLASSICAL MARKS OF THE CHURCH

Tim J. Crutcher

Introduction

The church found itself thinking about its identity and its nature from the very beginning of its existence. The first documents of what we now call the New Testament were written as letters to churches to help them figure out who they were and how they were to act. One of the gospel writers, Luke, even creates a "volume two" to his gospel, extending the narrative of Jesus into the earliest life of the church, as if the story of the church were somehow a continuation of the story of Jesus. New realities foisted new developments on the church as it early had to learn to organize itself (as it did by ordaining what we might call "deacons" in Acts 6) and deal with disagreements among its members (as it did with the so-called Jerusalem Council in Acts 15). It quickly became clear that the followers of Jesus were not going to be accepted as Jews, and the Romans weren't crazy about them either. And so the question of the church's identity was a matter of some urgency as Jesus' followers tried to figure out who they were in relation to each other and in relation to a world and culture that didn't know what to do with them and that handled that confusion violently as often as not.

As these reflections continued over the course of the next few centuries, a few ideas kept resurfacing. As various Christian writers and thinkers reflected on the nature of the church through its various internal and external struggles, consistent themes emerged that gave the church some broadly recognized anchors for its self-reflection. Through the fourth century, these reflections crystalized into a list of four identifying marks, attributed to the church by the Council of Constantinople in CE 381 and articulated in the Nicene-Constantinopolitan Creed (more commonly referred to as just the Nicene Creed). Those marks, distillations of three centuries of serious reflection by the church on its own nature and character, were articulated like this: "We believe in One, Holy, Catholic and Apostolic Church." It is our purpose here to briefly explore what each of those identifying marks means.

One

One early and consistent affirmation to arise out of the Scripture and be picked up by the writers and thinkers of the earliest church was the idea that the church was one. Drawing on the affirmations of Jesus (e.g., John 17:11) and Paul (e.g., 1 Cor. 12:12-14; Eph. 4:4-6), early Christian writers proclaimed that the church, by its very nature, was something of which there could only be one. If you start counting churches, you get to one, and then you stop. The church is united quantitatively, meaning that all who participate in church participate in the same, singular reality. Consequently, anything that threatened the unity of the church was seen as threatening the very being of the church.

The early church quickly recognized that the unity of the church was a function of its grounding in Jesus Christ. There was only one church because there was only "one Lord, one faith, one baptism; one God and Father of all" (Eph. 4:5-6). In fact, the statement in the Nicene Creed that introduces the church is parallel to the statements that introduce God ("We believe in *one* God") and Jesus Christ ("And in *one* Lord Jesus Christ"). Just as we believe in one God and one Lord, we believe in one church. Note, too, that the language of "believing in" connotes trust and not just the acknowledgment of some truth. An equally valid way of translating the creed would be to say that we trust in one God, in one Lord, in the Holy Spirit and in one church.

The early church also saw this oneness of the church revealed in the best biblical metaphors for church. In his earthly life, Christ only had one body, so there can be only one continuation of that body in the church. At his second coming, Christ will have the church as his one bride. Multiple churches would make Christ a polygamist! The oneness of the church was thus affirmed as a "derivative reality," one that flowed from God's reality and the nature of God's relationship to the world down into our own reality and experience. The church's oneness depended on the oneness of God and on the uniqueness of the incarnation. That also meant that this oneness did *not* depend on the oneness of its members. It was not the case that the church created unity by its doctrinal agreement or commonality of practice, a unity that would not exist in the absence of those things. Rather, the assumption of unity as a God-given gift was what motivated the early church to seek whatever level of commonality was necessary to display that unity to the world.

Still, as a sign of the church's unity—though not causes of it—the boundary lines between good and helpful doctrine and destructive ideas were very important to nearly all of the early church's leaders and thinkers. People who would hold certain ideas in a way that hampered the church's ability to live out its God-given unity were seen as a greater problem than those sporadic persecutions that merely ended up giving the church a chance to testify to the superiority of its Lord and Savior over the emperor. In practice this meant that there was a broad acceptance of many differing points of view in the early church on a whole array of doctrines, so long as those ideas did not cause schism or fracture. This was particularly true early on when the church was still sorting through which ideas worked to promote its life with God and which ones might hamper it. However, once the church discovered an idea or set of ideas that threatened the expressed unity of its fellowship, it clearly opposed them. Where no reconciliation was possible, most early church writers opted for believing that those who held divisive ideas had actually stepped outside the boundary lines of the one true church rather than believe that somehow the church itself could be split.

Holy

The second affirmation that the church makes about itself in the creed is that we believe in a "holy" church. This assertion may seem naive—even outright false—to many folks whose experience of church has been less than ideal. This happens because we often take the claim to be a validation of the activity of the church's members (as in "We are acting on behalf of the church, therefore what we are doing is holy"). This is not at all what the church fathers were saying, nor would the struggles we have with an imperfectly performing church have been foreign to the leaders and thinkers of that early church.

While we often use the word *holy* to refer to moral purity or sinlessness, we must remember that that is only a secondary meaning of the word. The original word in the creed is the descriptive form of a word that refers to religious awe or reverence, the attitude that recognizes the divine as above and beyond us, the divine as Other. In the strict sense, then, only the divine, only God, *is* holy; but the word can also be used of persons or things that have been set apart exclusively for God's use. To affirm something as "holy" in the ancient world was to affirm that it belonged to God alone, that only God could use it or that it was only to be used in God's service. Of course, if one has set something apart for God's exclusive use, then it ought also to be pure or spotless or blameless or the like. So the moral quality of holiness immediately comes along for the ride, but only because we think that anything less would be unworthy of the divine.

What the early church recognized about itself, then, was the fact that the church belonged to its Lord and to that Lord alone. In fact, the very word we use in English to refer to this reality, the word *church*, is derived from the Greek word *kyriakos*, meaning "belonging to the Lord." To say that we believe in a "holy church," then, is to say that everything the church is and should be doing is directed only by God. The church, then, is not a social organization or a self-help society or club designed to promote the best interests of its members. What the church is, at its very core, is that community that has its exclusive focus on God, a focus that also directs us to God's work in the world.

As a community designed by God to focus its attention on God and, through that, to draw other people's attention to God as well, the church is expected to behave in a way that reflects God's nature and character. But the priority here is important. The church is expected to live "holily" because it is "holy." It is not the case that the church's holy living is what makes it holy. The exclusive focus on God is God's gracious gift to the church; it is not something the church achieves on its own merit. Holy people do not come together and thus form a holy church. God creates a holy church in order to extend God's kingdom throughout the world, and because of that, those who participate in that church can become people exclusively devoted to God's service as well.

Of course, this does not mean that all of those who have been called into the church have already been adequately shaped into effective agents and examples of God's love and grace, but it does mean that that shaping is part and parcel of what it means to be the church and to be part of the church. As many early writers of the church would have affirmed, if one isn't interested in becoming more like God and better able to reflect God's character to the world, then one really isn't interested in being a part of what the church is all about.

Catholic

The word *catholic* bothers some Protestants because they only associate it with that part of the church they know as the Roman Catholic Church. In fact, in some Protestant versions of the Nicene Creed, the word *catholic* is replaced by the word *universal* or *Christian*. Neither of those words, however, says what the early church fathers wanted to convey by asserting that the church is catholic, and so it is probably better to clear up the misunderstandings surrounding the word and use it rather than try to find another word that might leave some of its important meaning out.

The word *catholic* is not a biblical term but is one the church developed in order to capture a biblical idea. It comes from the Greek phrase *kath' holou*, which literally translated means "according to the whole." So, where the mark of "oneness" refers to the church's quantitative unity, the "catholicity" of the church refers to its qualitative unity, its wholeness. Quantity and quality are, of course, not the same; one could, for example, have only one apple but it not be a whole apple. Therefore, the church wanted to affirm that the church was not just one, it was also whole. Everywhere the church was locally expressed, it was expressed in its totality. Likewise, every local expression of the church was to be understood "according to the whole," as a part of something that derived its significance from the larger reality it participated in. It was these ideas of the wholeness of every local church and also its interconnectedness with every other church that the church was trying to express with the term *catholic*.

To say that each church was a complete church was to say that each local expression of church expressed the whole of what it meant to be church. There was, in the minds of the early church fathers, no such thing as "half a church." However small, however composed, no gathering of believers focused on Christ was anything less than a full expression of Christ's body, knitted together in the Spirit, doing God's work in the world. It meant that all the resources for being church were available from God's uniting Spirit and did not depend on the various talents and abilities of individual members. All gifting and gracing for the work of the church came from the Spirit anyway. If the church needed leadership or any other empowerment for ministry, then it was assumed that what was needed was present. Again, this wholeness derived from God and was a gift to God's church; it was never something the church needed to work to achieve.

This view of catholicity did not mean, however, that each church was independent from all the others—quite the contrary! Each local church could express the totality of the body of Christ because each was integrally interconnected with that larger body. Each was part of a whole larger than itself. This interconnectedness was very important to the early Christians, and they symbolized it by sharing Communion, by praying for those other churches of which they were aware, and by displaying their unity in a geographical area under the leadership of a single bishop. Another expression of this qualitative unity was the popularity of stories about the martyrs, which were written as much to encourage the faith of those living as to celebrate the witness of the one who died. These martyrs were never seen as just expressions of the faithfulness of one particular locality (as in, "Wow, those Christians in Smyrna really are dedicated"). They were, in a sense, owned by the entire church. "This is us, all of us," the writers of these stories claimed. As with Paul's body of Christ metaphor, when one part suffers, the whole suffers. But when one part rejoices, the whole rejoices. That interplay of part and whole was part and parcel of what it meant to be a catholic church.

Apostolic

When the word *apostolic* is applied to churches today in Protestant circles, it is normally used to assert that this particular church is—or at least is trying to be—a so-called New Testament church, a church like the church of the apostles. Some leaders of these churches will even take the title of "apostle" for themselves, trying to say something about the immediacy of their connection to God and God's Word much like the original apostles would have had. While the association with the New Testament church is one of the major ideas the church had in mind when it first used this word all those centuries ago, there is one critical difference between the way the word is heard today and the way they intended it. Nowadays, when Protestants say they want a New Testament church, what is usually meant is that they want to jump back over nearly two thousand years of church history and get back to the way things were originally. So, in that frame of reference, an "apostolic church" would be a church that somehow managed to escape the centuries of tradition between the present day and first-century Palestine. That is certainly not what the word meant when the early church fathers settled on it as a mark of the church three hundred years after the time of the apostles.

In a world where many people were offering many different interpretations of the Scriptures about Christ, what it meant to be a follower of Christ and what Christ's ministry accomplished, the church realized that one—though certainly not the only—of its best measuring rods was the constancy of church tradition. If a new idea came on the scene and one could see that that idea did not trace its historical lineage back to those first followers of Christ—at least in embryo if not in a mature form—then such an idea was seen as suspect. It was the continuous tradition of trying to interpret Christ's life and then live it out that provided the church's main reference point when it came to guiding its thought and its ongoing interpretation of the Scripture. Therefore, it was precisely this intervening history that was important to them when they affirmed that the church was apostolic. The church was that group of people who could trace their historic roots from the present day right back to those original Galilean fishermen, Zealots, and tax collectors. It was continuity in history—not the ability to jump back over history as if it didn't happen—that showed the church for what it was. The one, holy, and catholic church was also the church that inherited the tradition first laid down by the apostles. Anything else couldn't be the church.

In addition to looking backward to its founding in the past, the mark of apostolicity invited the church to look at the present and the future and its mission to the world. Those first disciples of Christ were called "apostles" after Pentecost because the word means "one who is sent out." In anchoring its historical identity in the persons of the apostles, the church was also reminding itself that it existed to fulfill that original mission. Everywhere the one, holy, catholic church was found, it was to be continuing the apostolic mission of making disciples, even to the ends of the earth. A church that isn't interested in being sent out by Christ into the world isn't really interested in being church.

Conclusion

"We believe in one, holy, catholic, and apostolic Church." By saying that, the Council of Constantinople—and everyone who recites the creed from that time on—was affirming that we place our trust in that single continuation of Christ's incarnation that God designed as God's agent in the world, knit together through the work of the Holy Spirit, interconnected with one another, historically linked back to Jesus' original followers, and continuing the mission of those followers into the world. While there certainly are many other things that can and should be said about the church, these are the affirmations that rose to the top first. But while they do not say everything that needs to be said about the church, they do say a lot. When the church ignores these marks of its identity, tries to live as if all followers of Christ are not united, for example, or allows its focus to fall on something other than reflecting God's nature into the world and working for God's mission, it certainly suffers. On the other hand, a church that truly strives to live out the grace given to it to be one, holy, catholic, and apostolic will certainly make a difference, both in the lives of its individual members and also in the world. All in all, that's not a bad place to start.

Questions for Discussion

1. All of these marks of the church derive from the church's relationship to God (the church is one because God is one; the church is holy because God is holy, etc.). What are the practical consequences of saying that the church's identity is rooted in God rather than in the values or orientations of its members? How does that affect things like the church's worship, its educational work, or its missionary activity?

2. The anchoring of the church's identity in God also raises the question of how the members of the church treat their God-given "church identity" in relationship to their other identities—identities rooted in family, culture, or nation. How should our attempts to live out our oneness, holiness, catholicity, and apostolicity be related to the other identities that form our lives?

3. Given that the church is supposed to be one and catholic—quantitatively and qualitatively united—how important are the various efforts (usually labeled "ecumenical") to bring churches of different

denominations together? How important are things like agreement in doctrine or commonality in practice? How ought the church to deal with the fact that its members do not always agree?

4. Identifying the church has "holy" has implications for the way we talk about holiness among its members. As John Wesley himself noted, "There is no holiness which is not social holiness." What are the implications of recognizing that this quality we call "holiness" is rooted in the community and extends to its members (as opposed to seeing it as an individual quality first)?

Suggestions for Further Reading

Many books on the church will use the four marks of the church in organizing some or all of their material, but here are a few references for those who want to delve deeper into the issues raised in this chapter.

>Gaillardetz, Richard. *Ecclesiology for a Global Church: A People Called and Sent*. Maryknoll, NY: Orbis, 2008. This book contains good and sustained reflections on catholicity and apostolicity.
>
>Lathrop, Gordon, and Timothy Wengert. *Christian Assembly: Marks of the Church in a Pluralistic Age*. Minneapolis: Fortress, 2004. This book has an overview of the history of the marks of the church and extends the discussion through the Lutheran tradition into the present day.
>
>Madges, William, and Michael Daley, eds. *The Many Marks of the Church*. New London, CT: Twenty-Third Publications, 2006. The first section of this book contains two contrasting essays on each of the four classical marks of the church, each other wrestling with a different aspect of their meaning.
>
>Oden, Thomas. *Systematic Theology*, vol. 3, *Life in the Spirit*. New York: HarperCollins, 1994. In the long chapter on the church, this book contains essays on each of the classical marks of the church, along with copious quotations and references to the early church sources, making it an excellent resource for learning about the marks in the original context in which they were elucidated.

seven
CULTURAL CORRELATION
THE "POSTMODERN" MARKS OF THE CHURCH

Deirdre Brower Latz

I think it interesting that in a section relating to the core of the church, the editors asked for a chapter on "postmodern" marks of the church. Do such marks exist? Are they or can they possibly be core to the church? Should they be? In what way do such marks (if they can be seen to exist) reflect a Wesleyan ecclesiological stance?

In order to consider adequately these questions, there are several angles that need to be explored. First, what does postmodernism have to do with the church? Surely, if the previous chapters are correct (the church is always shaped in ways that reflect the kingdom, the triune God, ways that are christological and pneumatological), surely then there are marks of the church that resonate through time and history. I do think, however, that (without prejudging what the other contributors are saying) in the realm of Wesleyan ecclesiology there are any number of realities at work that shape and form the church. But one such reality is that the church as we know and experience it is always located, always particular. And, as such, it is always engaged in the processes and realities, of being the church within an environment that we understand to be culture—or, more rightly, cultures. Complementing those elements delineated in the earlier chapters as marks of the church, there is a profound need for the church to be who she is in the present tense.[1]

The church, then—for all of its purposeful self-understanding, all of its Spirit-driven and Spirit-led mission, all of its historical richness—is always discovering how to be who she is in relation to the present/real world around her. That is, as relating to the culture. Richard Niebuhr's classic understanding of this (most recently elucidated in the Reformed tradition by Timothy Keller in his *Center Church*) argues carefully that Christ, and thus the church, relate to the culture in a number of ways and that the church ranges in its relation to culture from rejection to absorption/assimilation, or to transformation, with stopping places in between.[2]

For those in the Wesleyan tradition—with our profound reliance on an optimism of grace, an understanding of the way the Spirit works in, through, and beyond the church in what we know of as justifying, sanctifying, and prevenient grace; with a sacramental theology (that is, God-with-us in material, embodied ways); with an understanding of holiness as contagious, corporate, *and* personal—the attitude of relation to the culture seems clear: we cooperate with God who is at work in and around us. The co-laboring of the people of God (also referred to as co-creativity as agents of grace, etc.) within the world means that the Wesleyan stance toward culture is not rejecting it, nor assimilation within it, but is profoundly hopeful toward it as a type of *via media*. With Wesleyan theology as the starting point, my claim is that the cultural correlation[3] that Wesleyans undertake is one of engaging with culture.[4] Certainly Wesley's own way of engaging with culture—making inquiries of it with a genuine stance of curiosity and openness toward it—stands in the background.

This middle ground, this *via media*, of Wesleyan theology's approach to culture is one that leads to tension for the church. At points, the Wesleyan stance means that adopting the ways of culture to effectively communicate the gospel is a given (e.g., the Wesley brothers adopting public house tunes for their hymns, setting their catechism to music that would be memorable and understandable to their converts). At other points the Wesleyan stance prophetically confronts a received truth within culture (e.g., John Wesley engaging with John Bennet the Quaker and William Wilberforce MP regarding slavery). Discerning which points of culture to engage with and which points to stand against is not easy—the idea of cultural correlation becomes an area of profound wrestling—and typically, such wrestling means that the people of God can discover themselves maimed and limping. But before we decide how to engage culture, we must first ask, as the church, what culture do we find ourselves in today?

Postmodern, hypermodern, late modern are all descriptors for the tenor and trajectory of (some) culture(s) in the beginning of the twenty-first century. I want to be quite careful here, for my contention would be that not everyone is postmodern and that some definitions of postmodernism are better than others at depicting what is at the heart of quite a complex phenomenon. Furthermore, I am yet to be persuaded *against* the view that postmodernism is a luxury that is related (somewhat) to wealth, education, opportunity, consumerism, and access to globalized technologies that serve as a vehicle for ideas that form and shape the world. Nevertheless, assuming that there is *something* that undergirds some of the cultural trends, *some* idea or concept that shapes the world we live in, whether or not we are conscious of it, and some truth to postmodern thinking, how should the church relate or correlate with it? This is a question that does and should occupy those of us located in the settings described above as most likely to be "postmodern." Are there ways in which the church can correlate to postmodernism and are there ways in which the church must not? Why is this important?

I would contend that for most of the church in North America, Northern and Western Europe, and in parts of Asia-Pacific (Australia/New Zealand), and for church leaders almost anywhere educated within the last forty years (or so) in a university setting influenced by the US/UK systems, there are some elements of postmodernism that have been imbibed. This is obviously a generalization! Postmodernism as a cultural phenomenon is uneven, and yet, it appears to be here to stay, and its influence on our children and our children's children seems deeply rooted. That means that we ignore postmodern ideas at our peril and must give careful attention to how we relate to them, and how, within the church, we embrace, absorb, or reject them. We can engage postmodernism with a confidence located in God, and with the capacity we are given, by the Spirit at work within us, to discern ways we can (and should) engage with postmodernism and be shaped by it and ways we must disengage or prophetically speak against it. This is a significant task for those of us leading and forming Christians within the church, and, indeed, for the community of faith.

The cultural elements of postmodernism are really an abstraction. There are descriptions that can be given, but they vary from place to place, author to author, philosopher to philosopher. Yet the reality of postmodernism affects us. The descriptions below are mere caricatures when compared to the complex realities they represent; descriptions act merely as signposts.[5] Some caveats may also be helpful. First, I am suggesting the ideas below more as cud to chew on, and then chew on some more, rather than as facts to be implemented without consideration. Second, for all of the elements I outline below, it seems to me there is a "yes, but" that could be presented as almost equal and opposite. I am choosing to suspend the latter in order to outline some ways in which I think postmodern thought *can* help enable the church—some points of sympathy if you like, where if we listen closely to the culture we may find our eyes open in new ways to some fresh insights for the sake of the gospel; and so, these points are more hints than marks, shades than colors, ellipses than full stops. Third, there are points where what I am suggesting should probably provoke a "but this is perennial" response. That is, the church has always thought of *correlation* as important. I agree. At those points, however, I am suggesting that the "postmodern" mark brings a renewed emphasis or subtly nuanced perspective to the situation, and thus is helpful in the "translation" of the gospel to the contemporary situation. In this sense a primary "mark" of the church is this need for *cultural correlation*. If we accept that postmodernism is our culture, we will then find ways of correlation—of searching the culture, engaging the culture, relating to culture, rebounding from culture, chastening culture, and (at points) being chastened by culture. Correlation may mean that there are even some areas where postmodern thinking may well have something to teach the church.[6] What could be considered other "postmodern marks" of the church?

Postmodern Marks of the Church

1. Within postmodern thinking there is an emphasis on the "**linguistic turn.**" Language is now described as both helpful and limited[7]; it is in some ways adequate to the task of talking about God but is always seen as limited, fragmentary, and pointing toward that which cannot be comprehensively understood. The shift toward an emphasis on unknowing, uncertainty, mystery, and silence can be a valuable contributor to militating against an over-certain and under-nuanced understanding of God. This same move, toward an awareness of the complexity of language and away from the tendency toward compartmentalization, also means that it is perfectly possible for language to be both a barrier and a bridge—the importance of grappling with this

postmodern aspect of culture means that listening and epistemic humility become important. In other words, postmoderns will only listen to a gospel that reflects these.

2. **Close, attentive, and reflective listening**—to culture itself, to the other, to the marginalized and the outsider, to the elder and the younger—all become increasingly important as a mark of the church. The capacity to truly engage and truly hear what the other is saying (including, of course, God) becomes possible only because of the art of listening.[8] Such a move requires silence, presence, and embodiment and is a reflection of the way the church may truly become a mediator of God-who-is-love, whose first words were the inarticulate cry of an infant, and who is the final Word expressed in kenosis.

3. The **epistemic humility** that accompanies such listening is a learned posture not easy for the church birthed in modernism's demand for confidence and objective truth that has been expressed by the church at times as rigid concepts of dogma and orthodoxy. The posture of humility as it extends to conversation, listening, and forming lives finds itself wrestling with formerly taken for granted assumptions of faith and life. It also recognizes the truth that humans *always already* interpret text and have a frame of understanding. This mitigates against a sense that *my* truth is "pure" or "objective"; rather, it is seen as formed by my own socioeconomic context. Such humility delights in genuine exploration and perspectives that open the world to alternate explanations. *But*, such epistemic humility need not be nihilistic, nor without form. The form is often a deep grasping of the divide between Creator and creatureliness and a subjugation of certainty to the possibility of mystery, uncertainty and yet, still faith. A deep faith (if you like) that recognizes—with hope—that we "see through a glass, darkly." This humility is profoundly hopeful and mindful of the gap between the already and the not yet.[9]

4. This emphasis on *ways* of understanding is also supported by the postmodern mark that emphasizes the possibility of two horizons for understanding[10] or the **"the fusion of horizons."**[11] The theologies at work when attending to the various elements that form and shape engagement with Scripture and the world of the reader are seen as nuanced, reflective, carefully attentive to the settings of both. Additionally, these elements become attuned to the different theological voices at work themselves. Various theologies (the espoused theology: "the theology embedded within *a group's articulation of its beliefs*"; the normative theology: "Scriptures, the creeds, official church

teaching, liturgies"; the formal theology: "the theology of theologians" and "dialogue with other disciplines"; and the operant theology: "the theology embedded within *the actual practices of a group*"[12]) are all attended to—and the Christian reflects on the multifaceted and dynamic realities of grappling with the Living Word.[13]

5. Of course, such an approach to life, such an emphasis, points toward a further "mark." That is, the **willingness to question,** to "deconstruct." Such an approach enables deep truths to be arrived at, the questions of what we do (pragmatic) engaged with the questions of why we do what we do (practice) and the possible outcome of re-formation, or reenchantment with *who* we are and *how* what we do reflects who we believe ourselves to be. This question of espousing a belief and the practice of the church is one that confronts us at every point. The challenge of deconstruction is the perception that at the end of deconstruction is nothing. The reality may be the converse—deconstruction as embraced by postmoderns enables espoused theology to meet the gritty reality of practical theology and be refined into a holy wisdom; this wisdom sees the need for reengagement with practices that are Christlike-forming—that is, form us into Christ's likeness—and the rejection of practices that have seeped in and may destroy.[14]

6. This possibility of reengagement, retelling, or **reenchantment** is a further mark of postmodernism. By this I mean the possibility of a renewed playful stance that reconnects story with imagination, faith with feeling, and hope with reality. It seems that for all the bad press postmodernism has received, the possibility of a revitalized faith is almost tantalizingly present. Such a faith, however, demands a deep renewal of what it means to be whole, or fully human. The vision of the good life and the possibility of a life marked by wisdom and inhabited by God-who-is-love seems alluring to postmodern culture. The question postmodern culture then asks the church is: is your vision of the good life, of wisdom, and of wholeness compelling? The gospeler's response is "yes"—for Christ is good news. The retelling of that good news is a further demand made upon the church by the postmodern turn.

Story, storytelling, and the rediscovery of *truth as discovered through narrative* is a further aspect of the mark of reenchantment in its postmodern influence upon the church. Hand in hand with the possibility of reenchantment with the gospel is recognition that story acts upon humans to shape and form them with a power that is undisguisable. The reading of Scripture as a narrative and the interpretation of it within narrative is powerful, and the importance of teaching through parable and poetics resonates with postmodern thinkers and culture. From narrative preaching, to film and TV, from blogs and books to Facebook and Google Plus, the narrative arc helps people locate themselves in relation to the world around them. The compelling story is matched by a sense of quest—for meaning, reality, *home*.

7. This sense of at-oneness seems to point to a further mark of postmodern hope.[15] That is, **the return to virtue**—an understanding that the question "how should I live my life?" directs the questioner at one and the same time to being shaped by practices that will form him or her ethically, and to the need for authentic relationships that will teach the way. This recurring note sounded within postmodern thinking is useful as a marker for the church in the sense that *phronesis* (practical wisdom) and *sapentia* (wisdom) are vital for faith. That is, faith is a lived-out and practiced expression of wisdom and an affective and beauty-forming wisdom that shapes reality and develops in real everyday life. The vision, then, for the good life, is one that denotes that such understanding is not automatic for humans but needs to be embodied, practiced, and passed on. This resonates with the premodern tradition.

This reality of *embodiment*—learning virtue, being "clothed" in righteousness, practiced and transmitted, handed over, and handed down—is a further dynamic of postmodern markers on the life of the church. The quest of personhood is matched by the *quest for community* that is simultaneously and paradoxically manifest in both tribalism (*our* community) and diversity (our *community*). The role of the Christ-formed community in interpreting Scripture is vital. The historical role of the Christ-formed community in shaping creed and church is drawn upon. The present role of the Christ-formed community as a people practicing life together as wise together is emphasized. And to the global Christ-formed community questioning and sharpening, the marginalized and outside voices speak and call the Christ-formed community to justice and to its senses; such is vitally important here. The open-handed community that welcomes all—from the least, the outcast, the widow, the orphan, the alien (in whatever forms these take culturally) to the most worldly-wise is a formidable representation of the body of Christ. The Christ-formed people of the community that live out their lives visibly alongside each other; thus challenging and shaping, grating and dreaming, diverse and uniquely compelling is the call made upon the church in a new way by postmoderns. The phrases of challenge handed on to the church in new ways[16] (e.g., "don't tell me what you believe, I will watch your life and tell you what you believe" or "if I saw people practicing the Sermon on the Mount, I would know they were followers of Jesus") are exercising as a marker drawn for the church; the call from those outside the church to the church to be the Christ-formed community she should be is startling and evocative. Likewise, within the church herself there are myriad of authors calling to the church to return to some ideal (or another): in the US from Keller, Jones, and McLaren to UK-based Cray, Murray, Tomlin, and Tomlinson, from the Australian/US context of Frost and Hirsh (to name but a few) there are a plethora of voices holding out a vision for a new kind of community. Often an element of this community is its centered-setness. That is, the strong core that holds the vision that is compelling and welcomes those on a fuzzy edge—sinners are welcome here as friends first, then companions, then as "us."

The "us" of this kind of community leads to a further element—*a renewed holistic care*; first, for self (in the form of Sabbath, work in its place, love and balance), then for others (the family, the fictive family and the other, the least and the last) and then for the world (its creation, its people, its being).[17] Such a triad of emphases is profoundly connected to the narrative sweep of Scripture, to an understanding of the world as potentially profoundly good, and to God's project as restorative not destructive. This then speaks, too, to the eschatological predilection of the postmodern mark of the kingdom—the already inaugurated kingdom and the not yet fully realized kingdom that will restore the world to wholeness in every dimension. This leads to a practice and an approach that calls for the church to be a prophetic and just community.

The mark of the church as a *community of justice*, then, aligning herself with God's desires for the world and for *shalom* in all its dynamic reality, is a perennial part of Christlike community; however, it is brought into a nuanced expression as part of the marks of the postmodern upon the church. Such an approach should always lean toward a suspicion of authority that oppresses, or dominates the landscape, and a desire to decouple the church from power in all its forms.[18] The realities of the church's relation to powers (small p) and the polis and politics of her age (small p again) are alive, and the challenge to the church to *reconsider her primary allegiance* and citizenship is a profound one. The need for the church to explore her failures, repent, confess, and keep check on her own real desires are increasingly part of the postmodern voice speaking to the church.

The church and cultural correlation, then, is controverted. I maintain in this chapter that the church *must* correlate to the culture it finds itself in. In fact, it can do no other; this is in keeping with Wesleyan ecclesiology as it plays out in the twenty-first century. However, the manner of this correlation must be dynamic, alert, open, and discerning. The culture at hand in this chapter is postmodern. I have chosen, however, to relate the church and postmodern culture as friendly dialogue partners—shaping and being shaped, engaging and being engaged. By the power of the Spirit I believe the church in the Wesleyan tradition can and should and must engage with postmodern elements—and furthermore, that the church in our tradition will, by so doing, discover herself enriched, revitalized, and reinvigorated as able participants and agents of change for the sake of Christ in the twenty-first century.

Questions for Discussion

1. In what ways does a Wesleyan ecclesiology engage cultural correlation as a means of discernment?

2. In what ways does Wesleyan theology engage in a postmodern culture? What are examples of adopting cultural norms to communicate the gospel?

3. As Christians, in what ways can we practice attentive listening, humility, and questioning as we are attentive to the culture?

4. In what ways does the church engage as a friendly dialogue partner with postmodern culture?

5. In what ways can the church retell Scripture through storytelling and narrative to shape and form persons?

Suggestions for Further Reading

Akkerman, Jay Richard, Thomas J. Oord, and Brent D. Peterson. *Postmodern and Wesleyan? Exploring the Boundaries and Possibilities.* Kansas City: Beacon Hill Press of Kansas City, 2009.

Caputo, John D. *What Would Jesus Deconstruct?* Grand Rapids: Baker Academic, 2007.

Caputo, John D., and Michael J. Scanlon, eds. *God, the Gift, and Postmodernism*. Bloomington, IN: Indiana University Press, 1999.

Concoran, Kevin, ed. *Church in the Present Tense*. Grand Rapids: Brazos Press, 2011.

Grenz, Stanley J. *A Primer on Postmodernism*. Grand Rapids: Eerdmans, 1996.

Murray, Stuart. *Church after Christendom*. Milton Keynes, UK: Paternoster, 2004.

Niebuhr, H. Richard. *Christ and Culture*. New York: Harper and Row, 1951.

Smith, James K. A. *Who's Afraid of Postmodernism?* Grand Rapids: Baker Academic, 2006.

Tomlinson, David. *Re-Enchanting Christianity*. Norwich, UK: Canterbury Press, 2008.

Vanhoozer, Kevin, ed. *The Cambridge Companion to Postmodern Theology*. Cambridge, UK: Cambridge University Press, 2003.

Volf, Miroslav, and William Katerberg. *The Future of Hope: Christian Tradition amid Modernity and Postmodernity*. Grand Rapids: Eerdmans, 2004.

Ward, Graham, ed. *Blackwell Companion to Postmodern Theology*. Oxford, UK: Wiley-Blackwell, 2005.

PART 2
The Church's Essential Functions

eight
THE CHURCH AT WORSHIP

Jeffrey T. Barker

Blessed be God: Father, Son, and Holy Spirit
And blessed be God's kingdom now and forever. Amen.

Essentially, worship is faithfully remembering God's cosmic salvation. And worship is essential to the meaning and practice of the church. Thus worship is one of the central practices of the church, and as such inherent to a robust ecclesiology. The church's pulse to share the saving, healing message of Jesus beats loudly. Each week pastors and congregations consider how to communicate Jesus' life, ministry, passion, death, resurrection, and ascension clearly with neighbors, coworkers, and friends. Participation in God's cosmic work of redemption (redemption for all) compels the church to adopt new and different avenues of dialogue. Quite frankly, the good news of Jesus is too important for poor communication! Yet, in our unbridled attempts to share the saving, healing message of Jesus, the church may have swung the gate too widely. No greater place has innovation reigned supreme than in the church's practice of Christian worship.

Consider today's landscape. Sheets of new music flood churches weekly. New songs are downloaded or viewed on YouTube regularly. Candles and incense invite one congregation into silence and reflection, but stage lighting and a pulsating bass rhythm pull another congregation into rapturous praise and hand clapping. Innovation in worship has become the norm. As a pastor, I often feel adrift in the face of so many options.

Without a formal book of worship, many in the free-church tradition (like myself) are left to make decisions in isolation. Sometimes the criteria for "good" worship are reduced to celebrating ingenuity and innovation or to counting the number of people gathered. This must not be. Pastors, trained liturgists, and musicians must guide the congregation in offering their bodies "as a living sacrifice, holy and acceptable to God, which is your spiritual worship" (Rom. 12:1). Such is the vision of Christian worship![1]

James F. White, in his classic text *Introduction to Christian Worship*, suggests that a phenomenological approach to study Christian worship is most helpful. This approach notices order and words, space and movement. It observes the actual practice of worship among the ecclesia.[2] It looks at the form, structure, and content of a service of worship to describe Christian worship. We will not be able to describe and define worship completely, but we must acknowledge that we "know" worship only when we enter into the holy space of God's encounter with God's people. "Woe is me!" "I am undone," and "Thanks be to God!" may be the most apt words in worship, for they invoke the awe and thanksgiving essential to Christian worship.

The following essay arises from both the formal study of worship *and* the practice of leading congregations in worship. This essay opens with a discussion of how the people of God remember their identity. Remembering is much more than recollecting the past. In Christian worship, past, present, and future crumble in a radically public act of bearing witness to God's ongoing redemption of all creation. Since I serve in a tradition without a formal book of worship, this essay reviews the Christian Scriptures as the master script for the practice of Christian worship. These Scriptures identify the God these Christians worship and chronicles their on-again-off-again relationship. This essay then reviews the structure and content the church employs to act out the drama of worship. Finally, this essay concludes with a few guiding questions to help pastors and congregations worship more faithfully.

Worship as Remembering

In worship, God's people remember the cosmic scope of God's salvation and their personal (never individual!) reception of this gracious gift. This remembering is anamnestic. Anamnesis is more than the absence of amnesia. Rather, in this remembering, God's salvation becomes present to us again as a new reality.

The various acts of rehearsing salvation history give us anew the benefits of what God has done for us in these past events. Christ's birth, baptism, death, resurrection, and so on are all given to us again for our own appropriation through corporate reenactment of them. These events become no longer simply detached data from the past but part of our own personal history as we relive salvation history by rehearsing it in our worship.[3]

Each week in worship, the ecclesia participates anew and bears witness again to God's cosmic-shaped salvation. Christian worship proclaims God's salvation through the person and work of Jesus the Christ witnessed to by the Spirit.

Christian worship is fluid and rhythmic as it dances in the shared life of the triune God who so loved the cosmos that self-emptying became the modus operandi.[4] Brent Peterson articulates the centrality of this Trinitarian proposal. "Within a robust theology of worship it becomes evident that God's invitation to and purpose of creation is so that all things may participate in the very love and intimacy of the triune God."[5] In worship, the church is gathered up into God's self and then poured back out into the world with an impulse to offer herself as a living and loving sacrifice on behalf of all. Christian worship makes visible a critical theological affirmation: God's love remains directed toward the entire cosmos.

This anamnestic remembering links doxology, soteriology, and the *missio Dei* together. The church, created and formed by God, remains chronically dependent upon God's being. Thus, Christian worship articulates an important reality—the ecclesia is because God is. The church's being is and will always be a response to God's gracious gifting. Worship expresses this response.

Reading the Master Script—the Christian Scriptures

John Wesley identifies the master script when he proclaims himself as *homo unius libri*, "a man of one book." The greater context situates Wesley's commitment to the "one book" in questions of the eternal. In the opening preface to the initial volume of his *Sermons on Several Occasions*, Wesley writes,

> I am a spirit come from God and returning to God; just hovering over the great gulf, till a few moments hence I am no more seen—I drop into an unchangeable eternity! I want to know one thing, the way to heaven—how to land safe on that happy shore. God himself has condescended to teach the way: for this very end he came from heaven. He hath written it down in a book. O give me that book! At any price, give

me the Book of God! I have it. Here is knowledge enough for me. Let me be homo unius libri.[6]

The thrust of his commitment to this particular *unius libri* (the Christian Scriptures) was to know (both content and experience) God's salvific activity. It seems, then, as children of Wesley, we already have the master script for our worship—the Christian Scriptures.

"In the beginning God." Chaos ordered by God. A people created by God. A covenant established by God. The people identified as God's people. God spoke. The people listened for a while. God called. The people responded for a while. God invited. The people followed for a while. God commanded. The people obeyed for a while. Back and forth the relationship moved. God's people forgot God's way of being in the world. In love God pursued the people. Time and again God remembered and restored. God's faithfulness to the covenant remained steadfast.

Evidence of God's remembering and restoring of the people unfolded in a tremendous scene following the Exodus from Egyptian slavery. God invited the people back into relationship and reframed the covenantal obligations to Moses on Mount Sinai. With the rearticulated covenant in hand, Moses descended the mountain. To the people, Moses rehearsed the covenantal responsibilities. Speaking God's word to the people, Moses proclaimed:

> I am the LORD your God, who brought you out of the land of Egypt, out of the house of slavery; you shall have no other gods before me. You shall not make for yourself an idol, whether in the form of anything that is in heaven above, or that is on the earth beneath, or that is in the water above the earth. You shall not bow down to them or worship them. (Exod. 20:2-5)

From the outset, worship framed the relationship between God and God's people. Yet the covenant obligated the people to living a particular way in the world. Samuel Balentine writes that "the Torah understands that covenant-making, from Israel's perspective, require[d] a solemn partnership commitment that places Israel in harmony with the liturgy of creation."[7] This insight suggests that the people's identity was to be evidenced in both their worship and their stewardship and care of all creation. The covenant linked worship of God, identity as God's people, and stewarding God's creation together.

Generations later, this covenant became particularized and made new again in the death, resurrection, and ascension of Jesus the Christ. In the new covenant, the perceived exclusivity of God's people is reconstituted as inclusivity. Jew and Gentile. Slave and free. Male and female. Parent and child. All are brought into the new covenant. The apostle Paul expressed this relentless love and commitment of God to an unfaithful people with the insertion of "but."

> You were dead through the trespasses and sins in which you once lived, following the course of this world, following the ruler of the power of the air, the spirit that is now at work among those who are disobedient. All of us once lived among them in the passions of our flesh, following the desires of flesh and senses, and we were by nature children of wrath, like everyone else. *But God,* who is rich in mercy, out of the great love with which he loved us even when we were dead through our trespasses, made us alive together with Christ. (Eph. 2:1-5, italics mine)

A people made alive in Christ! These made-alive people are because God loves, forgives, and reconciles. As God's "called out ones," the ecclesia proclaims God's resurrection power at work in the world. Eugene Peterson suggests that this ecclesia occupies a new landscape and speaks a new language. "We are in the country of salvation, the land of resurrection, in the company of resurrection men and women."[8] These resurrection people live a particularized way and speak a particular language as God's body in the world. Love, forgiveness, peace, reconciliation, justice, and hospitality evidence this new resurrection landscape. Grace and hope frame this new language.

In worship, then, the church tastes, albeit as a small sample, the fullness of God's glory and humanity's sanctification. John's apocalyptic writing envisions the cosmic-shaped scope of God's salvation through christological doxology. The angelic choir's gospel singing begins and ends with a tribute to the slaughtered Lamb.

> Grace to you and peace from him who is and who was and who is to come, and from the seven spirits who are before his throne, and from Jesus Christ, the faithful witness, the firstborn of the dead, and the ruler of the kings of the earth. To him who loves us and freed us from our sins by his blood, and made us to be a kingdom, priests serving his God and Father, to him be glory and dominion forever and ever. Amen. (Rev. 1:4-6)

Pulling back the curtain on this heavenly vision pictures the final constitution of God's people offering their bodies "as a living sacrifice, holy and acceptable to God, which is your spiritual worship" (Rom. 12:1). The new creation is a priesthood loving and serving God.

In this cacophony of divine cosmic-shaped salvation, voices bellow loudly, "Holy, holy, holy, the Lord God the Almighty, who was and is and is to come" (Rev. 4:8). The singing continues. "Worthy is the Lamb that was slaughtered to receive power and wealth and wisdom and might and honor and glory and blessing!" (5:12). This eschatological vision becomes present in the church's anamnestic worship. Sunday's dress rehearsal acts out this heavenly vision. Christ has died. Christ is risen. Christ will come again. Such is the vision of Christian worship!

Rehearsing the Master Script—Blocking and Staging[9]

James White surveys several definitions of Christian worship to describe the encounter that happens among the worshipping congregation.[10] One way of capturing the encounter in Christian worship is as revelation and response (Luther). Another way describes the happening as union with God (Calvin). Still another describes worship as that which brings glory to God and rectifies humanity (Cranmer). "The glorification of God and the sanctification of humanity" is yet another way of naming what happens in Christian worship (Roman Catholic).[11] John Wesley suggested that the telos of worship is God's honor and the church's edification.

> In divine worship, the first thing to be considered is the end, and the next thing is the means conducing to that end. The end is the honor of God, and the edification of the Church; and then God is honored, when the Church is edified. The means conducing to that end, are to have the service so administered as may inform the mind, engage the affections and increase devotion.[12]

For Wesley, worship honors God, transforms the worshipper, and subsequently compels one to acts of love and service in the world. Each of the above definitions contributes to, but fails to exhaust, the mysterious encounter in worship. In worship, something beyond language and movement happens. At times we may be more aware of it than at other times.

Over the last quarter century, the worship renewal movement led by Robert Webber has reintroduced the basic fourfold structure of worship back into (primarily) evangelical churches to map out and make visible what takes place in services of worship. This retrieval helps us prepare and order our services of Christian worship. Situated in the larger conversation that understands worship as revelation and response, each act in worship—Gathering, Word, Table, and Sending—begins with God and invites response. God speaks. The people respond.

In gathering, the people are called to worship God. Conversations about the trivial end. A word from God is imminent. The service of the Word mandates the reading and interpretation of the Christian Scriptures. The people respond to God's Word spoken into the life of God's people. The Table of the Lord—the Great Thanksgiving—invites the worshippers to rehearse and reenter God's salvation once again. The death and resurrection of Jesus is no longer remembered from afar. Sacrificial salvation is encountered anew at the Table. In the final act of worship, the people are commissioned and sent into the world as God's "agents of reconciliation" (see 2 Cor. 5:11-21). These "agents of reconciliation" now understand their ministry through the lens of sacrifice.

We must always be cautious. The temptation to believe our task is accomplished if we plot out the four acts of worship fails to respect the piercing, penetrating movement of God's Spirit. We can never tame the Spirit! Even as we try to describe and define Christian worship, we're reminded that much of what goes on in worship is not visible—revelation, union with God, glorification, sanctification. The Spirit works on us. The Spirit gnaws at us. The Spirit works in us. The Spirit makes us new.

Consider the work of the Spirit. Paul, being charged with misrepresenting the Christian message, suggests that the new covenant is being written by the Spirit. "And all of us, with unveiled faces, seeing the glory of the Lord as though reflected in a mirror, are being transformed into the same image from one degree of glory to another; for this comes from the Lord, the Spirit" (2 Cor. 3:18). Our work of ordering worship attempts to render visible that which is veiled. Our modest attempts at ordering our worship, while very important, merely invite God's Spirit to convict, transform, enliven, and compel God's people into the world to participate fully in God's mission. Such is the vision of Christian worship!

Stages Notes—First Questions for Christian Worship

In the absence of a formal book of worship, pastors, liturgists, and others within the free-church tradition need to be particularly mindful and reflective about the congregation's worship. For many of us, a framework for making certain the master script is read and rehearsed faithfully is needed desperately. Certainly there is room for creative and interpretive license. However, the central message never changes: Christ has died. Christ is risen. Christ will come again. It is imperative we make certain the good news of Jesus is never reduced to privatized religious experiences or psychological prescriptions.

Recently, Lester Ruth articulated a basic framework for worship service planning.[13] Ruth suggests two primary areas of attention: (1) content and (2) structure.[14] Those planning a congregation's worship must attend to both the message proper as well as how the message is organized. Ruth further parses the question of content in two ways: "personal-story churches" and "cosmic-story churches." A personal-story church focuses on interaction between God's story and the personal stories of parishioners. On the other hand, a cosmic-story church remembers "the grand sweep of God's saving activity" throughout history and in all places.[15]

Structure, for Ruth, has to do with where the most time is spent in a worship service. Yet this is more than just chronological time. The structure reveals a congregation's theology of Christian worship. How the congregation tells God's Story reflects what the congregation actually believes about God and God's purposes for creation. Ruth's three categories within the structure are: music, Word/preaching, and Table. Chronological time isn't the only consideration in structure. Actual words, music, and table elements matter.

This introductory "framework" for analyzing and preparing congregational worship situates the pastor, liturgist, or musician for theological reflection. A first step is to answer three sets of questions:

1. In what ways does the congregation's worship explore God's Story expressed through personal stories? In what ways does the congregation's worship proclaim the grand scope of God's activity in the world?
2. What structure or order guides the proclaiming of God's salvation? How does the congregation spend time in worship (music, Word/preaching, Table)?
3. In what ways do the local congregation's liturgical decisions reveal and reflect her denominational and theological identity? In what ways is the unique, localized context exhibited in the congregation's worship?

Pastors, liturgists, and others must engage in liturgical theological reflection. In doing so, each congregation will tell the cosmic story of God in ways that maintain a sense of continuity with Christians throughout the ages while experiencing the joy of speaking in contemporary, fresh ways. Telling the message of God's salvation is far too important to be lax in this work.

A Final Comment—Benediction

Worship is never about making us feel better about ourselves nor about elevating our station in life. Neither the pastor nor the gathered congregation is the ultimate subject in worship. Rather, Christian worship witnesses, if the congregation faithfully remembers, to God's cosmic-shaped salvation. The subject of Christian worship is always and only the Christ who acts in and through God's church. That is, worship remembers and experiences anew the God who so loved the cosmos. As we worship, God is glorified and we are changed from "one degree of glory to another" (2 Cor. 3:18). Then, receiving the benediction, we are sent into the world as Christ's body, "priests serving his God and Father" (Rev. 1:4-6). Such is the vision of Christian worship! This practice is indispensable to the development of a Wesleyan ecclesiology.

> And now, O God, send us out to do the work you have
> given us to do, to love and serve you as faithful witnesses of
> Christ our Lord. To him, to you, and to the Holy Spirit,
> be honor and glory, now and forever. Amen.

Questions for Discussion

1. Given that the pastor is a primary decision maker in the ordering of a congregation's worship, to what degree do you share the author's conviction that the ecclesia participates in and bears witness to God's salvific activity?

2. In what ways do you/does your congregation remember God and God's salvation in worship?

3. In a denomination devoid of a formal book of worship, why is it essential to remain faithful to the biblical narrative in framing the structure and content of a congregation's service of Christian worship? What features of the biblical narrative are underrepresented in the author's chapter?

4. Using the three sets of questions for considering worship, how does your congregation practice worship? Personal stories evidencing God's Story? The grand scope of God's Story? What space is given to music? to Scripture? to Table? How does your congregation reflect a denominational/theological identity?

Suggestions for Further Reading

Balentine, Samuel E. *The Torah's Vision of Worship.* Minneapolis: Fortress Press, 1999.

Johnson, Todd. *The Conviction of Things Not Seen: Worship and Ministry for the 21st Century.* Ada, MI: Brazos Press, 2007.

Peterson, Brent D. *Created to Worship: God's Invitation to Become Fully Human.* Kansas City: Beacon Hill Press of Kansas City, 2012.

Wainwright, Geoffrey. *Doxology: The Praise of God in Worship, Doctrine, and Life.* New York: Oxford University Press, 1984.

White, James F. *Introduction to Christian Worship,* 3rd ed. Nashville: Abingdon Press, 2000.

nine
THE CHURCH'S SACRAMENTS

Brent Peterson

It is fitting that a conversation on the essentials of the church in the Wesleyan tradition includes space for the church's sacraments. John and Charles Wesley embodied a close intersection between the church (i.e., ecclesiology) and the soteriological healing found in the sacraments of baptism and the Lord's Supper. Moreover, the sacraments of baptism and the Lord's Supper are primary occasions where God grows (baptism) and sustains (the Lord's Supper) the church, even as its healing and sanctification precipitates the further redemption of the world. This chapter will explore the gift and healing of the sacraments as a means of grace and then look more specifically at the healing of baptism and the Lord's Supper.

Sacraments as a Means of Grace

While it is beyond the space of this chapter to explore with great depth, it can still be said that for too many churches in the Wesleyan tradition, their understanding of the sacraments is perhaps more Zwinglian than Wesleyan. Ulrich Zwingli was a sixteenth-century Reformer who celebrated the importance of the sacraments. The main emphasis for Zwingli was not specifically what God was doing in the sacraments, but that the sacraments were "public acts proclaiming the community's faith."[1] While the importance for the community to proclaim its faith is to be celebrated and indeed practiced, too many Wesleyans have not affirmed that God is offering present healing in the sacraments. In the Wesleyan tradition the sacraments are occasions of God healing.[2] In one of John Wesley's sermons on the sacraments, "The Means of Grace," he claims that it has truly been the orthodox position that "Christ has ordained certain outward means for conveying his grace into the souls of [people]."³ Wesley was then in a debate with Moravians who were not convinced the sacraments were important or necessary for one's salvation. Wesley is clear that in the sacraments God offers healing and transforming grace and that they are soteriological.

Before moving forward to discussing the celebrating the sacraments as a *means of grace,* a word needs to be said about what is meant by the phrase "means of grace." While *grace* is a term used frequently, there is often some confusion as to precisely what grace is. In the Wesleyan tradition grace should be understood as God's undeserved presence offering transformation and healing. It is very important that Wesleyans do not conceive of grace as some thing or object outside of God. Grace is God's own presence offering to heal, redeem, transform, and sanctify God's people.[4]

Responsible Grace

Within the Wesleyan tradition it must also be celebrated that while God offers healing to persons in the sacraments, persons must also respond to God's invitation of healing. It is not the case that the sacraments are only about what God is doing; persons are empowered and wooed by God to respond to this healing.[5] While God is the primary actor, the healing offered must be responded to. The church does not simply go around the streets of its community throwing water on random and unsuspecting people declaring them baptized. Grace in the sacraments participates in God's ongoing covenant with God's people in the world. Therefore, while God empowers persons to respond to the healing grace offered, the persons' ongoing response is significant in order to let God's healing flourish in their lives and in the world.

Sacraments as *the* Central Actions of the Church

John Wesley not only affirmed the centrality of the sacraments in communal worship but also considered them the primary practices of the church. In John's sermon "Of the Church" the church is not defined in terms of its institutional or organizational structure but in terms of its participation in the sacraments. Wesley claims he is doing nothing more than is found in the nineteenth Anglican Article of Faith on the church. "The visible Church of Christ is a congregation of faithful [persons], in which the pure word of God is preached, and the sacraments be duly administered."[6] It is fair to say for

Wesley if the Word of God is not preached nor the sacraments duly administered, the Christian church is not present. Wesleyan scholar Ole Borgen concludes that for Wesley, "These means of grace are constitutive of the Church, that is the Church exists that the means may be administered for the benefit of '[the] faithful.'"[7] In another setting Wesley clarifies who is properly part of the Church of England. Note his definition locates practices of communal worship as central. "But when they are visibly joined, by assembling together to hear the pure word of God preached and to eat of one bread, and drink of one cup, they are then properly the visible Church of England."[8] Wesley meant that "any congregation where the gospel was not truly preached or the sacraments truly administered was neither a part of the Church of England nor of the universal Church."[9] The communal worship gathering of singing, praying, preaching, baptizing, and communing is not simply a nice idea but testifies as to who is the visible church. The sacraments do continually constitute and renew the church by God. Clearly the church is to be much more than an individual dispenser of sacraments, but as will be noted below, the sacraments themselves are events of God's healing and transformation of the church in order that it might be more fully the body of Christ united, and sent out in mission. To put it plainly, the sacraments are constitutive of the church, and thus essential to a Wesleyan ecclesiology.

Who Can Administer the Sacraments?

For John and Charles Wesley who started missional communities in bands and societies, as the people called Methodists grew within the broader Anglican context, the issue of what persons were permitted to do in worship came up often. It is crucial to note that the Wesleys never desired to break away from the Church of England. Wesley articulated why God raised up the preachers called Methodists. "Not to form any new sect; but to reform the nation, particularly, the Church; and to spread scriptural holiness over the land."[10] In this sense the church as expressed in the societies were a sacramental expression of the broader church's eschatological vocation. For the spread of scriptural holiness the Wesleys, as Anglicans, affirmed the importance of the ordained offices. Only those ordained by the Church of England were permitted to celebrate the sacraments. While John did permit field preaching by laity on occasion, John and Charles were clear that only those who are ordained should preside at the Table or baptize.[11] To have allowed the nonordained to celebrate the sacraments would be a clear sign of schism with the Church of England and for Wesley a betrayal of the Church of England's teaching of ordination.

As Protestants and Anglicans, John and Charles Wesley were convinced that the only proper sacraments to be administered by the ordained were those that Christ instituted and commanded in the Scriptures.[12] While Wesleyans have no need to decry the other sacraments celebrated by our Orthodox and Roman Catholic brothers and sisters, the two primary sacraments discussed will be theirs—baptism and the Lord's Supper.

Baptism

This section will address the healing of baptism and then consider the theological issues of adult and infant baptism. Finally some questions regarding confirmation of baptism versus rebaptism will be addressed.

Drowning and Resurrecting with Christ

John Wesley celebrates the healing God offers in baptism, which serves as "the initiatory sacrament, which enters us into covenant with God."[13] Baptism is first and foremost an initiation into the church, the body of Christ.[14] In this way the church believes that baptism replaced circumcision as one's entrance into covenant with God into God's people. Baptism is this new "mark" whereby one bears the name of Christ.[15] Baptism is both a cleansing from sin and a healing initiation into the people of God. These two aspects should not be disjoined.

As shown by the apostle Peter in Acts and Paul in Romans 6, baptism celebrates that an aspect of repentance includes being baptized into Christ's death.[16] This death to sin leads to the invitation of an ongoing cleansing and healing from the disease of sin. This death is necessary in order that persons may then also join Christ in his resurrection and walk in the newness of life.[17] Baptism, therefore, is a joining with Christ in his death and resurrection, putting to death the deeds of darkness so that persons may be healed to join Christ in the way of light and righteousness. But it is essential that persons in the Wesleyan tradition affirm and practice that in baptism *God is the primary actor!* (This will have implications below for those who seek to be rebaptized.) Baptism, as a symbol of repentance, initiation, and healing, is always a means of *God's* grace.

Is Baptism Necessary for Salvation?

With the importance of baptism as part of one's repentance, healing, and initiation into the church as the body of Christ, the question then follows, if someone is not baptized, is he or she going to hell? When this question is asked, persons are quick to use the thief on the cross in Luke as an example of someone who did not receive a Christian baptism and yet Jesus proclaimed to him the words of salvation, "Today you will be with me in Paradise" (Luke 23:43). While this event is descriptive of the grace of God, it should not be seen as normative. Again, as Wesleyans, there is nothing but the grace and forgiveness of God that are necessary for salvation. But with that said, Wesleyans should affirm and train all Christians to be baptized. Baptism is considered by the church to be ordained by God as one's healing and entrance into the church and as a covenant with God. Any person desiring to become and be known as Christian should be baptized. A person not baptized who believes in the gospel of Christ is someone who is missing out on this peculiar means of healing grace God desires to offer all in the community of faith.

In a spirit of inclusivity, John Wesley, in following his Anglican roots, affirmed that baptism can be "performed by washing, dipping, or sprinkling the person, in the name of the Father, Son, and Holy Ghost, who is hereby devoted to the ever-blessed Trinity."[18] Therefore, Wesleyans can and should use all means for baptism. On a practical level some persons may actually fear immersion and this becomes a stumbling block. If churches regularly perform baptisms by immersion, pastors would also do well to let the congregation know that other modes are also available and efficacious.

Adult and Infant Baptism

While it is recognized that the early church practices of baptism varied, it is important to note that adult baptisms were the early norm. It is important to highlight that the sacrament of baptism was part of the process of initiation, but not the only part. There was a period of training, teaching, and discipleship called catechism. In some parts of the faith this lasted over three years. The issue was not simply about the length of time but about a time of readiness on the part of the one seeking to be baptized.[19] As persons felt ready they were then questioned by leaders in the church to verify their readiness. The time of preparation immediately preceding one's baptism, often at Easter, included fasting, exorcisms, denunciations of Satan, affirmations of the creed, and anointing of oil, all culminated with the celebration of the Lord's Supper.

Too often in the current climate, there is little preparation for persons who desire to be baptized. While an organized and set time for intentional catechism is advisable, it is also important to note that for all Christians one's catechism, one's spiritual formation and discipleship, never ceases. Furthermore, drawing upon the practices of the early church, baptism symbolizes not simply my desire to join but really the church letting me in. The church's opening the door is not about my worthiness but about my observed willingness to discipline myself in the ways of God. The issue is both an awareness and a willingness to give oneself to the covenant in Christ in the context of the church.

With the emphasis on measuring a person's willingness and awareness of the covenant, how does this work with infant baptism?[20] As baptism replaced circumcision as one's initiation into the covenant for eight-day-old Jewish males, it was not a surprise that the church began the practice of baptizing infants. While the infants cannot demonstrate a willingness or readiness, the parents and godparents respond for the children while also pledging to raise them in the ways of God. While God offers healing and saving grace for the infants, the infants are also empowered to respond to this grace as they grow and mature physically and spiritually. For these infants who have been baptized, it is important for the church to also have them go through the catechism offered to other persons seeking baptism. At the conclusion of this formal catechism, such persons should be brought before the congregation where they can make their pledge and confirm the covenant into which they were initiated.

Confirmation, Not Rebaptism

One problematic area regarding baptism is displayed when pastors rebaptize. This evidences a lack of emphasis that *God* is doing the work in baptism. While the examples are many, it often occurs something like this: A person was baptized as an infant and walked away from God in the teenage years and spent many years wandering, sinking deeper into the pit of sin. Yet God's grace did not give up on the person who comes back to God and then comes to the pastor desiring to be baptized again as a pledge and testimony of faith that "I am back." In this case the pastor should absolutely provide an opportunity for the person to share a testimony and celebrate the person's coming home and *confirm* his or her baptism. However, the larger universal church is crystal clear on this: rebaptism is not orthodox. To baptize again would be to say to God, "God, you were not quite good enough the first time, but this time I hope you can make it stick." Of course, no person is meaning to say this, but this is precisely what is being practiced theologically. Remember, God is the actor in baptism. One who has been baptized in the name of the Father, Son, and the Holy Spirit never needs to be baptized again. Moreover, persons can come forward at any time (and many times) especially during the celebration of baptism and confirm the covenant that they and God had made previously. There are many resources for pastors to lead persons to confirm and reaffirm their faith in front of the body without the unorthodox practice of rebaptizing. In fact, every baptism and Lord's Supper is to be an occasion for all the baptized to renew their covenant and commitment to God and to the body of Christ. In the end, what is essential is that there is one baptism. One in the sense that all Christians share in this experience, but also one as in the adequacy for one baptism in a person's life.

The Lord's Supper

The prominent place of the Lord's Supper for the Wesleys was grounded in Christ's command to do it and the early church's regular practice of it. Yet the Wesleys never intended the celebration of the Lord's Supper to simply be a dry rule from God to be followed. John Wesley asserted that the Lord's Supper was one of the chief ordained channels of grace. It is in the eucharistic encounter that the believers powerfully experience God in Christ by the Spirit and thus are weekly transformed and renewed into the image of God. For Wesley the Eucharist was the central sacrament to be celebrated weekly as the *primary* experience where the church is renewed as the body of Christ. It is essential to the life of the church and constitutive of the meaning of the church.

Furthermore, Wesley was clear that as an ordinance and a mercy to humanity, through the constant reception of Communion "we may be assisted to attain those blessings which he hath prepared for us; that we may obtain holiness on earth and everlasting glory in heaven."[21] Wesley understood the Lord's Supper to be the primary means of the continual growth in love and renewal in the image of God, individually and corporately, into the eschatological glorification of the church. Hence, the Lord's Supper is primarily the sacrament that offers ongoing sanctifying grace. While space does not permit a fuller discourse, the Lord's Supper is a divine-human encounter where the church offers itself as a living sacrifice that is joined with Christ's sacrifice; then united as one in the Spirit, it is sent out in mission.[22]

In other words, not only does the *Eucharist* continually renew the church as the body of Christ, but such a healing also implies a vocation into which it is blown by the Spirit to be Christ's body and blood in the world. At the Table the church is renewed as the body of Christ that is both a calling and the empowerment to continue the ministry of Christ as his broken body and blood given to love and serve the world. But it does not end there. The ultimate mission of the church is not simply to go out loving, serving, and caring for the world, but that the world might be invited by the church and gathered by God back to the Table and so find real life and full communion with God as Christ's body. It is God's life breath that inhales the church only to then be breathed out (exhaled) by God to be breathed in the very next Lord's Day. It is this liturgical rhythm that provides the very life of the church that lives for God. It is possible to do ecclesiology without sacramental theology. But it is impossible to be Wesleyan and ignore the essential place the sacraments hold in the church.

Questions for Discussion

1. What in this chapter did you find the most helpful in regard to the sacraments of baptism and the Lord's Supper?
2. How does this chapter affirm and challenge your previously held understandings of the sacraments?
3. What in this chapter do you struggle with?
4. How will this chapter add to your celebrations of the sacraments?
5. Are you encouraged to realize God is offering healing in the sacraments? If so, how and why?

Suggestions for Further Reading

Borgen, Ole E. *John Wesley on the Sacraments*. Grand Rapids: Francis Asbury Press, 1972.

Staples, Rob L. *Outward Sign and Inward Grace*. Kansas City: Beacon Hill Press of Kansas City, 1991.

White, James F. *The Sacraments in Protestant Worship*. Nashville: Abingdon Press, 1999.

ten
THE CHURCH'S PROCLAMATION

James N. Fitzgerald

In his seminal work in 1974, *Models of the Church*, Avery Dulles offered "The Church as Herald" as one of five ecclesiological models.[1] In this ecclesiology:

> The mission of the Church is one of proclamation of the Word of God to the whole world . . . The Church is essentially a kerygmatic community which holds aloft, through the preached Word, the wonderful deeds of God in past history, particularly his mighty act in Jesus Christ. The community itself happens wherever the Spirit breathes, wherever the Word is proclaimed and accepted in faith.[2]

Against the backdrop of Dulles's herald model, this chapter will address the role of preaching in the ecclesiology of John Wesley and the Church of the Nazarene. We will begin by considering John Wesley's ecclesiology—to what extent does the herald model describe Wesley's view of the church? Then the ecclesiology of the Church of the Nazarene will be considered in light of both Wesley's views and Dulles's herald model. Finally, we will offer some direction for further reflection on and refinement of the articulation of an ecclesiology for the Church of the Nazarene.

John Wesley's Ecclesiology

At first glance there is considerable evidence from John Wesley's life and ministry that would seem to align him with the herald model of the church. "I do indeed *live* by preaching," Wesley wrote in his journal,[3] and that certainly seemed to be the case. At the urging of George Whitefield, Wesley began field preaching in 1739, which opened the door for Wesley to preach multiple times each day. He did so at an amazing pace, preaching over forty thousand sermons in his lifetime.[4]

Although Wesley himself was ordained, Methodism was known for its widespread use of lay preachers, which unleashed a vast preaching army, first in England and later in the United States. Because of the urgency the movement sensed to preach the Word, men and women who sensed a call to preach were empowered to preach even if they would never pursue ordination. Wesley's admonition to his preachers was that "you have nothing to do but save souls. Therefore spend and be spent in this work."[5]

In his *Notes* on the book of Acts, Wesley emphasized the primacy of preaching in the early church. "In the first church, the primary business of apostles, evangelists, and bishops was to preach the word of God."[6] However, despite the undeniable emphasis that Wesley had on preaching, his ecclesiology was actually much broader than the herald model encompasses.

John Wesley's ecclesiology can only be understood in the context of his lifelong connection to the Church of England and the development of Anglican ecclesiology. Article XIX of the Articles of Religion of the Church of England reads:

> The visible Church of Christ is a congregation of faithful men, in the which the pure Word of God is preached, and the Sacraments be duly ministered according to Christ's ordinance in all those things that of necessity are requisite to the same.
>
> As the Church of Jerusalem, Alexandria, and Antioch, have erred; so also the Church of Rome hath erred, not only in their living and manner of Ceremonies, but also in matters of Faith.[7]

The wording of Article XIX closely follows that of Article VII of the Augsburg Confession, which reads in part, "The Church is the congregation of saints in which the Gospel is rightly taught and the Sacraments rightly administered."[8] It reflects the classical Protestant view that the marks of the true church are (at least) the Word and the sacraments. While the Church of England text had remained unaltered for more than 150 years before Wesley's birth, discussions about the church took on various nuances depending upon the opposing reference point. Thomas Cranmer's efforts to define the Church of England over against the church at Rome sounded different from Richard Hooker's efforts to define the Anglicans over against both Rome and the Puritans, and both sounded different from Jeremy Taylor's efforts to define the

Church of England over against the Continental Reformers.[9] John Wesley nowhere set forth a new doctrine of the church because he had no intentions of forming a new church. What he did offer, however, was his own nuanced reflections on Article XIX. Like his Anglican predecessors, Wesley's discussions on the doctrine of the church reflected both his intended audience and his opponents.

In his earliest full printed defense of the Methodist movement, "An Earnest Appeal to Men of Reason and Religion" (published in 1743), John Wesley discussed his view of the nature of the church. He refers to Article XIX of the Church of England and highlights three key parts of the statement on the church:

> The article mentions three things as essential to a visible Church. First: Living faith; without which, indeed, there can be no Church at all, neither visible nor invisible. Secondly: Preaching, and consequently hearing, the pure word of God, else that faith would languish and die. And, Thirdly, a due administration of the sacraments, — the ordinary means whereby God increaseth faith.[10]

Wesley goes on to make a distinction between the first part of the article (a company of faithful or believing people—*living faith*), which he defines as the *essence* of the church, and the latter two phrases (the pure word of God preached, and the sacraments duly administered), which he defines as the *properties* of the church.[11] Wesley's distinction between the essence and the properties of the church remained a constant throughout his life (he repeated it in a letter to his brother Charles in 1785),[12] but over the course of his lifetime he underwent a significant shift in his views on church order. Early in his ministry Wesley had very rigid views,[13] but he gradually began to incorporate practices that were considered a violation of church order.

What is particularly significant is the greater flexibility that Wesley exhibited on issues related to preaching in comparison to issues related to the administration of the sacraments. Wesley was much more resistant to the idea of lay administration of the Eucharist than he was to the use of lay preachers. Speaking of his lay preachers, he wrote, "None of them dreamed that being called to preach gave them any right to administer the sacraments."[14] He was willing to participate in field preaching, to use lay preachers, and to preach across recognized parish boundaries—all of which were considered to be violations of church order. Behind it all lay his reasoning that the message of the gospel must be proclaimed and that no barriers should be yielded to, ecclesiastical or otherwise, in the pursuit of that mission.

Over the course of his lifetime, Wesley's ecclesiology evolved in its emphasis, though it was always tethered to Article XIX of the Church of England. As Albert Outler notes, the "distinctively Wesleyan accent is that the church is best defined *in action*, in her witness and mission, rather than her form of polity."[15] That "mission" was clearly highlighted in the Methodist preaching services. Despite the fact that Methodist preaching services were considered the "glory of the Methodists,"[16] however, Wesley made a clear distinction between Methodist preaching services and proper worship. Part of that distinction was that proper worship includes the regular celebration of the Eucharist. Because the preaching services were not eucharistic services, Wesley considered them "essentially defective" worship.[17] So while Wesley emphasized the role of preaching, he was not willing to separate that from the broader scope of the life and work of the church. He always held to the importance of *both* properties of the church—the preaching of the Word and the administration of the sacraments.

In summary, the herald model of the church is not broad enough to encompass the whole of John Wesley's ecclesiology, but it certainly is descriptive of much of both his thought and practice. Many of his variations from the established order seem to lean toward, and be shaped by, the herald model. He refused to be bound by an ecclesiology that would inhibit the herald's task of proclaiming the kerygmatic message of the kingdom.

The Church of the Nazarene

The Herald Model

There are several characteristics of the herald model of ecclesiology which are clearly evident in the Church of the Nazarene. Dulles notes that "this ecclesiology goes with a strong evangelistic missionary thrust,"[18] and it is "radically centered upon Jesus Christ and on the Bible as the primary witness to him,"[19] both of which remain true for the denomination. Dulles also identifies the following strengths of the herald model, which have a strong affinity to both the implicit and explicit ecclesiology of the Church of the Nazarene:

- It has a good biblical foundation in the prophetic tradition of the Old Testament, in Paul, and elsewhere.

- It gives a clear sense of identity and mission to the church.
- It gives rise to a rich theology of the word.[20]

In the herald model there is a strong connection to the preaching ministry of Jesus, and a sense that as the church attends to the task of preaching it is continuing the ministry of Christ in the world.

> Jesus came preaching. The picture is drawn so clearly in the Gospel of Luke. It was in the synagogue of Nazareth that Jesus opened up the book of the prophet Isaiah and, reading from the passage that spoke of how the long-promised Messiah would preach the gospel, announced that the promise had been kept. At the center of Jesus' ministry was this reading and interpreting of the Scriptures, this proclamation that they had been fulfilled . . . Jesus came preaching because he had been sent for this purpose by the Father. Similarly, Jesus sent his disciples out to preach: "'As the Father has sent me, even so send I you'" (John 20:21). The earliest Church understood preaching to be at the heart of its mission. The Great Commission made it clear: "'Make disciples of all nations, baptizing them . . . teaching them to observe all that I have commanded you'" (Matt. 28:18-20). We find the same thing in the long ending to the Gospel of Mark: "'Go into all the world and preach the gospel to the whole creation'" (Mark 16:15). And still again Luke makes this same point: "'Repentance and the forgiveness of sins should be preached in his name to all nations'" (Luke 24:47).[21]

In all of these ways, the Church of the Nazarene exhibits many of the strong characteristics of the herald model of the church. It also reflects Dulles's description of the role of the sacraments in this model: "Sacraments in this type of ecclesiology, as contrasted with the institutional and sacramental models, are seen as definitely secondary to the word."[22] This did not prove to be the case with Wesley, who led both an evangelical and eucharistic revival. But while Wesley was able to be an exception to the rule, the Church of the Nazarene early on fell into the standard categories that Dulles described—an ecclesiology that emphasized preaching considerably more than the sacraments.

The Development of Nazarene Ecclesiology

While Methodism began as a movement within an established church, the Church of the Nazarene was the establishment of a church that came out of a movement—the American Holiness movement. From the start, then, there was a different ecclesiastical context for the two. At its inception, the Church of the Nazarene did not have a robust expression of its ecclesiology—nothing that clearly articulated the traditional Protestant marks of the church as being a place where the Word of God is preached and the sacraments are duly administered.

The denomination did not have Articles of Faith until 1923, but the early *Manuals* included Doctrinal Statements (which would later be designated as Articles of Faith) and an Agreed Statement of Belief. Neither of these contained a statement on the church. What there was, in its place, was three statements about the church that have consistently appeared in Nazarene manuals: "The General Church," "The Churches Severally," and "The Church of the Nazarene."[23]

The statement on "The General Church" is the assertion that "the Church of God is composed of all spiritually regenerate persons, whose names are written in heaven." The statement on "The Churches Severally" affirms the principle of churches being voluntary associations of believers: "The churches severally are to be composed of such regenerate persons as by providential permission, and by the leadings of the Holy Spirit, become associated together for holy fellowship and ministries."

The third statement on "The Church of the Nazarene" reads:

The Church of the Nazarene is composed of those persons who have voluntarily associated themselves together according to the doctrines and polity of said church, and who seek holy Christian fellowship, the conversion of sinners, the entire sanctification of believers, their upbuilding in holiness, and the simplicity and spiritual power manifest in the primitive New Testament Church, together with the preaching of the gospel to every creature.

It is worth noting that none of the three statements mention the role of sacraments in the discussion of the church. When the denomination adopted a constitution for the first time in 1923, the General Assembly voted to include these three statements as Articles of Faith.[24] When the *Manual* was published, however, these statements were not included in the Articles of Faith. They remained as three separate statements, sandwiched between the Articles of Faith and the Agreed Statement of Belief that was required for church membership.[25] The denomination did not develop an Article of Faith on the church until 1989.

Lacking an explicit ecclesiology in the early years, the Church of the Nazarene had an implicit emphasis on "living faith" as being essential to the church (with the two references to "regenerate persons") and an expressed emphasis on "the preaching of the gospel to every creature."

Like Wesley, the Church of the Nazarene was more likely to define the church in action rather than in polity. Unlike Wesley, however, the Church of the Nazarene did not produce a substantive Article of Faith on the church that would speak to the nature of the church. Lacking a statement that spoke of the *essence* of the church, the denomination's focus was on the *properties* of the church, and preaching was emphasized much more than the administration of the sacraments. Without a statement that named the administration of the sacraments as being constitutive of the church, the denomination had no theological foundation to recover the frequent sacramental practice of John Wesley. There was an Article of Faith on the sacraments, and administration of the sacraments was listed among the duties of the ordained minister. The preaching role clearly received greater emphasis, however, than the administration of the sacraments. At its inception, the Church of the Nazarene had an essentially preaching-based piety and was much more closely aligned with the herald model of the church.

Articulating the Role of the Sacraments

By the end of the 1960s, theologians within the denomination were calling attention to the need for an Article of Faith on the church. At the Nazarene Theology Conferences held in 1967 and 1972, the focus was on the doctrine of the church, and concern was expressed to see a *Manual* statement drafted articulating a doctrine of the church. It was not until 1985, however, that the General Assembly appointed a "Doctrine of the Church Commission" to draft a document. The commission presented a document to the 1989 General Assembly, which was adopted as Article of Faith XI, "The Church."

The original Article XI had four paragraphs. The first paragraph speaks to the nature and identity of the church and includes the phrase that the body of Christ is "called together by the Holy Spirit through the Word."[26] The second paragraph delineates these three marks of the church: (1) the unity and fellowship of the Spirit, (2) worship through the preaching of the Word, observance of the sacraments, and ministry in his name, and (3) obedience to Christ and mutual accountability.[27]

Article XI continues to be a work in progress, but its articulation has seen a parallel development—the Church of the Nazarene is broadening its model of the church beyond the herald model. This is resulting in an ecclesiology that more closely aligns with the denomination's Wesleyan roots.

Conclusion

While John Wesley's ecclesiology had many marks of the herald model of the church, it was broader than that model, particularly in Wesley's emphasis on the sacraments. The Church of the Nazarene began without a clearly defined ecclesiology. The various fragmented expressions of an ecclesiology were narrower than Wesley's ecclesiology and were closely aligned with the herald model of the church. As the denomination continues to consider the role of preaching in the life of the church, these guidelines can lead that reflection:

- Continue to embrace the herald model as a corrective to patterns of preaching that are more therapeutic or "good advice" than kerygmatic.
- Consider the question of whether preaching is simply a mark of the church or whether it is constitutive of the church.
- Clarify the preaching roles and the offices for ordained ministry.
- Include a statement on the church in the Agreed Statement of Belief and the Ritual for the Reception of Church Members.

The Church of the Nazarene continues to clarify its ecclesiology and more closely align itself with its Wesleyan roots. In this process, without rejecting any of the strengths of the herald model, the Church of the Nazarene can broaden the scope of its ecclesiology to reflect an emphasis on both the preaching of the Word and the administration of the sacraments.

Questions for Discussion

1. In what ways does your local congregation exemplify the model of the "church as herald of kerygma"?

2. The church's role as "herald" is often seen as being fulfilled through the proclamation of the Word in worship. Are there other venues for the church to fulfill this role? If so, what might those be?

3. How essential is preaching to a definition/doctrine of the church? Is preaching *constitutive* of the church or *a function* of the church?

4. One of Phineas F. Bresee's noteworthy mottos was, "In essentials unity, in nonessentials liberty, in all things charity." What essentials would you identify as you articulate the kerygma that the church proclaims?

5. As you reflect on the role of preaching in the identity of the church, what other images or models besides "herald" should be a part of the discussion?

Suggestions for Further Reading

Campbell, Ted A. *Wesleyan Beliefs: Formal and Popular Expressions of the Core Beliefs of Wesleyan Communities.* Nashville: Kingswood Books, 2010.

Cooke, Bernard. *Ministry to Word and Sacraments: History and Theology.* Philadelphia: Fortress, 1976.

Dulles, Avery. *Models of the Church*, expanded ed. New York: Doubleday, 1991.

Harper, Brad, and Paul Louis Metzger. *Exploring Ecclesiology: An Evangelical and Ecumenical Introduction.* Grand Rapids: Brazos Press, 2009.

Lischer, Richard, ed. *The Company of Preachers: Wisdom on Preaching, Augustine to the Present.* Grand Rapids: Eerdmans, 2002.

eleven
THE CHURCH AS CONFESSIONAL EDUCATOR
A CATECHETICAL APPROACH TO CHRISTIAN EDUCATION

Mark A. Maddix

The role of Christian education is central to the life of the church. Through the educational ministries of the local church, Christians are formed and shaped to live a life of faithful discipleship. Christians affirm the mandate to "go . . . and make disciples" (Matt. 18:19), but each faith tradition expresses what it means to be a follower of Christ and the role the church plays in shaping faithful disciples. Some faith traditions view Christian education primarily as Christian nurture; some view Christian education primarily as the transmission of knowledge through teaching, while others view Christian education as the process of spiritual formation. All of these are valid expressions of Christian education, but in themselves they do not provide a holistic approach to Christian education.

The Church of the Nazarene, which finds its roots in the Wesleyan-Holiness tradition, has often struggled with the development of a holistic approach to Christian education due to the emphasis on revivalism and instantaneous experience. In more recent years there has been a growing interest in the development of a holistic approach to Christian education, rooted in the theology and practice of John Wesley that informs Christian education for the church today. A more holistic approach to Christian education can be found in the theology and practice of John Wesley. Wesley, a practical theologian, understood the need to establish Christian educational practices that aided people to grow toward "holiness of heart and life."

Catechesis

Developing a holistic approach to Christian education can best be described as *catechesis*. Catechesis is the process by which Christians are formed, educated, and instructed. Catechesis is a broader term than Christian education because it includes all intentional learning within the faith community. Catechesis, according to John Westerhoff, is a pastoral activity intended to transmit the church's tradition and to enable faith to become living, conscious, and active in the life of maturing persons and a maturing community.[1] It is concerned not only with conversion and nurture, commitment and behavior but also with aiding the community to become Christian. It is about passing on the living tradition in the form of story and vision as well as for all those who share in the life and mission of the Christian faith community.[2]

A catechetical approach for Christian education is reflected in John Wesley's focus on the "means of grace."[3] Wesley describes the means of grace as, "By means of grace, I understand outward signs, word, or actions, ordained of God, and appointed for this end—to be the ordinary channels whereby he conveys to mean, preventing, justifying or sanctifying grace."[4] Wesley uses the word "means" with the word "ordinance" on occasion as an indicator that this participation was expected by God.

Wesley divided the "means of grace" into three divisions: instituted means of grace, the prudential means of grace, and the general means of grace. The instituted means of grace are practices given directly by Jesus Christ. They are: prayer, searching the Scriptures, participating in the Lord's Supper (Eucharist), fasting, and Christian conferencing (spiritual conversation).

The prudential means of grace are practices that are wise and beneficial to do. They include obeying Christ, small groups, special prayer meetings, visiting the sick, doing all the good we can to all the people we can, and reading from the devotional classics of the rich tradition of two thousand years of Christianity. The prudential means of grace were designed to meet the person at his or her point of need, thus they are adaptable to a person's particular historical situation or context. The general means of grace include watching, denying ourselves, taking up our cross daily, and exercising the presence of God.

Wesley didn't confine God's grace to just these practices. Because he understood grace to be God's loving uncreated presence, he believed many other activities could be means of grace. Thus, grace is still active even among those who have no access to specific means like Christian baptism, the Eucharist, or the study of Scripture.

Formation, Discernment, and Transformation

Wesley's categories of the instituted and prudential means of grace, along with the acts of mercy, suggest a way of ordering educational practices into three complementary approaches to Christian education: *formation, discernment,* and *transformation.*[5] Coupled with Wesley's sacramental theology and his desire for a transformative holiness of heart and life, these three complementary approaches provide a catechetical process for Christian education.

Formation

The process of formation takes place as persons are assimilated into the Christian culture through a series of established Christian practices. This is reflected in Wesley's understanding of the instituted means of grace where persons are formed and transformed as they participate in the total life of the faith community. Through intentional participation in communal practices persons are shaped in Christian character and transformed by their new identity.[6] This formational process does not take place individually but through participation in the communal practices, such as worship, the Eucharist, and small groups. Through these communal practices persons are socialized into the Christian faith.[7] For Wesley, by God's grace, the goal of participation in these communal practices is holiness of heart and life.

There are a variety of practices that are formational, but some that reflect John Wesley's theology and practices include childhood formation, adult formation (small groups), and worship (Eucharist).[8]

Childhood Formation

The approach of John Wesley to the Christian education of children follows logically from his theology. According to Wesley, both young and old are lacking in God's natural and moral image. Sin dislodged the image of God in all humanity and brought alienation from God. Wesley was primarily concerned about the salvation of children. He believed that one of the primary means to this end was through Christian education. In his sermon "On the Education of Children," he states:

Now, if these are the general diseases of human nature, is it not the grand end of education to cure them? And is it not the part of all those to whom God has entrusted the education of children, to take all possible care, first, not to increase, not to feed, any of these diseases (as the generality of parents constantly do)?[9]

It was to this end that Wesley spent much of his ministry educating children. He believed that the first step in the redemption of the child was baptism.[10] The new birth, the beginning of spiritual transformation, was reached by adults through baptism, only on the condition that they repent and believe the gospel; that spiritual life is reached by children through an outward sign of baptism without this condition, for they can neither repent nor believe.[11] This does not mean that infant baptism is without effect. Infants are in a state of original sin, and in the interpretation of some Wesley scholars, they cannot be saved ordinarily unless this sin is washed by baptism. Baptism regenerates, justifies, and gives infants the privileges of the Christian religion. This is a thoroughly Anglican interpretation that Wesley seems to follow. Another interpretation of Wesley on infant baptism focuses not on the guilt of original sin being washed away but on the prevenient grace given that will call the child to a relationship with God and that will keep the child safe in God's arms until the child "sins away its baptism."

The next step in Wesley's view of Christian education of children is conversion. Wesley believed that anyone who had sinned after baptism had denied that right of baptism and, therefore, must have recourse to a new birth. He judged conversion to be universally necessary for children as well as for adults.[12] Prince states, "Wesley did not hold that religious education makes conversion unnecessary, but that religious education and conversion supplement each other."[13] Prince's seminal work on Wesley and childhood education states the purpose of Christian education as expressed by Wesley:

> The goal of all work with children at home, in the schools, in the Methodist society is to make them pious, to lead to personal religion, and to insure salvation. It is not merely to bring them up so that they do no harm and abstain from outward sin, not to get them accustomed to the use of grace, saying their prayers, reading their books, and the like, nor is it to train them in right opinions. The purpose of religious education is to instill in children true religion, holiness and the love of God and mankind and to train them in the image of God.[14]

For Wesley this took place in the home, in the schools, and in the societies to make children Christians, inwardly and outwardly.[15]

Once a child reaches the age of accountability, around age twelve, the child goes through a catechetical process of confirmation to learn more about theology and the doctrines of the church. Through this process the child can either affirm or reject his or her baptism. Congregations should include a service of confirmation for children to affirm their baptism and their faith in Jesus Christ.

An important catechetical approach, based on Wesley's ecclesiology, includes the formation of children through their participation in the practices of the faith community. As children are engaged in the practices of the church, including important spiritual encounters like baptism and confirmation, they become members of the covenant community.

Adult Formation (Small Groups)

For Wesley, living a holy life required one's life in intimate fellowship on a regular basis. His development of small groups provided an educational framework to help people grow in "holiness of heart and life." The groups provided a context for seekers to receive support, accountability, and encouragement. Wesley's system of mutual accountability included three formative aspects: societies, classes, and bands.

Societies were primarily focused on teaching or educational channels by which the tenets of Methodism were presented. These tenets were taught in a large classroom setting primarily through lecture, preaching, public reading, hymn singing, and "exhorting." Societies consisted of people seated in rows, women and men separated on each side, where they listened to a prepared lecture. Societies were led by John and Charles Wesley, but later as the movement expanded, lay assistants were delegated oversight in the absence of ordained clergy. Naturally, considering the impassioned preaching and fervent singing, there was an affective dimension of instruction. But the major aim was to present scriptural truth and have those truths clearly understood.

Class meetings were the most influential instructional unit in Methodism and probably Wesley's greatest contribution to spiritual growth. Class meeting gets so much credit because of its radical transformation of England's working masses. Its success centers on the instructional design of behavioral change.

Classes were intimate gatherings of ten or twelve people who met weekly for personal supervision of their spiritual growth. Class meetings were coeducational experiences, which included women in leadership. The classes were heterogeneous in terms of age, social standing, and spiritual readiness. Wesley wanted the classes to represent a cross section of Methodism. Some were at very different points in their spiritual maturity. Also, the classes provided a place to accept people from a variety of social backgrounds. This helped break up the rigid classes of eighteenth-century England.

The leaders would share honestly about their failures, sins, temptations, or inner battles. They were the role models for others. Class meetings consisted of personal experience, not doctrinal ideology or biblical information. Perfect love was the goal of the class meetings. Leaders were fellow strugglers who started the meeting, provided spiritual oversight or pastoral care to others—subpastors in the Methodist organizational hierarchy—and were to carry the concerns of the class through the week. Leaders created an atmosphere of trust for all members to "bear all things." Class meetings provided community and the development of relationship and spiritual accountability for those who were struggling with habitual issues.

Bands facilitated affective redirection. Unlike the classes, it was a homogenous grouping by gender, age, and marital status. Bands were voluntary cells of people who professed a clear Christian faith and who desired to grow in love, holiness, and purity of intention. Bands included ruthless honesty and frank openness, in which its members sought to improve their attitudes, emotions, feelings, intentions, and affections. The central function of the band was what Wesley termed "close conversation," by which he meant soul-searching examination, not so much of behavior and ideas, but of motive and heartfelt impressions.[16]

The development of the societies, classes, and band meetings provided an educational system that formed and shaped faithful disciples. David Michael Henderson develops a taxonomy that provides an external framework for identifying psychological conditions in Wesleyan groups, which include three primary "modes," or that include societies (cognitive mode), class meetings (behavioral mode), and the bands (affective mode).[17]

Certainly it is difficult to replicate Wesley's process completely, but these principles can be included in our local congregations. Gathering in groups for spiritual accountability can help foster faith and growth in Christlikeness. It is through these groups that formation takes place that leads to holiness of heart and life. Congregations, who want to reflect a Wesleyan ecclesiology, are to include groups that help to facilitate learning, relationships, and accountability toward holiness of heart and life.

Worship as Formation

Since faith communities are the "natural agency" for communicating Christian faith, liturgy and worship is a vital avenue for this communication. Westerhoff says that "the fundamental issue for Christian nurture is ecclesiology, the nature of the Church or Christian community."[18] The faith community has a "narrative character" where the liturgy and rituals are rich, the memories are handed down to generations, and the "common vision" connects the present to the past and will connect the present to the future. Worship is the heart of the faith community and is its authority, and thus essential in defining the meaning of the church. "Christian nurture . . . is dependent upon experience and reflection within a faith community."[19] To facilitate socialization there must be catechesis in the church because it assumes a communal understanding of human nature and the necessity of a faithful community. A community shares a common memory and vision; it is conscious of its roots and committed to the vision of the future.[20]

In worship, the people of God gather to give praise and thanksgiving to the triune God. Worshippers respond to God's grace through the proclamation of the Word and the Eucharist. Debra Dean Murphy believes "Christians are formed and transformed through worship, praise, and doxology: All efforts at forming and discipling Christians should presume the centrality of worship."[21] Word and Table were central to Methodist worship during the time of John Wesley but are not as common today in many Methodist and Holiness congregations. Most evangelical congregations identify with the proclamation of the gospel through preaching. These congregations see Scripture as central to formation and proclamation. This reflects the influence of the Protestant Reformation, which placed a high value on Scripture and proclamation. Many of these congregations are less likely to participate in Holy Communion (or the Eucharist) on a regular basis. One of the primary reasons is that many Wesleyan-Holiness congregations consider themselves Low-Church, with a diminished view of liturgy, lectionary readings, and sacramental theology.

The Eucharist, according to Wesley, served as a channel of grace that formed and transformed the believer. Wesley's sermon, "The Duty of Constant Communion," asks why Christians should participate in Communion on a regular basis and then provides a response. He said we are to participate in Communion as much as possible because Christ commanded us to "do this in remembrance of me" (Luke 22:19). Some fear that regular participation in Communion will be diminished over time, but Wesley argued against those who feared that its frequency would diminish its impact. He argued that the benefits of Communion for all who participate in obedience to Christ include the forgiveness of past sins and the present strengthening and refreshing of our souls. Wesley stated,

> The grace of God given herein confirms to the pardon of our sins, by enabling us to leave them. As our bodies are strengthened by bread and wine, so are our souls by these tokens of the body and blood of Christ. This is the food of our souls: This gives strength to perform our duty, and lead us on to perfection.[22]

For Wesley, the Eucharist was an opportunity to experience and commune with Christ. Through Communion persons experience the very presence of Christ. For Wesley, since Christ was present, everyone was invited to participate, believers and nonbelievers alike. Christ was present spiritually, immediately, and independently, interacting with the recipient to convey grace. Eucharist could therefore be a conversion experience for non-Christians if they responded in faith. Wesley's view of the Eucharist as a sacrament reflects his belief that a person may receive forgiveness and reconciliation through obedient response to God's grace, including participation in the Eucharist. He believed that something divine takes place when a person comes with an open heart to receive the life-giving gift of the bread and wine as the Word of God.

In this respect, Wesley believed that the Eucharist was a converting element for those who confessed and believed *during* the Lord's Supper, as well as a sustaining and sanctifying one. Wesley's desire to see Methodist followers take Communion regularly was based on both obedience to Christ and the hope that blessing and holiness would follow the use of this essential means of grace. Communion, as a means of grace, is formative for those who are being drawn toward holiness and those who have been sanctified. For those desiring to grow in God's grace, which is a deepening of love for God and neighbor, Communion is the ordinary means of such growth. The sacrament serves not only to preserve and sustain but also to further progress and growth in faith and holiness.

Centrality of Scripture in Worship

Christians can encounter the transforming reading of Scripture in worship through a variety of practices. First, Christians engage Scripture through the preaching of the Word. Historically, preaching in the early church preceded the writing of the New Testament texts. The eyewitnesses of the Christ event testified to what they had seen and heard.[23] Preaching touched and transformed the lives of the early Christians. In similar ways, when the Scripture is preached today, the hope is that lives are changed and transformed through the work of the Holy Spirit. The proclamation of Scripture emphasizes the spoken Word of God that bears witness to the incarnate Word of Jesus Christ. But there is more to this than bearing witness. Through the proclamation of Scripture, the spoken Word becomes a fresh expression of the living and active word of God. In this sense, the spoken word becomes a "means of grace."

The preacher speaks *for* God, *from* the Scriptures, *by* the authority of the church, *to* the people. God speaks through the proclamation of the Word, through the inspiration of Scripture, to provide healing and reconciliation. As Marva Dawn writes, "Sermons should shape the hearers by bringing the transforming Word to nurture the development of the character and pattern of Christ."[24] When preaching is maintained as central to liturgy, through the following of the lectionary and the Christian calendar, preaching is the Scripture-driven, worship-centered act that makes meaning for a community's life as it strives to bear witness to the truth of the gospel in the world.[25] The preacher interprets Scripture for the community, placing it within the larger narrative of the biblical witness, and helps congregants make meaning for life. Scriptural preaching allows the congregants to hear and discover their role in the broader narrative of God's redemptive work in the world.

Second, Scripture is encountered through the worship service or liturgy. It is the Word of God, read and preached and received, that calls the Christian community together to worship. When the people of God gather around Scripture, this reveals something of the heart of Christian worship. Without Christian worship there would be no Bible. The Bible, in a very real sense, is the product of the early church's common prayer. The earliest Christian communities circulated among themselves and read in common worship stories of the life and ministry of Jesus and the early apostles so that they could hear and respond. Similarly, the interrelationship between worship and the Scriptures is evident today as Scripture is preached, read, and experienced in worship.[26]

Through worship, as the community of faith gathers, Scripture comes to life. Congregations that follow the Christian calendar and lectionary readings provide congregants with opportunities to participate in the story of God. The reading of Scripture is an interpretative act that provides an opportunity for worshippers to encounter the living Word of God. In order for Scripture to be formative in the life of the church, Scripture must be read, experienced, and interpreted as a central aspect of the worshipping community. Also, through responsive readings, hymns, and choruses (assuming they have a biblical basis), the faith community provides various avenues for worshippers to interact with God's message through Scripture.

A Wesleyan ecclesiology, then, includes Word and Table as significant practices that form and shape faithful disciples. The combination of the weekly participation in the Table with the reading and interpreting of Scripture in worship creates a setting in which persons are being formed and shaped into faithful disciples.

Discernment

The prudential means of grace include a variety of contextual practices that can become a means of grace. Wesley's provision for a contextual set of prudential practices invites Christians to the ongoing task of discerning what practices truly convey grace.[27] Discernment begins with the awareness of God at work in our lives through Christ and moves to inquiry about how to live a more faithful life as a result of God's grace.

Often the process of discernment begins with Scripture and how we are to interpret Scripture in our context. As believers gather in communities to study Scripture, they seek God's guidance in discerning how to understand and interpret Scripture. The process of Bible study is a means of grace that forms and transforms. The process of discernment prepares Christians to hear more fully what Scripture has to say to challenge the church and our Christian walk.

Studying Scripture in community includes a wide range of methods and approaches. The process of discernment is practiced best through the inductive process instead of a deductive process. The inductive approach to Bible study is more objective and impartial because it demands that a person examine the particulars of Scripture and then draw conclusions. The inductive approach to Bible study produces people who hear and listen to the text. An inductive approach to Bible study allows the reader to interpret the Bible through observation and reflection, by drawing out ideas and truths in Scripture. Inductive Bible study is an approach to inquiry in which persons learn by examining the objects of the study themselves and drawing their own conclusions about these materials from their direct encounter with them (Maddix and Thompson). The deductive process is more subjective since the reader comes to the Bible with conclusions and then proceeds to the text to find proof for those ideas.[28]

This inductive approach allows the interpreter to discover what God may say through the biblical text as Scripture and to allow those discoveries to be internalized, resulting in formation and transformation. It is important to note that no person can read the Bible purely inductively. The reader's life experiences, context, and personal bias impact the interpreter's study of Scripture. A Wesleyan approach to Bible study does not begin with deductive presuppositions *per se*, but rather seeks a creative engagement and inductive encounter with God through Scripture—which takes the faithful reader to a deeper level of understanding and experience than simply the gathering of factual information.

Another process of scriptural discernment is the practice of *lectio divina* (sacred reading). This ancient practice that originated with the desert fathers and mothers consisted of prayerful rumination on biblical texts. Today many Christians and faith communities are regaining the significance of this ancient practice as a means to make Scripture reading exciting and meaningful. *Lectio divina* is a process of scriptural encounter that includes a series of prayer dynamics that move the reader to a deep level of engagement with the chosen text and with the Spirit who enlivens the text. It includes reflective listening and silent reading followed by a time of meditation and prayer. *Lectio divina* can be a personal or corporate spiritual practice. In either case, *lectio divina* provides a direct and subjective encounter with Scripture that forms and transforms Christians.

As Christians seek the guidance of the Holy Spirit, in the context of community, they can discern the meaning of Scripture and how it applies to their lives. The discernment of Scripture, both individually and corporately, is an important part of the catechetical process. As Christians encounter Scripture they are formed and transformed into holiness of heart and life.

Transformation

Wesley confirmed his emphasis on works of mercy by his own practices for those on the margins.[29] As an educational approach, the purpose of transformation is to heal and liberate persons, Christian communities, society, and ultimately all of creation. A Wesleyan approach to ecclesiology seeks to accomplish these goals through educationally transformative activities.[30] These activities include evangelism, discipleship, and mission.

Historically the church has embraced a variety of approaches as valid forms of discipleship. But Christians often struggle with how discipleship is related to evangelism. Evangelism is viewed as a process of getting someone converted, and discipleship is the process of educating and equipping new believers into becoming faithful disciples of Jesus Christ. Those who emphasize evangelism are often concerned primarily about a person's decision of faith. The focus is on ensuring that person is saved. What sometimes suffers, however, is the longer-term growth that takes place through the process of discipleship. Likewise, Christian educators often focus on aspects of nurture and education without giving emphasis to mission and service.

As Christians today are called to be faithful disciples they are to engage in God's mission in the world. Missional discipleship includes both engaging in mission and being intentional about faithful discipleship. Given this reality, many congregations are refocusing to embed the gospel through acts of compassion, justice, and love of both neighbor and community. This missional church movement is deeply connected to a theology of the church that is expressed in the very nature of God as mission. The very heart of the triune God is mission. In fact, *missio Dei* simply means the mission of God. The missional pattern of the triune God is captured in the words of Jesus, who told his disciples: "As the Father has sent me, so I send you" (John 20:21). God the Father sent Jesus Christ to redeem all of humanity and creation; Jesus sent the Holy Spirit to empower and guide us; and the triune God sent the church into the world to participate in the new creation. God's mission in the world calls, gathers, and sends the church into the world to participate in God's mission. The nature of the church remains to seek and follow wherever God continues to be active in the world.[31]

A Wesleyan ecclesiology includes the engagement in God's mission in the world. Wesley's emphasis on social reform is a reminder of both evangelizing to "save souls" and to participate in the redemption of all of creation. The consensus is that Wesley's social reform was intentional, taking definite structures that involved others in its execution and providing for its continuance. His life was a model for all Methodists. He wanted to model how they might apply themselves to similar projects within their sphere of ministry. Henry Abelove states that wherever Wesley traveled he provided medical services to people without charge.[32] When the poor were sick, they could seldom afford to go to a physician or an apothecary. Instead they would go to the back door of a nearby rectory or great house where they could get broth, wine, common drugs, advice, or a favor.[33] Wesley deployed genteel and openhanded charity, not only providing coal, bread, and clothes for the needy, especially among his followers, whom he visited house-to-house and oversaw closely, but also creating make-work for the unemployed and, on one occasion, assuming responsibility for an orphaned child.[34]

Wesley's missional engagement is a reflection of his mission to being sent into the world to partner with God in the redemption of all of creation. As Christians today are called to be engaged in faithful discipleship, they engage in God's mission in the world through acts of compassion, social justice, and caring for the poor and oppressed.

Conclusion

Based on a Wesleyan understanding of the means of grace, a holistic approach to Christian education can best be expressed through a catechetical process that includes *formation, discernment,* and *transformation.* As pastors and church leaders develop this catechetical process in their local congregations, it can help persons grow in holiness of heart and life. Also, as Wesleyan-Holiness churches seek to regain an ecclesiology, rooted in the theology and practice of John Wesley, a catechetical approach provides the church with a holistic approach to Christian education.

Questions for Discussion

1. What are some examples of catechesis in your local church? Do they include aspects of formation, discernment, and transformation?

2. How can your local church develop a catechetical process of Christian education that forms and transforms persons into faithful disciples? What needs to be adapted and changed in your congregation to incorporate this catechetical process?

3. In what ways is your local congregation shaping childhood faith through the practice of infant baptism and confirmation?

4. How does your approach of adult formation relate to Wesley's small groups? What can we learn about faithful discipleship from Wesley's small groups? In what ways can they be applied to our context today?

5. In what ways are the communal practices of worship forming and transforming persons into holiness of heart and life? Do they include both Word and Table?

Suggestions for Further Reading

Blevins, Dean G., and Mark A. Maddix. *Discovering Discipleship: Dynamics of Christian Education.* Kansas City: Beacon Hill Press of Kansas City, 2010.

Foster, Charles R. *Congregational Education: The Future of Christian Education.* Nashville: Abingdon Press, 1994.

Henderson, Michael D. *A Model for Making Disciples: John Wesley's Class Meeting.* Nappanee, IN: Evangel Publishing House, 1997.

Maddix, Mark A., and Richard Thompson. "Scripture as Formation: The Role of Scripture in Christian Formation," in *Wesleyan Theological Journal* 46(1) (Spring 2011): 134-49.

Maddix, Mark A., and Jay R. Akkerman, eds. *Missional Discipleship: Partners in God's Redemptive Mission.* Kansas City: Beacon Hill Press of Kansas City, 2013.

Matthaei, Sondra H. *Making Disciples: Faith Formation in the Wesleyan Tradition.* Nashville: Abingdon Press, 2000.

Murphy, Debra Dean. *Teaching that Transforms: Worship as the Heart of Christian Education.* Grand Rapids: Brazos, 2004.

Westerhoff, John. *Learning Through Liturgy.* New York: Seabury Press, 1978.

twelve
THE CHURCH AS FORMATIONAL FELLOWSHIP

Dean G. Blevins

Introduction: Why Fellowship?

Since the early Christian church, *koinonia,* or fellowship, has characterized the nature of a community that gathered in care and support. However, does Christian fellowship exist primarily for the sake of the emotional care and nurture of believers, or might believers expect more of Christian community? Do congregations gather as community, either in all-church gatherings or in smaller groups, primarily to emotionally support each other in times of trial and need? Can fellowship define another purpose, one that moves beyond meeting emotional needs alone and spurs people to something greater within and among themselves?

A Wesleyan perspective offers a broader framework for *koinonia* gatherings, one that provides a habitus for deeper, spiritual healing and empowerment. For Wesley, Christian community provided the context and the means for spiritual formation through an accountable discipleship anchored in shared story, shared practices, and relational bonds. Ultimately this Wesleyan combination of devotion and discipline provides a view of ecclesial fellowship, both in the congregation and through small-group accountability. This view reminds Wesleyan-Holiness people that discipleship, or formation, exists primarily as a community endeavor, one less concerned with individual mentorship or private, emotional consumption. Wesleyan fellowships ultimately form believers into holiness of heart and life both as persons and as communities.

To understand the formative power of Wesleyan fellowship, this chapter explores Wesley's own endeavors to combine communal discipline and devotional action through different expressions of community: church, society, classes, and bands. Following the review of Wesley's varied fellowships, the chapter summarizes Wesley's efforts to connect these various fellowships through the practice of the means of grace and through relationships forged in Christian accountability. The chapter then discusses how congregations, anchored in worship and fellowship, might incorporate the principles of a shared Christian story, Christian practices, and covenant relationships. This approach results in a theologically sound view of fellowship, one that pushes beyond either personal nurture or corporate socialization, to insure a Wesleyan pursuit of holiness of heart and life for persons and for communities.

Wesley's Fellowships

Wesleyans often concede that Christian fellowship constitutes much of John Wesley's ministry to the people called Methodists. Methodism started primarily as a renewal movement, born out of evangelical preaching, but sustained first as a religious order within the Church of England and later as a denominational church.[1] Wesley's own sojourn with different forms of fellowship included his early involvements with religious societies, fellowships established for religious renewal. These societies predated John and Charles's own participation but eventually constituted the core of later Methodist fellowship.[2] Richard Heitzenrater notes three prominent communities that shaped John Wesley's spiritual life and public ministry: the Holy Club of John and Charles Wesleys' days at Oxford, the missionary societies and Moravian community influences in Georgia, and finally the development of the Fetter Lane society and Foundry Societies in London, which combined Anglican, Moravian, and Methodist improvisation into a unique community fellowship that would mark future Methodist gatherings.[3] Beginning in Bristol and Kingswood in 1743, Wesley combined itinerant preaching and the societies throughout his ministry.[4]

The societies provided a primary form of fellowship for the Methodist movement (Methodism organized as the United Societies); however, these groups by no means served as the only form of communal accountability. Wesley also imported the use of Moravian bands (smaller core groups designed for personal renewal) prior to the establishment of uniquely Methodist societies.[5] Later, Wesley adopted and improvised the better known class meeting structure that guided most of the Wesleyan accountability known today.[6] The class meetings, comprised of twelve people and one class leader, grew out of an effort to raise funds for the Bristol preaching chapel, the New Room. Originally the leaders met individually with members. However, the expediency of meeting together, coupled with the power of relational accountability, soon established the "classes" as the central communal gathering within the society even as bands and larger society gatherings continued.[7] The structural importance of these communities will be reviewed below. Collectively these fellowship gatherings (including penitent bands for those seeking rehabilitation back into the groups), alongside other events like the watch night and love feast services, provided a constellation of theologically informed, missionally guided, communal gatherings, all designed to renew the church.[8]

The church, particularly the local congregation, also merits consideration as a formative fellowship. John and Charles Wesley, both ordained ministers within the Church of England, considered their tradition an important, but not exclusive, expression of the church universal.[9] Wesley's own accounting of the church included several distinctive traits, including the Anglican emphasis of preaching the true word of God and administering the sacraments.[10] However, Wesley also understood that the congregation served as a holy fellowship. Wesley writes,

> Lastly, that his followers may the more effectually provoke one another to love, holy tempers, and good works, our blessed Lord has united them together in one—the Church, dispersed all over the earth; a little emblem of which, of the Church universal, we have in every particular Christian congregation.[11]

Wesley's sermon "Of the Church" expanded on Ephesians 4:1-6 by including key dispositions or traits that marked both individual and congregational life: humility, fortitude, love, and unity.[12] A review of Wesley's engagement with differing forms of fellowship reveals Wesley envisioned the Christian life as one of holy love, or holiness of heart and life.[13]

The local church, among other things, served as the primary fellowship to provoke the transformation of people toward both holy tempers (holiness as attitude or disposition) and good works (holiness as expressed lifestyle toward others).[14] Smaller fellowships, societies, classes, and bands all served as strategic fellowships to help congregations, and the church at large, accomplish this mission. To accomplish his intended goals through these fellowships, Wesley employed both specific Christian practices and modes of relationships, shaping participants into John's vision of holiness of heart and life.

Formation within Fellowships: The Means of Grace and Accountable Discipleship

How might Wesleyans connect the smaller Methodist communities (societies, classes, and bands) with the congregation as a formative fellowship dedicated toward holy love? Perhaps the best place to begin would be to explore the practices within these settings, often known as the means of grace, that form and transform believers.[15] Wesley combined a number of key Christian practices (what we might call acts of devotion and charity) alongside strong levels of accountability (what we might call disciplined relationship). This combination of devotion and discipline provided a basis for Wesleyan formation in Wesley's day and potentially in our own.[16]

John Wesley defined a number of religious practices, such as fasting, prayer, worship, and engaging Scripture, as means of grace. His use of the term to encompass a broad array of devotional and compassionate activities seemed rather new, although the concept behind the means of grace proved undoubtedly much older.[17] John's most explicit definition is found in his sermon with the same title. "By 'means of grace' I understand outward signs, words, or actions, ordained of God, and appointed for this end—to be the *ordinary* channels whereby he conveys to men, preventing, justifying or sanctifying grace."[18] Wesley preached this sermon in the midst of a dispute with a group of Moravians who embraced quietism and challenged the value of any participation with God's redemptive work.[19] This dispute provided the catalyst for Wesley emphasizing the means of grace. Albert Outler notes the term appears for the first time in the 1662 edition of the Book of Common Prayer in "The General Thanksgiving."[20]

Wesley categorized the means of grace in several writings. Sometimes John emphasized either personal spiritual formation (works of piety) or specific compassionate acts toward others (works of mercy). Other times he stressed stable practices he believed instituted by Christ and sustained by the church (instituted means of grace); other times John allowed for more contextual practices that proved prudent or wise to adopt and adapt (prudential means of grace). Collectively, as members participated in these practices, Wesley believed they would be shaped into a people of holy love.

Congregations serve as a primary context for practicing the means of grace, particularly participation through corporate prayer, preaching of Scripture, and celebration of Communion, all which Wesley expected as part of weekly worship. However, Wesley also envisioned Christian practices occurring in smaller fellowships. Particularly John saw a life of mutual accountability emerging in the smaller fellowships that provided a relational framework for people's gatherings. Wesley incorporated questions and guidelines to guide the class and band gatherings, specifically questions that invited transparency concerning a person's spiritual journey. People were invited not only to share their journey but also to submit to other people's inquiries, always under pastoral guidance by the class leader.[21]

The power of this form of relational, mutual accountability rested with simple conversations of a religious nature. Indeed, Wesley incorporated Christian conversation as a primary means of grace, instituted and sustained within the church. Alongside prayer and fasting, engaging Scripture, and partaking the Lord's Supper, Wesley asked Methodist lay preachers (or "helpers") to consider their conversations a means of grace.[22] Wesley writes,

> Christian conference: Are you convinced how important and how difficult it is to "order your conversation right"? Is it "always in grace? seasoned with salt? meet to minister grace to the hearers?" Do not you converse too long at a time?[23]

Wesley insisted Christian "conversation" must be plain but gracious speech endowed with truth.[24] Such conversation mirrored and stood alongside holiness of heart and life.[25] Tom Albin notes that the power of these communities is accountability. Surveying early Methodist diaries, Albin discovered that many Methodists underwent transformations within these groups rather than at the field preaching or demonstrative congregational gatherings.[26]

Overall the ongoing level of accountability insured that these groups maintained an intentional focus on the goal of Christian living, holiness of heart and life. To be sure, even the church was understood as a means of grace, providing a form of "social grace," while the fellowship gatherings within Methodism collectively served as an *ecclesiolae in ecclesia* (little churches in the church), or evangelical gathering within the church catholic.[27] Later Methodism struggled to maintain consistency in providing sound leadership for the groups, but Methodists never lost sight of community for the sake of spiritual vitality.[28] This perspective linked the varied intentional gatherings with corporate worship and congregational life.

Formative Fellowships: More than Nurture

To be honest, one must acknowledge that many in the Wesleyan tradition see fellowship as a key component of emotional nurture and therapeutic healing.[29] Nurture does occur through *koinonia* gatherings, particularly as people come to know and care for each other. People struggling with particular problems found healing and new freedom that often marked future self-help or recovery groups.[30] However, this freedom emerges within a disciplined fellowship shaped by a committed community beyond personal needs.[31] Wesley's vision of healing included the possibility of the spiritual transformation of the whole person into holy love, transforming the affections or dispositions of people (their very attitudes and desires) by shaping their habits and practices to express those holy desires toward God's people and God's creation: holiness of heart and life.[32]

The formation of holiness of heart and life occurs first through the broadest expression of fellowship, the life of the local congregation.[33] Christian educators often stress the cultural power of the congregation through socialization or enculturation. As people participate within the life of the church they are shaped by that community's shared values, communicated in language, specific ritual or communal actions, the arrangement of space, the use of time, and the incorporation of symbols.[34] As people embrace the congregational culture, their Christian identity becomes shaped by the actions and expectations of that culture. A congregation that tends to adopt market language for outreach and nurture, one that focuses on individual needs, tends to shape people into the identity of a consumer. A congregation anchored in demonstrable religious experiences like radical conversions tends to shape people's expectations so that only those types of spiritual experiences matter.[35]

A Wesleyan approach to congregational life begins first with worship as the central practice of formation.[36] The arrangement of worship invites participants to enter into the very presence of God through praise, prayer, and confession; to hear the power of the Christian story in Scripture, song, and preaching; to respond and celebrate God's good news at the altar and through Communion; and to be sent to live out God's holy love in the world. For Wesleyans, worship shapes both the order and the life of the church, guiding the other processes that constitute congregational life. For Wesley, worship provided the logic that governed the whole life of the early Methodist movement.[37] However, this corporate practice also deeply penetrates the identity of persons who participate in the narrative and practices that constitute worship.[38]

Similarly, Wesleyans believe that people's lives are shaped in smaller communities. Reviewing the different Wesleyan groups, theorists such as John Drakeford and David Michael Henderson argue the societies, classes, and bands served differing functions that emphasized different relational connections and different cognitive, behavior, or affective learning demands.[39] Other scholars assert group gatherings need to incorporate commitments to specific practices anchored in devotion to God or service toward other people.[40] Regardless of purpose or practices, each group requires careful leadership; and some fellowships, like the selective societies, provided specific leadership training.[41] Through these varied smaller fellowships people partnered together to participate in the means of grace and also to bring their shared spiritual vitality into relationship with each other so they might grow together in holiness of heart and life.[42]

Whether anchored in structure of worship or the relational accountability of disciplined discipleship, ultimately the story at the center of these communities proves central to both holding and guiding fellowship.[43] Within Christian fellowship, this narrative rises from Scripture and the history of Christian tradition, and the story incorporates the contexts that shape the local congregation's mission and ministry. Charles Foster notes this common story allows fellowships to exist across generations, link people into partnerships for ministry, and invite strangers into community.[44] The story may be expressed in worship and testimony, explored in the study of Scripture and tradition, and demonstrated in ministry and missional living.

Alongside the common power of the Christian story, it should be noted by now that formation occurs through shared Christian practices (the means of grace) and through shared accountability to each other, a graceful but disciplined interdependence as people grow together in love. Ultimately, people need to covenant together and enter into some agreement—one that integrates shared practices and communal accountability.[45] The nature of this type of covenant agreement begins as one joins a local congregation both as a testimony of saving faith and as a commitment to Christian community. In Wesley's day, and in ours, such a commitment often requires prohibitions, or the willingness to avoid certain destructive habits that challenge any pursuit of holiness of heart and life.[46] In addition, the commitment means the acceptance and adoption of other practices, like those listed as means of grace. These practices meet fundamental spiritual needs concretely, they are done with others as they continue over time, and they implicitly provide a sense of accomplishment as one engages each practice.[47] Overall, these practices link our lives in Christian fellowship to everyday life, demonstrating how God is at work in the world.[48] In this sense, the liturgical practice of worship and the communal engagement of the means of grace provide a "liturgy of life" in general, recognizing God is at work in the world as well as in gathered fellowship.[49]

The uniqueness of these covenantal relationships in small groups revolves around the sense of transparency and accountability that emerges in community. Wesley recognized not only the power of one-on-one mentoring but also the strength of mutual accountability within groups where transparency existed alongside varying gifts and graces through different individuals. Wesley always envisioned a believer's personal relationship with God through the framework of multiple relationships. A classic example surfaces in his sermon "The Means of Grace." In that sermon Wesley provides an evangelistic encounter of conversion. However, the person is transformed only after encountering several means of grace through his engagement with different relationships including the corporate life of the church.[50] Wesleyan formation occurs primarily through community, whether in the worshipping community or through smaller fellowships of disciplined discipleship—fellowships where people covenant together in a common Christian story to practice differing means of grace and lovingly hold one another accountable through transparent but disciplined relationships.

Questions for Discussion

1. Have you ever had a small-group experience that includes both devotion and discipline (spiritual enrichment but also accountability)?
2. Why is it important to incorporate both congregational life alongside small-group ministry for a truly powerful model of fellowship?

3. Can you name a time where you saw the intersection of the Christian story, Christian practices, and covenant relationships within the life of the church?

4. Can you name examples where congregational practices (worship, compassion, service, discipleship) fostered holiness of heart and life? What were the key factors that stimulated this type of deep discipleship?

5. What are the dangers of pursuing community only to fulfill personal needs?

6. How might congregations order their practices to encourage a culture that reflects Christian identity?

Suggestions for Further Reading

Bass, Dorothy C., ed. *Practicing Our Faith*, 2nd ed. San Francisco: Jossey-Bass, 1997, 2010.

Blevins, Dean G., and Mark A. Maddix. *Discovering Discipleship: Dynamics of Christian Education*. Kansas City: Beacon Hill Press of Kansas City, 2010.

Chilcote, Paul Wesley. *Recapturing the Wesleys' Vision*. Downers Grove, IL: InterVarsity Press, 2004.

Henderson, D. Michael. *A Model for Making Disciples: John Wesley's Class Meeting*. Nappanee, IN: Francis Asbury Press, 1997.

Watson, David Lowes. *Covenant Discipleship: Christian Formation through Mutual Accountability*. Nashville: Discipleship Resources, 1991.

thirteen
THE CHURCH AS EGALITARIAN LIBERATOR

Kristina LaCelle-Peterson

To claim that one of the church's essential endeavors is to be an egalitarian liberator would probably strike some Christians—and non-Christians for that matter—as a bit strange. After all, many churches seem comfortable with the role of conserving culture, of bolstering the status quo whether it comes to women's place, race relations, or the economic structures that oppress many in our society. The danger in this, of course, is that people, both inside and outside of the church, begin to confuse more traditional social mores with the message of the church. Instead of hearing the liberating gospel of Jesus, people perceive the church as a place of preservation of privilege. This chapter attempts to break open the assumption that the message of Christ and the church is safe; the gospel message turns the world upside down.

When I was in graduate school, for instance, I frequently had women ask me how I could stand to be part of such a male-centered church. They could not hear the gospel in churches that treated women as second-class citizens, auxiliaries to the main story, men. They did not realize that there were traditions, such as the Wesleyan-Holiness tradition of which I am a part, that challenged this erroneous view of Christianity as inherently anti-woman. Obviously it is a very serious thing to allow cultural assumptions about religion, for example, to stand in the way of people hearing the true, liberating gospel. Christians should not be like the people standing in the doorway so that the paralyzed man and his friends couldn't get near to Jesus.

But another no less serious result of the church pushing a culturally conservative view of women, in this instance, is that it binds the very ones Jesus freed and it hamstrings the church and its effectiveness. Far too often women are encouraged by the church, even the evangelical church, to bury their talents in the ground despite the express teaching of Jesus against that sort of thing. Ultimately, as Pew and Barna polls show, many women are leaving the church. It's not that the work world is perfect, but many women have positions of responsibility and are treated as competent adults during the week. But then on Sunday they are patronized and often assumed to be less capable in many areas. (For instance, where are the women treasurers, women trustees taking care of property, women on building committees, women in the regular preaching rotation, women elders, etc.? Why isn't all of this completely normal given the preponderance of women in church membership and attendance?) It isn't surprising that they are leaving in droves.

The good news here, as one of my seminary professors used to say, is that at least in the church there is a standard to call people to live up to; Scripture as our shared text has authority in how we construct our Christian life in community. As people in the Wesleyan tradition we have our theological heritage to call people to as well. First, let's look at Scripture. The interpretive moves that follow are in line with our tradition, even if some of our members are unaware of them and their implications.

The first affirmation in Scripture regarding humanity—that we were created in the image of God—is the foundation for thinking about our identity as human beings, and therefore the foundation of any discussion of how the church is to function as egalitarian liberator. If, then, in our society any class of people is deemed inferior, less worthy of attention, they should find in the church a different attitude, a different treatment, because we affirm that all of us, male and female, bear the image of the Almighty. In Genesis 1 we learn another thing about female and male humans: that God invests them with a job to do together. They are to be fruitful, multiply, fill the earth, subdue it, and so forth. The list obviously applies to both male and female since one of them cannot be fruitful without the other. Significantly, neither is depicted as the boss, but they are simply commissioned to do God's work together. In the next chapter, the text offers us a picture of woman's creation (or the splitting of the original unsexed human), and if assumptions about male superiority hadn't clouded our reading and turned Eve into an afterthought or a little helper for Adam, we would see that the drama revolves around the essential equality of the two human beings. As we know, God takes note of the man's need for a partner since he is a social being and won't flourish in a solitary environment. Then God parades the animals before him and Adam names them, recognizing them for what they are: God's creatures but not beings capable of the fellowship he needs. In other words, the animals fail because of their innate inferiority to Adam, whereas the woman, created from a piece of Adam's body, shares his substance as well as the image of God, with the man. Where the animals were rejected on the basis of their lack, the woman is affirmed because she is a full and complete human. It is not a story about her inferiority but her being on Adam's level. To underscore the point further, the text gives us Adam's reaction: "bone of my bones"! Finally someone who can be a partner comparable to him. That's why they cling to one another: they give one another life-sustaining help. (The word for help, as in helpmate to describe Eve, is used primarily in the Old Testament for God helping Israel or helping people. It is not a word that denotes a subordinate or auxiliary helper role.) A text that underscores their delight in being human together has been twisted to portray women as lesser in value and even peripheral to God's story.

The fall narratives have also been read problematically so that sin entering the race is blamed on Eve, and the ensuing punishment is assumed to be what God intended in the first place. Neither of these represents a straightforward reading of the text. With regard to blaming Eve for the fall, it is important to read the entire verse, Genesis 3:6, to keep the scene in better focus: she ate and gave some to her husband *who was there with her* (italics mine). If he is there with her and they are eating together, how is she the only blameworthy party? Besides, when Adam blames Eve for the whole thing, God is not especially impressed. So why did the church get in the habit of perpetrating Adam's accusation? The text suggests, rather, that just as they were equally created in God's image, they are now together in the fall, equally fallen. Furthermore, they share the results of sin, the difficulty in tilling the soil (farming as a human task), the pain of bearing (and raising?) children, the interruption of their relationship. The celebration of mutuality and clinging to one another has been changed to domination and subservience as a result of sin, not as the perfect will of God. Her desire will be for him, but he will rule over her and this ruling over her will be expressions of the brokenness of humanity after the fall. Clearly this is not part of the design of God for humanity and as such it is right we work against it, just as it is right to use plowing tools and tractors to work the soil. After all, in the words of Isaac

Watts, "[Christ] came to make his blessings flow, far as the curse is found." He came to mend what was broken at the fall, not just the intimacy between God and the humans but also the intimacy between them. In Christ we are redeemed and renewed in Christ's image as individuals; we are made a new creation together (2 Cor. 5:17). Part of our work is to be reconcilers, renewing what sin broke; doing God's work together. This reversal of the fall is seen in how the Holiness movement understood Pentecost. They believed strongly that the Holy Spirit was given, for one, so that all persons would be treated with equality and dignity.

Of course, this is what Jesus modeled for us. He showed us what egalitarian welcome and liberation would look like with real people, in fact, with social outcasts of many kinds. For instance, he has his disciples call blind Bartimaeus to him for healing despite the fact they had told the blind beggar to be quiet. The same thing happened with the Syrophoenician woman who had enough faith to believe her daughter could be healed at a great distance and enough spunk to spar with Jesus as he highlighted the bigotry of those around her. He healed people with skin ailments and commended the Samaritan in particular for his coming back to express his gratitude. In both of those stories he addresses grace to ethnic minorities, despised minorities at that, and highlights their faith, underscoring their belovedness before God.

He was moved with compassion for a crippled woman in the synagogue and with anger for those who cared more about order and religious rules than about her well-being. He welcomed the touch of a ceremonially unclean woman and welcomed her voice in public conversation about the grace of God that had been given to her. He took the hand of a little girl who had died. He not only heals but welcomes Mary Magdalene, Susanna, and other women into his circle of followers (Luke 8). And perhaps most comforting of all, he extended kindness, love even, to sinners: the "sinful woman" at the Pharisee's table and Matthew the dirty rotten tax collector.

Even though Jesus did address his preaching to the religious elite of his day and to the wealthy, he concentrated on the masses, especially the social outcasts, including women and the poor. By transgressing social boundaries Jesus thereby calls them into question. He rejects societal assumptions about the inferior value of people in particular groups. In other words, he extends the extravagant love of God to all and in so doing redefines them as worthwhile in God's eyes. Of course, this is one of the things that irritated his critics most: he was profligate with God's grace. And that's where egalitarian liberation begins, with the overflowing grace of God that bursts out of the restrictive social categories that we use to define people and "their place" in our social hierarchies.

In the rest of the New Testament we see this theme revisited. For instance, Paul reminds the Corinthian church that God gives gifts as God wills. For them, for us as well perhaps, the distribution of gifts seems a little inconvenient, calling into question as it does our ideas of who should do what. Take the example of widows, for instance. Jesus' teaching often included widows but demonstrated their status as a despised group in the society: as preyed upon by the wealthy, as despised by a judge, as folks easily overlooked when piety is being judged at the temple offering box. In Acts 6 they are depicted simply waiting for a fair distribution of food, but by the end of Paul's ministry, widows are a particular class of women who are devoted to ministry and have foresworn further marriage. Their status morphs even within the years in which the New Testament documents are being written, and it develops in the next few centuries into the biggest ministry group in the church. It began with welcoming members of a despised class into the fellowship who eventually become indispensable in the ministry of the church.

And this leads us to consider the history of the church, for a moment. Obviously the church has not been perfect, but neither has it been without its inspiring, sacrificial, empowering movements and individuals. Writing about the early church, for instance, Glen Hinson discusses some of the reasons people joined the church early on: not just almsgiving, but assisting the poor, even burying the dead; buying people out of slavery; hospitality networks all over the empire. Many have noted that in the early centuries of Christianity this new faith appealed to slaves, to women, to the poor, to the ethnically marginalized because it was in Christ that they found their full selves affirmed. In creation and in redemption people stood on level ground before almighty God and the church was that place, more and less perfectly, of egalitarian liberation. Grace extended to the "least of these" and then welcomed them into a community of the redeemed called to serve together.

One could also point to the egalitarian ideal that suffused the development of monasticism. In *The Rule of St. Benedict* (the guide for most monastic communities in western Europe for many centuries), everyone was to engage in *ora et labora*, that is, prayer and work. All have to pray; all have to work.

And not only that, but everyone was supposed to take a turn at each type of work; no one was to consider himself or herself above the most menial tasks, mopping the kitchen floor or peeling onions, whatever it may be. With regard to their ministry in their communities, many monastic houses approximated the ministry of Jesus, providing a place of education, care for the poor, health care, and evangelism.

This radical egalitarianism was a feature of Wesleyanism early on. The outreach of the Holy Club, John and Charles Wesley's small group at Oxford, and later the Methodist revival chapels, was typified by a concern for those who struggled with lack of resources. Wesley didn't believe simply in sending money but believed in going to the places where poor people lived, interacting with them as human beings. He fought against the use of grains to make whiskey and rum when it should be used to make bread cheaply so no one had to go hungry. He decried the use of "strong drink" because of the vulnerability of women and children in a system where they were only one alcoholic family member away from utter ruin. And, as many know, he was an outspoken critic of the evil of presuming to *own* another person, someone made in God's image. Rather, they are God's children.

Related to this is the Wesleyan tradition's affirmation of women's leadership. It is beyond the scope of this chapter to examine this in detail. May it suffice to say that Methodists and other Wesleyans during Wesley's day and a hundred years later would concur that the impulse to address the gospel to people at all levels of the social hierarchy is egalitarian by its very nature. If we believe that all are deemed equally worthy recipients of God's grace (by God), then it follows that all are welcomed to participate in the redeemed community. Roles in this new community are based on the gifts given by the Holy Spirit, not on social markers imported from the cultures in which the church functions.

We are to be a new family. Remember the story in Mark 3 where Jesus' family members come to talk with him? When he was told his mother and brothers were there to see him, Jesus responded: "Who are my mother and my brothers?" Then he answers his own question: "Here are my mother and my brothers! Whoever does the will of God is my brother and sister and mother" (Mark 3:34-35). Jesus uses an image that accentuates the even ground that we stand on and the basis on which we approach God. We are welcomed—a divine condescension, to be sure—as family members, and a diverse family, not just the paired opposites (mother isn't opposite to sister or brother). For this reason, in early American Methodism the only term to refer to each other in the body were "Sister" and "Brother" and not, reverend, father, rector, and so forth.

Ultimately one could argue that ideas of egalitarian liberation are grounded in an understanding of the Trinity. Rejecting the theologies afoot among some conservative Christian groups that teach a subordination of Jesus to the Father as a way of arguing for women's subservience to men, this tradition affirms that the triune God is not in hierarchical relationship within the Godhead. Rather, the Trinity is a community of powerful, loving personae working together in creation and new creation. This serves as a model of the egalitarian and shared nature of the church's task. We, too, empowered by the Holy Spirit, work together lovingly toward God's new creation. This does not require us to "keep order," as if the social order we have been socialized into is somehow universal anyway, though that's what nineteenth-century slaveholders claimed and twenty-first-century male headship or male-only church leadership advocates also claim. (Truly, this should give contemporary headship advocates pause, that they are using the same failed—let alone frightfully unloving—arguments that slave owners used.) Rather, following Wesley, the Wesleyan tradition has pictured God's activity revolving around the fecund, energetic, and even messy work of creating and re-creating.

One further note on order—those who believed that women (or blacks, or whatever marginalized group was at hand) were truly inferior had legitimate cause to assign them a lesser role in God's name. Modern folk, though, who affirm the equality of women but argue that God wants them to take a secondary role to men are suggesting that God cares more about order than about justice. In this schema, God cares more about order than about women using the gifts that God put there! For instance, in many churches women are taught to take the back seat in church decision-making and in their marriages or even to assume the child's role of allowing someone else to decide what's best for them. We can and should ask: In what way does this mirror how Jesus treated women? Jesus freed women to follow him around the countryside; he challenged women theologically; he redefined them, refusing to make Mary join Martha in the kitchen and rejecting the comment: "blessed is the womb that bore you and the breasts that nursed you" (Luke 11:27). No, rather, those who do God's will, those who do God's work are the blessed. If Mary herself wasn't to be honored because of the baby she bore, why does the church so often communicate that women's highest calling is in raising children? Rather, the church should be that place that promotes the fullest flourishing of everyone's gifts, for their own spiritual health and the new creation these gifts would assist in building.

A number of years ago a chapel speaker at the college challenged us with this thought: we should endeavor to read the Gospels not always as if we were the faithful disciples but as if we were those who were confused or even opposed to Jesus. Let's go back again to the stories of blind Bartimaeus or the Syrophoenician woman, both people at the bottom of the socioeconomic ladder and both told to leave Jesus alone—by his own followers. Jesus modeled a different type of ministry, and he gently but consistently invited his disciples to join him. Rather than push Bartimaeus away, they are instructed to call him, tell him that Jesus wants to see him. That is the same challenge for our churches now: don't push away the Syrophoenician woman—or any woman—but welcome her. Don't push away those who are different—the economically challenged, those from other ethnicities, the disabled, to name a few. Let's celebrate that it is God who formed us, forgave us, redeemed us, called us into a new family and empowers all of us for service. Rather than being viewed as one of the more restrictive institutions, let ours be a community known for its liberating welcome and extravagant grace to all.

Questions for Discussion

1. The first question for each of us might be: in what aspect of life do I feel like an outsider? Where do I need the egalitarian welcome of God and the liberation Jesus came to bring? Can I let these stories encourage me to receive grace from Jesus, the one who extends grace to all?

2. Who in your community is like the Syrophoenician woman or blind Bartimaeus? Would these folks feel like Jesus wants to help them, or that he doesn't have time for them because the church doesn't have time for them?

3. In what ways has your church welcomed all equally to the Table and equipped them for usefulness in Christ's kingdom?

4. In what ways has your church perhaps mirrored the power dynamics of society, allowing it to seem that men are naturally "in charge" and more suited to represent God?

Suggestions for Further Reading

Chilcote, Paul. *She Offered Them Christ: The Legacy of Women Preachers in Early Methodism.* Nashville: Abingdon, 1993.

Dayton, Donald. *Discovering an Evangelical Heritage.* New York: Harper and Row, 1976.

Hardesty, Nancy. *Women Called to Witness: Evangelical Feminism in the Nineteenth Century.* Nashville: Abingdon, 1984.

LaCelle-Peterson, Kristina. *Liberating Tradition: Women's Identity and Vocation in Christian Perspective.* Grand Rapids: Baker Academic, 2008.

Stanley, Susie. *Holy Boldness: Women Preachers' Autobiographies.* Knoxville, TN: University of Tennessee Press, 2004.

fourteen
THE CHURCH OF COMPASSION AND JUSTICE

Stephen Riley

The Church's Central Mission

The central mission of the church is the proclamation of the good news, the truth that God is redeeming all creation. Because of God's great love—most fully shown in the life, death, and resurrection of Jesus Christ—all are invited to participate in a new family that models what has always been God's design for creation.

When the church is faithful to this central mission, lives are transformed and the possibility of right relationships is opened. Response to the good news brings with it the opportunity to live not only in right relationship with God but also in right relationship with other humans and with all creation. When we are able to live in right relationships we are freed to live as God intended. This way of life is described in a number of ways in our tradition. Words such as *salvation, holiness,* or even *glory* may be used to describe parts of or all the process that follows when people respond to the good news. However, I would like to suggest a helpful concept for us to consider as we think about what it looks like when people respond to the good news, the concept of *shalom*.

Shalom as God's Desire for All Creation

Shalom is a Hebrew concept that is often translated into English as "peace." Unfortunately, although the word *peace* is an important part of *shalom*, by itself *peace* does not capture the fullest meaning of the concept. *Shalom* is best understood by capturing a range of ideas such as wholeness, justice, compassion, righteousness, and security. As one author put it, *shalom* is a place where "all of creation is one, every creature in community with every other, living in harmony and security toward the joy and well-being of every other creature."[1] Therefore, I would suggest that when the church is faithful to its central mission, the possibility of *shalom* occurs here on earth as a vision of what life will be like in the world to come.

This vision of *shalom* is central to our canon of Scripture. Scripture bears witness that *shalom* has been God's hope from the beginning, is what God continues to work for throughout history, and will be God's final victory. Evidence that *shalom* has been God's first desire comes from the very first covenant God made with humans. Genesis 1:26-31 gives a poetic account of the first covenant God made with humanity and creation. "God created humanity in God's own image, in the divine image God created them, male and female God created them. God blessed them and said to them, 'Be fertile and multiply; fill the earth and master it. Take charge of the fish of the sea, the birds in the sky, and everything crawling on the ground.' Then God said, 'I now give to you all the plants on the earth that yield seeds and all the trees whose fruit produces its seeds within it. These will be your food'" (vv. 27-29, CEB). God's covenant with humanity is based on their good care for all creation. Right relationship would bring about flourishing for all as God desired. Likewise, God's covenant with Abraham, recorded in Genesis 12, is rooted in the vision of *shalom*. Abraham and his descendants are chosen and blessed in order that the whole world will be blessed. God's desire for *shalom* is also visible in the giving of the Torah, the law for community life. These instructions set boundaries for right relationships, ordered the community, and provided a way that all creation could thrive.

Our Canon also witnesses to God's ongoing work to sustain the possibility for *shalom*. When Israel was oppressed and enslaved to Pharaoh, God raised up Moses to lead the people in the exodus to freedom. In the land, God charged Israel's kings with the responsibility to care for the people in such a way that the Torah was fulfilled and *shalom* was possible. When the kings and the people of Israel failed to live up to their covenant with God, prophets were sent to exhort the people back to faithfulness. These prophets offered words of judgment and hope so that Israel might respond to God's call and return to the offer to live in *shalom*.

Within Israel's life with God, the clearest example of what it means to live in *shalom* is found in the life, death, and resurrection of Jesus Christ.

Jesus' life among the people brought about opportunities for others to see the very image of *shalom*. When Jesus was present love reigned and people were healed of physical, emotional, and spiritual brokenness. In his death and resurrection, God swallowed up the sting of death as the enemy of *shalom* once and for all. By doing so, Jesus Christ not only modeled a way of living for us all but also initiated a new family that moved the boundaries of *shalom* beyond the family of Abraham to all people. As the missionary Paul would later say, "There is neither Jew nor Greek; there is neither slave nor free; nor is there male and female, for you are all one in Christ Jesus. Now if you belong to Christ, then indeed you are Abraham's descendants, heirs according to the promise" (Gal. 3:28-29, CEB). Jesus Christ has broken down the barriers to *shalom* and it is possible for us to live in right relationship with one another as God intended.

While we believe that Jesus Christ has made it possible for us to live in *shalom* here and now, we also recognize that there will be a final victory where God's *shalom* will be complete. This is the final witness of Scripture. The Canon closes with a vision of a new tomorrow where there would be no more broken relationships, no more abuse, no more death. The Revelation of John ends with a portrait of a new heaven *and* earth where God will rule and make all things new. All of creation will live in right relationship in that new tomorrow. *Shalom* will be the final victory of God. Our tradition's great hope is that because it is God's desire that initiates and completes *shalom*, we are not alone in our work here on earth. We are guided and supported by the power of God at work in us that will bring it to completion.

Roadblocks to *Shalom*

Even though God's desire is for *shalom*, not all creation fully participates in it yet. Sometimes individuals do not participate because of choices they have made. Other times it is because of structures, policies, or institutions of the community that inhibit people and creation from participation in God's *shalom*. This is the beauty of our tradition, which affirms that our freedom to choose comes with both positive and negative fruits. Scripture gives witness to how the destructive, selfish choices by both individuals and communities can bring about the loss of *shalom*. One example of this comes during the prophet Isaiah's life. Isaiah 6 recounts a vision that the prophet has of the holiness of God. This vision occurs during a time of political and social unrest in Israel. Foreign influences were pressing hard against the monarchy, and the people were faced with difficult choices. Many, including the monarchy, had made choices that led away from *shalom*. It is into this situation that Isaiah received his vision and was convicted to the point where he proclaimed, "Mourn for me; I'm ruined! I'm a man with unclean lips, and I live among a people with unclean lips. Yet I've seen the king, the Lord of heavenly forces!" (Isa. 6:5, ceb). Isaiah recognized that his lips were unclean, that he was responsible for the mess in which Israel found itself. Likewise, there are some today who fail to participate in God's *shalom* because of their own choices.

Our tradition has a wonderful history of talking about the individual sin that separates us from living in a loving relationship with God, humanity, and creation. However, the prophet also recognized that the community to which he belonged was responsible for structures, policies, and institutions that had brought about the loss of *shalom*. Unfortunately, our tradition has not talked about the communal aspect of responsibility as much as the individual, at least in certain contexts. This is particularly sad given the fact that our spiritual parents understood that individual and community could not be separated. John Wesley and his followers understood that if one did not take responsibility for the community, then one's spiritual life was not complete.

We must not dismiss the fact that some fail to participate in *shalom* because of powers that are beyond their control, powers that work against God's desire. As long as such powers exist in our communities, this communal aspect of responsibility, which is just as important to the biblical witness as the individual's, must be emphasized if *shalom* is to be a possibility.

Shalom Comes by Justice

Therefore, when any part of creation fails to fully participate in *shalom*, we have work to do. The work we have to do is the work God has always wanted from the covenant people. The prophet Micah sums up this work best when he recorded these words of dialogue long ago, "He has told you, human one, what is good and what the Lord requires from you: to do justice, embrace faithful love, and walk humbly with your God" (Mic. 6:8, ceb). The things God desires in order for all creation to participate in *shalom* are justice, faithful love, and humility. When rightly understood, the last two could be combined into a single category: compassion. When people embrace faithful love (the Hebrew term is *hesed*—a broad term that encompasses much more than feelings of love for someone) and walk in humility they become compassionate toward all of God's creation. Thus, the work of the church becomes the work of compassion and justice. By engaging in this work, we help create the space so that all creation can participate in God's *shalom* here on earth and eventually in God's final victory.

What does working for justice look like? Too often the term *justice* is linked exclusively with legal categories, such as individuals "getting what they deserve" in the eyes of the law. While this is certainly an important aspect of our modern conception of justice, it is not all that the biblical witness holds, especially when it comes to the work of *shalom*. Justice, broadly understood as a biblical concept, is a frame of reference where people are able to flourish and become fully human as God intended. In a short but compelling book, Carol Dempsey points out that Scripture witnesses to a number of ways justice can be accomplished. There are occasions when justice is wrought by liberation, such as when God delivered the Israelites from slavery in Egypt. There are other times when justice is brought about by laws enacted to care for those often overlooked by society, such as the commands for Israel to care for the orphan, widow, and foreigners in their midst. Still yet, there are opportunities for people to speak out against injustice and dehumanization, such as when the prophets of Israel decried their community's failure to be a blessing to the nations. All of these, Dempsey argues, are ways in which God and God's people may work for justice in the world. In our day we must discern what things inhibit creation from participating in God's shalom. What forms of injustice are present, both on an individual and a communal level, that must be dealt with so that *shalom* can reign? Perhaps, it is a form of oppression in your community. Is there a group of people marginalized and dehumanized by certain forms of economic or societal oppression? Some churches have become involved in work with immigration or people caught in the oppression of human trafficking. Others have identified underpaid workers or underserved schools in their communities as groups to work alongside for justice. People caught in the destructive cycle of domestic, sexual, or chemical abuse might be another area that requires your attention. These are just some of the communal structures that must be addressed if *shalom* is to be realized.

Shalom Comes Through Compassion

We must work for justice in its multiple forms; however, justice on its own falls short of all that is required for *shalom* to fully reign. Justice can surely be administered without compassion, as is often the case in legal situations. Yet, as Dempsey writes, "If one desires to live a life rooted in the Spirit of God and the Spirit of Jesus, then one's response to life—to creation—calls for a response that roots justice in something that is far deeper than what would be required by law."[2] This is very much like what the apostle Paul said in his letter to the Corinthians when he wrote, "If I give away everything that I have and hand over my own body to feel good about what I've done but I don't have love, I receive no benefit whatsoever" (1 Cor. 13:3, CEB). When Paul speaks about this kind of love, he is speaking of something much deeper than good feelings and kind actions. He is speaking of a core conviction that motivates people to live in a certain type of relationship to others. It is what Jesus modeled when he walked among us. A great example of what it means to have compassion for another is recorded in Luke's gospel in the parable of the compassionate Samaritan. In Luke's telling of the parable, Jesus invites his listeners to consider the relationship between compassion and justice. A nameless man was robbed, beaten, and left for dead on the side of the road. Two leaders of the people, a priest and a Levite, pass the man on the other side of the road as they walk by. They would have been restricted by purity laws from contact with others, especially one who was "unclean." The third person, a Samaritan, is moved with compassion and not only touches the man but cares for him at great expense. Many times we focus on the Samaritan's ethnicity as the main point of the parable. We say, "Oh, the point is we should look for the undesirable who does good work?" That may be part of the point; however, I think the bigger issue is that the Samaritan had compassion and that the one who asked Jesus the question was told to "go and do likewise." Ultimately, we, too, must go and do likewise. Like the Samaritan, we have to work for justice with compassion for whoever is in need. Our tradition is insistent on the fact that our work for justice must be done from a heart of compassion that has been transformed by the love of God. More importantly, Jesus was clear; those who want to follow him must have a heart of compassion.

Shalom Breaks Down the Boundaries between Us

One of the most difficult issues in working for God's *shalom* is overcoming the "us/them" mentality. This is the thinking that there is a divide between those who have and those who do not have. It is often set between people of different ethnicities, geographical regions, social status, or gender. The unfortunate consequence of this mentality is that it perpetuates a wrong way of thinking that there are some who are more desirable and, perhaps, in a better position to dispense God's love to others. However, our Canon gives witness to the fact that we are to live as if there is no us/them mentality. Jesus lived this way as he welcomed all who came to him and gave each one the dignity of being equal in the eyes of God. The apostle Paul stated the good news this way in his letter to the Galatians, "There is neither Jew nor Greek; there is neither slave nor free; nor is there male and female, for you are all one in Christ Jesus. Now if you belong to Christ, then indeed you are Abraham's descendants, heirs according to the promise" (Gal. 3:28-29, CEB). Paul understood that in Christ there were no more dividing walls. Thus, as people working for *shalom* we must overcome our propensity for division and see each other through the eyes of Christ. This will mean some changes in the way we view others. No longer will we be able to say things like "They're poor and dirty" or "She's just a woman" or "They can't help because they're from the third world." These ways of thinking have no place in God's *shalom* because they limit our brothers and sisters and their ability to participate fully. No, in God's *shalom* we will live into a new way of thinking about ourselves and our neighbors. We will live without fear of the other. We see the other as a possible ally rather than an enemy. In doing so we will catch on to what Paul understood and what Desmond Tutu has tried to capture when describing the African concept of Ubuntu. Ubuntu, he says, is a concept that means a person is "open and available to others, affirming of others, does not feel threatened that others are able and good, for he or she has a proper self-assurance that comes from knowing that he or she belongs in a greater whole and is diminished when others are humiliated or diminished, when others are tortured or oppressed."[3] We must be able to see each other as God's children, each one with incredible worth and invited to participate in God's new family. When God's love enables us to live into this way of seeing each other, new possibilities will arise for partnerships in working toward *shalom*. Those once seen as recipients or adversaries of our work will now be possible partners in our work for justice through compassion. Ones we once thought could offer nothing or were simply the target of our ministries can now be our partners in Christ to accomplish God's work in the world.

Localizing *Shalom* First

Once we understand that we are all God's creation, one in Christ, we can begin our work for *shalom* right where we stand. Too often, for a variety of reasons, the church has felt the need to share the good news somewhere across the globe rather than around the corner. However, for *shalom* to have any sort of global impact, we must first localize it before moving outward. We might even start with our own community of faith. Our local church might need some justice and compassion in order to become a place of *shalom* where the good news can gain traction and grow outward. From there we must move out into our local communities, looking for those places where the roadblocks to *shalom* are placed and join hands in compassion to work for justice so others may join our family. It is only then that we should think about moving outward beyond our community.

Some might ask if this localized *shalom* is contrary to the Great Commission of Matthew 28. There Jesus commanded his followers to make disciples of all nations. It is true that Jesus instructed his followers to make disciples, baptize them, and teach them to obey everything he commanded. However, often there is a sense that mission work must occur somewhere "over there." The "over there" is often looked upon as a poor group of people in desperate need of the good news. We send money and people "over there" and forget that they are made in the image of God, just as we are. They often want to share with us and do not think of themselves as poor or desperate. If we are able to allow God to transform our hearts in such a way as to really see each other as equal partners in the good news, then we could rethink global mission in such a way that we might creatively cooperate to work for justice locally and globally without the unfortunate assumption that one hemisphere's model is particularly correct.

The Three Rs of *Shalom*

When we begin the work for *shalom* it is not enough to wish for it to happen. Very practical steps must be taken in the work of justice through compassion. Often such work will involve very small but serious steps in a community. In a very important book about ministry in urban Atlanta, Robert Lupton discusses the three Rs of community development that he believes are necessary for justice to be accomplished. The three Rs are relocation, reconciliation, and redistribution. I believe that these three Rs are especially helpful for the church as we seek to work for God's *shalom*.

The first R is relocation, by which Lupton means that a ministry must be incarnational, it must live among the people, to be effective. We must recapture an understanding that our community is our parish. We have to incarnate the good news among the people we wish to invite into the family of God. In some cases this may mean physical relocation of our homes or church facilities. In other cases it may simply mean a shift in our thinking about the community to which we are ministering. Either way, if we have no sense of belonging to the community in which we work for *shalom*, we will fail to fully participate in the healing and wholeness that God desires for all creation.

The second R is reconciliation. It seems self-evident that the good news of God should bring about healing in relationships. Indeed, *shalom* is about right relationships. However, because of our brokenness there is much work to be done. The work of justice through compassion requires that the church become a place where people can be reconciled not only to God but also to one another and to creation. For *shalom* to be a possibility, we must consider our relationship with God's creation, both human and nonhuman. Doing so will often include the difficult work of forgiveness, which requires the work of restoration between alienated parties. Restoration is not easy work. Often we are much more willing to "forgive and forget" than to actually engage in the courageous endeavor of healing that will bring about new relational possibilities by acknowledging the hurt and pain of the past but also the powerful transformation possible in the love of God.

The final R is redistribution, by which Lupton means the just distribution of resources among everyone. For God's *shalom* to reign, there must be an availability of resources to all creation. This means that if we are serious about seeing God's purposes accomplished here on earth, we will have to become serious about helping the flow of economic and human resources into underserved areas in our communities so that everyone can have the opportunity to participate in *shalom*. Jesus' instruction in Matthew 25 is particularly important in this regard. He reminds his followers that when they care for the stranger, the homeless, and the prisoner, they are doing so as if they did it unto him. In our day these same people are those that are often marginalized by our community's structures that inhibit people from fully participating in *shalom*. Jesus reminds us that we must work, often by redistributing resources so that even those on the margins have the opportunity to enjoy God's desire for *shalom*.

Shalom Looks Like...

A final question should be, "What would *shalom* look like, if we were faithful to our central mission?" I think an appropriate starting point for the discussion comes from Paul's letter to the Ephesians. In chapter 2, verses 11-22 he writes a sustained vision of what Christ has done. In it he describes the fact that in Christ those who were once far away, the "uncircumcised" or Gentiles, are now reconciled and at peace with the commonwealth of Israel. In the cross, God has made the two into one and there is no division, no alienation. Now, in Jesus Christ, we are all one being built into a dwelling place for God. When the church is faithful to its central mission, God works in and through us to make *shalom* a reality for all creation.

Questions for Discussion

1. How is *shalom* a helpful concept for thinking about the church's central mission?
2. Consider some of these biblical passages in relationship to the concept of *shalom*. What aspects of peace, justice, and compassion are highlighted in each?
   a. Psalm 72
   b. Isaiah 11:1-9
   c. Ezekiel 34:25-29
   d. Matthew 12:15-21
3. What roadblocks to *shalom* are present in your life and community?
4. How would your community look if *shalom* broke down the us/them barriers?

5. What aspects of the three Rs of *shalom* do you believe your community should work on?

Suggestions for Further Reading

Brueggemann, Walter. *Peace*. St. Louis: Chalice, 2001.

Dempsey, Carol J. *Justice: A Biblical Perspective on Justice*. St. Louis: Chalice, 2008.

Lupton, Robert D. *Compassion, Justice, and the Christian Life: Rethinking Ministry to the Poor*. Ventura, CA: Regal, 2007.

Miles, Sara. *Jesus Freak: Feeding, Healing, Raising the Dead*. San Francisco, CA: Jossey-Bass, 2010.

Nouwen, Henri J. M. *Creative Ministry*. Garden City, NY: Image, 1978.

Perkins, Dr. John M. *Let Justice Roll Down*. Ventura, CA: Gospel Light, 2012.

Woodley, Randy. *Shalom and the Community of Creation: An Indigenous Vision*. Grand Rapids: Eerdmans, 2012.

fifteen
THE CHURCH AS A WITNESSING COMMUNITY

David Busic

I was driving down a main street one summer and stopped at a traffic light. It was dusk and just beginning to turn dark. Suddenly, over my air conditioner and radio, I heard someone calling out from the corner. I turned to see a young man, Bible in hand, wearing a sandwich board with something religious written on the side. He was barking out a sermon that sounded very much like a Mayan prediction about the end of the world. Not wanting to be obvious, I slowly cracked my window to hear what he was saying. I will admit that at first I was a little embarrassed for him, until to my surprise I looked around and noticed that nobody was listening. Nobody stopped on the street to evaluate his message. There was no heckling or ridicule. They simply drove past him as if he were the invisible man. I am not questioning his motives. In fact, there is a part of me that admires his tenacity and courage. But is this what witnessing of the kerygma looks like?

The Purpose of Pentecost

The book of Acts describes Pentecost with powerful images: freight train sounds of wind from heaven; tongues of fire dancing on disciples' heads; and United-Nations-style language interpretation. Luke is trying to describe a phenomenon that had never been experienced before. He does it by offering metaphors that picture the purpose of Pentecost: the image of wind, the image of fire, the image of tongues of fire. It is important to observe Luke's exact words. He does not say a mighty windstorm came blowing through the room. He said, "There came a sound *like* the rush of a violent wind" (Acts 2:2, italics mine).

It was something that was heard, but it was a completely unique and a divine event. He also does not say that fire fell from heaven and singed the hair of the disciples. He said, "Divided tongues, *as of fire,* appeared among them, and a tongue rested on each of them" (Acts 2:3, italics mine). It was something that was seen, but it was a completely unique and divine event.

Luke's purpose was not to scientifically depict what happened at Pentecost, but to reveal the deeper spiritual meaning behind the events. What happened was *like* wind and *like* fire. It was an extraordinary invasion from heaven that could not be explained in ordinary terms. Therefore, Luke draws word pictures with descriptive meanings. To interpret, wind is descriptive of power. Fire is descriptive of purity. But it was not power for power's sake or purity for purity's sake. Rather, the power and purity given was intended to *do* something. That something is expressed in the next image employed by Luke: the image of tongues. Tongues refer to language. Here is one of the most important purposes of Pentecost—the proclamation of Christ.

The last words Jesus spoke to his disciples before ascending into heaven were: "But you will receive power when the Holy Spirit has come upon you; and you will be my witnesses in Jerusalem, in all of Judea and Samaria, and to the ends of the earth" (Acts 1:8). It was a missional mandate. But how were they going to do that? They did not have the power, courage, or the passion to be witnesses. These were simple men and women who, for the most part, could only speak one language, and when it came to sharing the gospel, were probably afraid to do even that. They needed something they did not previously have to fulfill the Great Commission given by Jesus. They needed a gift.

It is striking to note that in all three of the Pentecost images there is a reference to speaking or hearing. They *heard* the sound. They were given the gift of language to *witness.* Even the flames of fire were in the shape of tongues. Why was the church born? It was born to bear witness to the good news of Jesus. What does the Holy Spirit give to the church? He gives an empowered life that brings witness to speech. Not a mystical, ecstatic language with unclear meanings, but language that empowered the church to preach and proclaim the gospel to every nation, tribe, and people to the ends of the earth. And when Peter mounts the pulpit to proclaim the kerygma, everything changes. The church is born.

Heralds and Witnesses

A *herald* is a person who proclaims important news. *Kerygma* is the Greek word for proclamation or preaching. It is a cognate of the Greek verb *kerusso,* which means to proclaim as a herald. When the two words are put together, it refers to proclamation, announcement, or preaching of the good news. A herald of kerygma is a messenger of hope (see Matt. 3:1; Luke 4:18-19; Rom. 10:14). That was the proclamation of the original Pentecost. But Pentecost remains as a symbol to us today. Pentecost is what gives the church the passion to care, the boldness to move out, and the power to speak. Pentecost is what purifies believers, sets their tongues on fire, and enables them to communicate a clear proclamation of the gospel. The gift of the Holy Spirit gives the church her voice!

When the Holy Spirit was poured out on the first Christians, they poured into the streets. The Spirit compelled the church outward. With this newfound power they were able to witness and communicate in ways that were previously impossible. God's timing for the launch of the church could not have been better. There were thousands of people in Jerusalem for the Feast of Pentecost from many different nations and language groups.

This brings to mind the story of the Tower of Babel (Gen. 11). At Babel God confused the languages of the people and dispersed the nations around the world in order to stop their evil intentions from multiplying. There was a type of confusion among the nations again, only this time it derived from the fact that everyone heard ordinary men and women, filled with the Holy Spirit, speaking in the mother tongues of their own people. "In our own languages we hear them speaking about God's deeds of power" (Acts 2:11). This was a miracle of witnessing. Pentecost was a reversal of Babel. The result was the birth of an international, multilingual church.

Luke finds it important to tell his readers that there were no less than sixteen world areas represented at Pentecost. What is interesting about the list is that several of the nations had ceased to exist. The Parthians and Medes, for example, were kingdoms in history that were no longer in existence. Luke delivers a message that this gospel good news is for every tribe and tongue and nation—past, present, and future. Young and old, close and far, men and women get in on the blessing. Everyone can hear the good news and everyone can find a voice to bear witness.

That is Peter's big idea for his sermon: "In the last days it will be, God declares, that I will pour out my Spirit upon all flesh, and your sons and daughters shall prophesy, and your young men shall see visions, and your old men shall dream dreams. Even upon my slaves, both men and women, in those days I will pour out my Spirit; and they shall prophesy" (Acts 2:17-18). Because of what happened at Pentecost, every Spirit-filled person is given a voice to witness about Jesus Christ!

These in-breaking signs of power, purity, and Spirit-enabled communication threw the entire population into turmoil. Rather than ignore the heralding disciples and their message, everyone wanted to know what was going on. They were amazed and perplexed with questions—two to be exact. These two questions function as bookends between the beginning of the account and the end of the account.

Question 1: "What does this mean?" (v. 12) and question 2: "What should we do?" (v. 37). The answer to the first question came as a gospel sermon from Peter. The convicted response of the hearers to the sermon precipitated the second question. Peter's answer is the heart of kerygmatic witnessing: "Repent, and be baptized every one of you in the name of Jesus Christ so that your sins may be forgiven; and you will receive the gift of the Holy Spirit" (v. 38). That very day three thousand people were baptized and added to their number.

The Church as Witness

Essential to the church is the proclamation of the gospel. This happens in two ways. First, churches that are filled with Spirit-filled people bear spiritual fruit, "And day by day the Lord added to their number those who were being saved" (v. 47). All Christ followers are heralds of the gospel in this sense of being witnesses. But the church has also recognized that there are those who are called to the particular vocation of proclamation. There are those who are called to preach.

Augustine, who is often considered to have written the first textbook on preaching, said that the purpose of preaching is to teach, delight, and move. The teaching and moving aspect of preaching seems fairly self-explanatory. But what does it mean to delight? At the very least to delight is to make the preaching interesting, certainly. But if we take Acts 2 seriously, it necessarily has something to do with a life compelling enough to capture others' attention to hear the message. Thus both witnessing and preaching involve more than the message. They involve the lives of the messengers. Only when the church reflects Christ will her witness be "delightful."

As I remember the young preacher on the street that summer night, it is not with any sense of condescension. While I am not inclined to agree with his methods, I must at least also acknowledge that tens of thousands drive by churches every day and just ignore them. They drive by without ever stopping to think, much less ask, "What does this mean?" Perhaps if the lives of the people of the church were today filled with the Spirit of Pentecost, more would be open to hearing the message of the church's witnesses.

I was having a conversation with someone who was very happy to have found our church. He introduced himself to me after the service and said: "I've been bouncing around some other churches but haven't found one that I was really comfortable being a part of." I was glad to hear him say he felt comfortable to our church. But then, in an attempt to encourage me, he continued: "This church is one of the best-kept secrets in the city." That "encouraging" comment has been like a stone in my shoe. Why are the church and the message of the church a secret? I realize that the events of Pentecost are unique and unrepeatable in salvation history. Nevertheless, I am convinced that when the Spirit of Jesus (the same Holy Spirit who was poured out at Pentecost) is empowering his church, then at least *some* of the people *some* of the time should be asking the question: "What does this mean?" If not, heralds and witnesses of the gospel will spend nearly all of their time answering "What should we do?" to people who already know the answer and have heard it for many years. In other words, the church sometimes preaches only to itself. Preaching and witnessing exclusively to the already converted is not the goal or the mission of the church.

Salt of the Earth

Being and doing are intricately connected in Christian witness. Christians cannot effectively do what they have not internally become. What we do rises from who we are. This is the proper order of the Sermon on the Mount. The indicative (being) beatitudes precede the imperative (doing) commands. Transformation precedes lifestyle. We must become persons of the message before we deliver the message.

Jesus said, "You are the salt of the earth" (Matt. 5:13). To modern ears, Jesus might say, "You are distinctive."

I heard a pastor tell the story about a wedding he conducted for a fine young Christian couple in his church. It was a society wedding with about 250 people in attendance. The guest list included several high-ranking government officials and professional athletes. It was a wonderful occasion.

The reception speech was given by the bride's father. He related to the guests how the young groom had come to ask for his daughter's hand in marriage. The father (who was not a Christian) liked the young man very much. He recounted telling the young man (who was a Christian), with the best of intentions: "You are still very young. You have just graduated from college, and marriage is a lifelong commitment. So why don't you just get an apartment and live together for a while and see how it works out?"

The father continued, "I was immediately made aware that I had made a big mistake. My future son-in-law said to me, 'There are three people involved in this marriage: your daughter, myself, and God. And because that is true, I could not even think about just moving in together.'"

At this point in the speech, the guests, most of whom were not Christians, burst into applause. The father finished his speech by saying, "There is one more thing I have to tell you, and I have their permission to share it, they have still not slept together!"

This astounding piece of news was greeted with even louder applause and my pastor friend said, "I had some very interesting conversations after the meal with people who wanted to know: Tell me about this strange thing that you Christians believe?"

The further our society moves from the teaching and practice of Jesus, the more distinctive the beliefs and lifestyle of his followers should be. Moreover, the more distinctive the lifestyles of Christ followers are, the more frequently people will ask the question: "What does this mean?"

The biblical category for that distinctiveness is "holiness," which means: *different, set apart, unique in character, like the Father, like the Son.* This is not about being weird or obnoxious. This is not about being irrelevant, eccentric, or out of touch. Sometimes, in our attempts to be distinctive, the church has been prone to limit our distinctiveness to what we *avoid* and are *against*. The first Christians, on the other hand, were distinctive for what they *did* and what they were *for*. (Read Acts 2:42-47; 3:1-10; 4:32-37.)

They gave gladly and sacrificially until there were no needy persons among them. They were fearless witnesses undaunted by threats and beatings, and even imprisonment and death. Their worship was not confined to special days and places. They broke bread in their homes and ate together with glad and sincere hearts, praising God and enjoying the favor of all the people. And their selfless love, magnanimous generosity, and unbounding compassion set them apart from what those outside the faith were accustomed to seeing.

As a result, the "fear of the Lord" and the "joy of the Lord" came together in such perfect harmony that nonbelievers were simultaneously attracted to them and afraid to join them. That is holiness in practice! They were God's holy people. They were different. They were distinctive. They were the salt of the earth. And their lives begged the question: "What does this mean?"

Light of the World

Jesus also said, "You are the light of the world. A city built on a hill cannot be hid" (Matt. 5:14). Again, what does that mean to modern ears? "You are visible."

When Christians are in the world and *of* the world it negates their witness. But conversely, when Christians are not of the world and not *in* the world it also negates their witness. There are disturbing indications that many Christians are retreating from the world as fast as they can.

A pastor friend of mine took a sabbatical that provided an opportunity for him to visit various churches over a period of three months. One particular Sunday, following a very serious event in the world, he visited a small church in the area he was staying. Given the seriousness of the issue and the closeness to home, he expected something of it mentioned in the service, or at the very least during the prayer time, but there was nothing. Furthermore, on the Tuesday following that Sunday, there was a presidential election taking place. But again there was no mention of the upcoming election, and nothing that had anything to do with the outside world whatsoever, except the death of one elderly member of the congregation. What he said next was revealing: "It could just as easily have been 1904 as 2004." As he visited various other churches, he discovered that this was not the exception, but the norm. Many of the churches seemed to focus on themselves and their needs, to the exclusion of anything outside their orbit. When the church begins to believe that what happens on Sundays has little or nothing to do with the rest of the world, our voice has been lost, and with it our visibility.

Jesus' reference to a city on a hill may seem to have no connection with the theme of light. However, in the ancient world many cities were built in elevated places for defensive purposes, also making them highly visible. Additionally, because there was no electricity in the first century the light of any city at night was clearly visible, regardless of its elevation. Imagine a town with hundreds of fires and lights burning, and now place that town on top of a hill. You could not miss it! It could be seen from miles away! "A city built on a hill cannot be hid."

Jesus' message is obvious. In the moral darkness of the world, my followers are to be head and shoulders above the rest, clearly visible to everyone around them. The church's light is to shine so that people will see and hear the message and finally praise our heavenly Father.

If the house is dark at night, there is no sense in blaming the house. That is what happens when the sun goes down. The question is: Where is the light? If meat goes bad, there is no sense in blaming the meat. That is what happens when bacteria breeds unchecked and the preservative does not inhibit decay. The question is: Where is the salt? If society is dark and corrupt, there is no sense in blaming society. That is what happens when a sinful, fallen world is left to itself and human evil is unchecked. The probing question is: Where is the church?

The first Christians could have turned their upper room into a protective sanctuary and invited people to come to them. Instead, they spilled out into the streets, into all of the decay and corruption and darkness and became salt and light. They were distinctive and visible, and God was glorified and the church grew.

If the church is not distinctive and visible, there will be no witness. And when there is no witness there can be no kerygma. "What should we do?" will not be asked until "What does this mean?" is made compelling.

Natasha grew up in an atheistic family in the Soviet Union. She studied Marxism and Dialectical Economics at Moscow University, graduating with honors in all her classes. During the cold war, she traveled the world teaching Russian and spreading her belief in Marxism. She lived in many countries in Europe and Asia, including India where she encountered the major religions of the world firsthand. Her conclusion was that they were a waste of time.

Eventually, she arrived in Scotland to teach at Harriet Watt University. Peter Grainger, a pastor in Edinburgh, was privileged to baptize her in his church. He asked her, "Natasha, you studied all the major philosophies and major religions of the world, and found them to be lacking. What changed your mind?"

Her answer was very revealing. She did not say his sermons (although I'm sure the Lord used them)! No, she said, "I met Peter and Margaret Martin. And they were different."

Peter and Margaret Martin were senior adults in Peter's church. And because Margaret had a burden for the spiritual condition of Russia, in her late sixties she decided to learn the Russian language. She showed up in a class being taught by (guess who?) Natasha. She learned a little Russian, got acquainted with Natasha, invited her to her home, and they became friends. One day Natasha asked her, "What is it about you and Peter? You're just very different." Margaret explained that she was a Christian and extended an invitation, "Why don't you come to our church where you'll hear the Christian message explained clearly every week?"

And so one Easter, several years ago, she did. The Holy Spirit opened her heart to the message of the gospel, and she came to a deep and living faith in Jesus Christ. Since then Natasha has had an incredible impact on her friends and family in her return visits every year to Russia.

How did she become a Christian? Through a herald called Pastor Peter? Yes, thank God. But she would have never heard the gospel preached unless she had seen it lived out in the life of an ordinary, Spirit-filled Christian who caused her to ask, "What does this mean?"

Questions for Discussion

1. What are the fruits of a Spirit-filled Christian and what are some examples of how their fruits are made evident in the kerygmatic witness of the church?

2. In what ways are you engaged in kerygmatic witness? What are the challenges you face in being salt and light?

3. What are some examples of how your congregation is engaged in kerygmatic witness? In what ways can your church be more effective in witnessing the good news of the gospel?

4. Since all Christians are called to engage in kerygmatic witness, what role does the pastor play in kerygma (proclamation) and what role does laity play? How are they similar but also different?

Suggestions for Further Reading

Jones, Scott J. *The Evangelistic Love of God and Neighbor: A Theology of Witness and Discipleship.* Nashville: Abingdon, 2003.

Pohl, Christine D. *Making Room: Recovering Hospitality in the Christian Tradition.* Grand Rapids: Eerdmans, 1999.

Pointer, Lyle, and Jim Dorsey. *Evangelism in Everyday Life: Shaping and Sharing Your Faith.* Kansas City: Beacon Hill Press of Kansas City, 1998.

Stetzer, Ed. *Living the Missional Nature of the Church.* Nashville: Lifeway Publishing, 2008.

Stone, Brian. *Evangelism after Christendom: The Theology and Practice of Christian Witness.* Grand Rapids: Brazos Books, 2006.

PART 3
The Church as Organized Organism

sixteen
THE BODY OF CHRIST
A THEOLOGY OF ECCLESIAL RELATIONSHIPS

Richard P. Thompson

The poem on the children's lips in their Sunday school class is familiar to most of us. They were sitting in a circle around their teacher, clutching their hands together with all but their index fingers pushed into their palms. "Here is the church, and here is the steeple," they chanted. And then, turning their hands over and revealing their wriggling fingers, they cried out, "Open the doors, and see all the people!" It is a simple message, to be sure. Yet it tells children at an early age that church is not identified by a sign out near the street, a mailing address, or a Web site. The church really is about people!

There is nothing new about that affirmation. When we hear the word *church* most of us do not think first about a church building or even an institution, even though we *do* associate such things *with* the church (since, after all, they have typically come along with how we have "done" church for centuries). In fact, when we use the word *church* or even just have the idea of church in our minds, most of us probably do not give much thought about our assumptions (or lack thereof) that tag along with that word (or idea) and that inform how we use it. For we may know *that* the church is ultimately about people rather than a building or address or Web site, but often we give little or no attention to *what* the assumptions—theological or otherwise—that actually shape our understanding of church (our ecclesiology) may be. And the first place where we see the influence of our "assumed" ecclesiology is in the different kinds of relationships embodied within the ecclesial context. For instance, the frequency of biblical instructions about loving or living at peace with one another may tell us that, in these general yet basic relational issues, there may ultimately be ecclesiological reasons behind them that have gospel implications. That is, there is more to loving one another than meets the eye!

As Wesleyans in theological orientation and heritage, we look to Scripture as our primary source for theological reflection. And we should acknowledge several things about ecclesiology and the Bible from the beginning. First, the Bible's contributions to discussions about ecclesiology and the church are mostly indirect rather than specific in nature. That is, whereas the biblical texts may offer us different ecclesiological insights, few if any biblical texts offer an explicit or comprehensive ecclesiology. Second, the Bible offers a variety of perspectives regarding ecclesiology. Of course, the Old Testament contributions focus on the role of Israel as the "people of God" (and should be considered in discussions of ecclesiology), with the New Testament texts both drawing on these Old Testament texts and building upon them in light of the coming of Jesus as the Christ. However, we should also not assume a unity of thought among either the Old Testament or New Testament texts themselves, since these different texts were written by different authors and addressed different contexts, situations, audiences, and the like. Because of the diversity inherent within the biblical Canon, we should not be surprised by the many different images used to describe aspects of the church in the New Testament: "a chosen race, a royal priesthood, a holy nation" (1 Pet. 2:9); branches of the vine (John 15:5); God's holy temple (1 Cor. 3:16); the bride of the Lamb (Rev. 19:7); the circumcision (Phil. 3:3); God's field (1 Cor. 3:9); and Christ's letter (2 Cor. 3:2-3), among others. This variety indicates the rich diversity in expression and thought, not a unity in perception. Third, biblical contributions to discussions about ecclesiology sometimes come from those texts that include little if any "ecclesial" terminology. Thus, narrative texts may have wonderful input into our thinking, even when the "default mode" is to turn to New Testament letters because of their direct means of discourse into specific church contexts. For instance, although the term *church* never appears in Luke's gospel, the meal scenes that frequent the narrative landscape offer significant pictures about what it means to be and relate to one another as the church.[1] Because at the heart of the biblical Canon is the belief that God speaks through these texts as sacred Scripture to guide and instruct the church (which is the point of inspiration as emphasized in 2 Tim. 3:16-17),[2] we may make the bold claim that *all* biblical texts to which the gathered church listens in worship potentially add to these ecclesiological discussions.

These points being stated, the Pauline metaphor of the church as the "body of Christ" (1 Cor. 12:12-31; see also Rom. 12:4-8) stands out among other biblical images and contributions to a Wesleyan (and biblical) ecclesiology. There are two reasons for this. On the one hand, the passage itself indicates a more developed sense of ecclesiological thought, rather than mere reliance on stated images (like many other biblical metaphors) left to stand on their own. On the other hand, and perhaps more importantly, there are indications that this "body language" that Paul appropriates in 1 Corinthians 12 provoked further developments or thought regarding its implications for other churches in later years (see, e.g., Eph. 4:1-16; Col. 2:16-19).[3] The contributions of this particular metaphor in terms of its depiction of a theology of ecclesial relationships become even more striking when that image and passage are explored in relation to the overall letter. Thus, this chapter examines the "body of Christ" metaphor in 1 Corinthians 12 in terms of two types of ecclesial relationships: the ecclesial relationship between God and the church and the ecclesial relationships between those who comprise the church. The final section briefly explores some implications of these biblical concepts for a contemporary Wesleyan ecclesiology.

The Ecclesial Relationship between God and the Church

Although the apostle Paul describes the church as the "body of Christ" later in the letter known as 1 Corinthians, this follows his general assessment of the situation in the Corinthian congregation in the first four chapters of the letter. In these opening chapters, Paul reveals the theological orientation of the letter,[4] which is assumed when the apostle appropriates the "body of Christ" metaphor as he addresses questions about spiritual gifts within the church. Here he reflects about knowing God (see, e.g., 1 Cor. 1:21; 2:8, 11, 14) and belonging to Christ (see, e.g., 1:9; 3:23), which are significant and related themes that weave their way throughout the letter. What is particularly noteworthy is the apostle's focus upon God and God's salvific activity. One should not miss the fact that, in these four chapters, the apostle mentions God almost as often as in the remaining twelve chapters. It was God who "called" and "chose" the Corinthian church (1:9, 24, 26-28). It was "the grace of God" that this church had been given (1:4). This church was the beneficiary of "the wisdom of God" that confounded human wisdom in the cross of Christ (1:18-31).

For our purposes, two expressions accentuate the relationship between God and the church that the apostle Paul understands as central to the gospel message. First is his identification of the Corinthian believers as "the Church of God," *ekklēsia tou theou*. Although the expression has been understood or translated in this Christian sense, it originates from the Septuagint and translates the Hebrew *qahal Yahweh* or "assembly of the Lord" (e.g., Deut. 23:2-4, 8; 1 Chron. 28:8; Mic. 2:5); the noun *ekklēsia* may even refer to the equivalent *qahal Israel* (e.g., Deut. 31:30; 1 Kings 8:14, 22, 55; 1 Chron. 13:2, 4; 2 Chron. 6:12-13). In other words, Paul borrows a description for the assembly of Christian believers from the Scriptures of his day, thereby linking or placing the church in continuity with those identified in the Old Testament as the covenantal "people of God."[5] Just as a central feature of the covenant was the understanding of God's gracious calling of Israel to be God's possession and people (see, e.g., Exod. 19:5; Deut. 7:6; 14:2; 26:18), the appropriation of the expression *ekklēsia tou theou*, which literally means "those called by God,"[6] affirms a divine gathering and calling of believers, not unlike what Israel experienced centuries before.[7] Of course, what made Paul's claim so radical was that these Corinthian believers would have also included those of Gentile background. Nonetheless, the apostle reiterates their divine calling, even though it defied society's arguments to the contrary (see 1 Cor. 1:26-31). That calling means that they are to be formed as a believing community—a people—that (*a*) belongs to God and (*b*) does not belong to the world as it once did.

Related to this divine calling is another Pauline expression that describes this relationship between God and the church, which focuses on specific divine activities on behalf of the church. After depicting the Corinthian believers as the "church of God"—the *ekklēsia tou theou*, "those called by God" or the people of God in Corinth—he then states that they are "sanctified in Christ Jesus" and therefore called "saints" (1 Cor. 1:2). That is, God was responsible for the sanctification of the Corinthian church, thereby making *them* to be God's "holy ones" (*hagioi*) who, as a result of that divine work (note the perfect passive participle *hēgiasmenois*), are to live in ways that reflect God's holy character (that this church had all kinds of issues indicating their failure to live faithfully is a different issue). Because of what God had done, Paul desires the Corinthian believers to see themselves as formed into a faith community that is called to holiness. The prepositional phrase "in Christ Jesus" (1:2) should be understood as indicating both the means and the sphere of that sanctification: God's sanctifying work occurs *through* Christ and the believing community has life as God's holy people *in* him as well.[8] Thus, such an understanding of the church in terms of God's sanctified community recognizes what should be the cooperative roles of both God and community in the ongoing life and conduct of its members. God has called and formed this community through the cross of Christ, and that community shares its collective life as it gathers together and partakes in the eucharistic cup and broken bread (see 10:16-17).

The Ecclesial Relationships between Those Who Comprise the Church

It is with this important theological understanding of the church in relation to God that Paul addresses a number of ethical issues that plagued the Corinthian church (1 Cor. 5—14). Interpreters in the past have often confused these latter chapters as separate treatments apart from the initial theological discourse, but these materials actually reflect the apostle's natural thought progression or the "next steps" of his theological reflection as it relates to issues facing that specific congregation.

One particular issue, as Paul addresses it in 1 Corinthians 12—14, has to do with some members of the Corinthian congregation who apparently perceived some spiritual gifts as more important than others and who used those gifts for their own advantage (see 14:4, 6; cf. 10:23-24). Such practices and attitudes placed the unity of the congregation in jeopardy, a topic that coincides with the apostle's prior theological discourse (see, e.g., 1:10-17; 3:1-9). While Paul is quick to affirm the diversity of those gifts, from the beginning he reminds the Corinthian believers of the divine source of those gifts, which is consistent with their calling and founding as a church, as the people of God: "the same Spirit" (12:4), "the same Lord" (v. 5), "the same God who produces all of them in everyone" (v. 6, CEB). And this is where Paul compares the Corinthian church to a body: "For just as the body is one and has many members, and all the members of the body, though many, are one body, so it is with Christ" (v. 12). The analogy of the body was often used in that day to illustrate from nature the essential unity of the social order, as well as the role and importance of different persons within it.[9] And so Paul similarly appropriates the analogy of the body to affirm the church's unity in relation to what God has done and is doing through the Spirit (see esp. vv. 7-11). Within this theological context, that analogy depicts some basic ecclesiological concepts with regard to the relationships among those who make up the church.

First, we see in the Pauline image of the "body of Christ" that what is central to their relationships is not an ambiguous idea called "unity" but the common good of the church (v. 7; see 10:23). In other words, the body of Christ works together to accomplish its divine calling or its reason for existence in the world. Just as different parts of a body have necessary functions for the good of the whole body, different members of the church have active roles to fulfill in order for the church to be and do as God calls her as the people of God. Relating to one another in such dynamic roles of ministry is not due to the nature of the church as the "body of Christ" or, more specifically, as the extension of Jesus' own incarnational, bodily ministry. After all, Paul seldom emphasizes Jesus' life in his letters, and Jesus' incarnation was a reality not to be repeated again or confused with the ministry of the Spirit. Rather, the apostle affirms how the church's diversity may actually *serve* its unity as the body that belongs to Christ.[10] Paul makes it clear that these different roles or "gifts" (*charismata*) are given by divine appointment (12:11, 28). It is likely that Paul does not offer a conclusive, definitive list of spiritual gifts for the Corinthian Christians or for all other Christian readers. Both the ambiguity regarding the specific nature of some gifts and the differences among various listings (vv. 7-11, 27-30; Rom. 12:6-8; see also Eph. 4:11-13) suggest that the apostle is being more illustrative by presenting examples that speak to the specific situation. There is also no indication as to whether a specific gift should be understood as more durative or momentary in nature. Looking too closely here distorts the bigger picture: the purpose behind the divine provision of gifts was the common good of the church, which Paul emphasizes later as the upbuilding or edification of others (e.g., 1 Cor. 14:1-12). Conversely, treating something that is the result of God's grace as a private possession for personal benefit rather than a divine gift for the benefit of others is a gross misunderstanding of the essence of God's sanctifying work upon the church. According to Paul, the gracious act of Christ on the cross was the ultimate "gift" (see Rom. 5:6-9, 15-16) for the church to emulate.

Thus, in Paul's thought Christ's act transforms the body analogy so familiar in political circles of his day because of his selflessness in service to God and for the sake of others.[11]

Second, the image of the body of Christ suggests there to be a mutual interdependence among its members. There are two different sides of this one issue. On the one hand, no member should see himself or herself as dispensable or unnecessary. The apostle uses some comic relief to illustrate this point. He uses two "speaking" body parts—a foot bemoaning that it is not a hand and similarly an ear that it is not an eye—to illustrate how foolish it would be to reject the role that one has been given in the body of Christ (1 Cor. 12:15-16). On the other hand, no one should view another member as unnecessary. Paul in effect draws a cartoon of a body made up of only one eye to make the hyperbolic point of how ridiculous it would be to affirm or depend on only a few gifts, when by God's grace the church is comprised of various persons who respectively embody the diverse gifts that God has given (vv. 17, 19-21). The eight rhetorical questions in the latter part of the chapter (vv. 29-30), which are written to expect negative responses, clarify that not everyone (or anyone!) among the Corinthian congregation possessed all the listed gifts, which also insinuates that these believers may have embodied other gifts (perhaps even those that Paul had not explicitly mentioned). The point here is the mutual interdependence among those who comprise the church, the body of Christ.

Third, the image of the body of Christ relies on authentic love for all its relationships. Rather than favoring some in the church over others (see v. 21), Paul argues that love enables the relationships within the church to nurture one another so that all persons fulfill their place within the body. In Paul's use of the body metaphor, he refers to the different ways humans treat and clothe different parts of the body. Some parts are considered "private" (e.g., sexual organs), and we clothe and treat them with utmost care or honor due to culture and decorum (v. 23). Other parts (like the face or hands) need very different treatment. The apostle suggests that, in the body of Christ, something similar must happen among the various members if the body is to function in a healthy manner. Such a suggestion for the church goes against the prevalent cultural views of Paul's day, which was based on an "honor and shame" system that honored the powerful and wealthy while putting down the weak and poor. That Paul does not offer tips for identifying the respective "ranking" of various members but turns instead to describe love (13:1-13) as the "more excellent way" (12:31) insinuates that this nurture of one another within the context of the church may be *the* essential aspect of ecclesial relationships (see also Eph. 4:15-16).[12]

Some Implications for a Contemporary Wesleyan Ecclesiology

Contemporary understandings of the church—ecclesiologies, if you will—come from various sources. However, those of us who come from the Wesleyan theological traditions should resonate with the central themes that provide the basis for Paul's ecclesiological comments as he addresses the Corinthian believers. Rather than reading popular ideas into the image of the body of Christ that refer to an "incarnational theology" that may be foreign to Pauline thought, we may instead embrace Paul's emphases on (*a*) God's sanctifying work in setting apart the church as God's holy people and (*b*) our part in loving one another so that the church functions to live out what that divine work has transformed the church to be and do as the holy people of God. After all, such emphases also stand at the center of Wesleyan theology, as Wesley himself pointed to these texts in 1 Corinthians as affirming the central place of love in his teaching.[13] Thus, at the heart of who we are as Wesleyans are these Pauline emphases that are also at the center of his ecclesiology. And these remind us that our understandings of ecclesiology must be active in nature—lived out in loving relationship with those who comprise the church as God's people and who then are to live as conduits of the divine grace that has shaped us and now enables us to be a missional people.

As theological descendants of John Wesley, who described himself as a "man of one book,"[14] it is also essential that we allow the different contributions of the biblical Canon to speak into and provoke theological trajectories regarding contemporary understandings of ecclesiology. For instance, we need to understand the body metaphor and corresponding ideas as they appear in 1 Corinthians and see how the church has appropriated them in later times (see Eph. 4:1-16; Col. 2:16-19).[15] What often occurs is that similar metaphors and ideas in other parts of the Canon are simply grouped together to understand what Scripture has to say about a specific issue, with the negative result that differences and nuances are lost in the quest for gaining *the* biblical understanding of the church. A more robust understanding regarding the church and ecclesiology may require a more patient approach that exegetes and listens carefully to the different canonical "voices," not to mention an approach that considers the variety of materials and genres throughout the Canon and how they might contribute to these important biblical conversations about ecclesiology.

Questions for Discussion

1. How do you see other Pauline images of the church in 1 Corinthians—such as God's "field" (3:6), God's "building" (vv. 10-15), and God's "temple" (vv. 16-17)—as adding or contributing to what the apostle says about the church in chapters 12—14?

2. This essay suggests the "body of Christ" metaphor does *not* refer to the church as the extension of Jesus' own bodily ministry or incarnation, but instead focuses on the church's unity because of belonging to Christ. Why is this distinction important? And what does this suggest about the "body of Christ" metaphor in terms of a theology of ecclesial relationships?

3. After studying 1 Corinthians 12:1-31, read Ephesians 4:1-16. What additional concepts does the Ephesians passage add to the "body of Christ" analogy? What do you see as significant about those contributions? How does the Ephesians passage agree with or differ from the 1 Corinthians passage?

4. After studying 1 Corinthians 12:1-31, read Colossians 2:16-19. What additional concepts does the Colossians passage add to the "body of Christ" analogy? What do you see as significant about those contributions? How does the Colossians passage agree with or differ from the 1 Corinthians passage?

Suggestions for Further Reading

Banks, Robert J. *Paul's Idea of Community: The Early House Churches in Their Historical Setting.* Rev. ed. Grand Rapids: Baker Academic, 1994.

Brower, Kent E., and Andy Johnson, eds. *Holiness and Ecclesiology in the New Testament.* Grand Rapids: Eerdmans, 2007.

Furnish, Victor Paul. *The Theology of the First Letter to the Corinthians.* New Testament Theology. Cambridge: Cambridge University Press, 1999.

Hanson, Paul D. *The People Called: The Growth of Community in the Bible.* San Francisco: Harper and Row, 1986.

Harrison, John, and James D. Dvorak, eds. *The New Testament Church: The Challenge of Developing Ecclesiologies.* McMaster Biblical Studies Series. Eugene, OR: Wipf and Stock, 2012.

Twelftree, Graham H. *People of the Spirit: Exploring Luke's View of the Church.* Grand Rapids: Baker Academic, 2009.

seventeen
THE PRIESTHOOD OF ALL BELIEVERS
A THEOLOGY OF LAITY

Rebecca Laird

This is a telling story: A student active in ministry speaks of a desire to go to seminary and be ordained but is clear that a call to preaching or public leadership is not the motivation. When asked, "Why are you pursuing a professional ministry degree?" the student replied, "For the identity, I guess. So I could sit down next to someone on a bus who looked troubled and ask them how they were without them thinking I'm trying to hustle them. So I could be up front about what I believe, in public as well as private. So I would have the credentials to be the kind of Christian I want to be." Barbara Brown Taylor, the teller of this story, counters, "God help the Church if clergy are the only Christians with 'credentials,' and God help all those troubled people on the bus if they have to wait for an ordained person to come along before anyone speaks to them."[1]

This story underscores the need for the whole people of God to remember who we are and what we have been called to do. All Christians redeemed by love stand in the long line that reaches from that first group of disciples who were called out from common jobs and ordinary lives to imitate Jesus by following him for the love of others. Jesus chose religious novices then and now to reconcile all things to God.

Ministry is meant for amateurs—those baptized by confession of faith into Christ, who do what they do for love and out of love.[2] Of course, theological understanding, self-awareness, and spiritual maturity are necessary and progressive, but ministry is a natural overflowing response to the inexplicable, transforming, compelling love of God. God's blueprint of the church—the set apart and called out people who step out together in response to God's gift of grace with faith and love—assigns the work of the ministry to apprentices: those who are learning what it means to love by doing love in relationship to others who have been on this journey a little longer. In God's plan there are no black-belt-level Christians. No experts who have earned a terminal degree in loving God and neighbor. There are no specialists who have solved the mysteries of God and have been awarded an advanced degree or special prize for special knowledge of the mind of God. There are only saints-in-training who are grateful to be saved by grace and who regularly gather together to worship God in word and deed so they can carry that worship into their workaday lives—all to the glory of God.

So why do we often call church leaders "ministers" or commonly say that only religion majors or seminary students are "preparing for full-time ministry"? These questions uncover one of the most common misunderstandings in the Christian church. Many Christians wrongly assume that trained pastors who do their work in public are the ones who "do ministry" while the congregation members attend worship services and give a little time or money when they can to "support ministry." Many just assume that the clergy are meant to do the heavy lifting when it comes to church matters. Nothing could be further from the truth!

The New Testament Vision of Ministry

Paul in writing to the church at Ephesus offers one of the most well-known metaphors for the way the Christian church is designed to function. "There is one body and one Spirit, just as you were called to the one hope of your calling, one Lord, one faith, one baptism, one God and Father of us all, who is above all and through all and in all. But to each of us was given grace according to the measure of Christ's gift" (Eph. 4:4-7). After making it very clear that the church is "one," comprised of people unified in a single, shared calling, Paul continues to list some of the varied gifts before describing that each one is divvied out "to equip the saints for the work of ministry, for building up the body of Christ" (v. 12). In some versions of the Bible the phrases "equip the saints" and "for the work of ministry" are separated by what is sometimes referred to as the "fatal comma." This punctuation is not present in the original Greek and has served to wrongly divide the equipping of the saints and the work of the ministry. They were never to be put asunder. The saints—those called out from darkness into God's glorious light (1 Pet. 2:9)—are to serve each other and the world. There is no other class of people to get God's work done. Some members of the body are given public gifts for preaching, teaching, or leading, but these gifts are given only to equip the saints. These saints are *all* those that John Wesley might say "are going on to perfection" in seeking to love with a perfect motive of wanting what God wants for the world. A person who is called and ordained to the public ministry has a certain functional role to train others for ministry in the world. Yet a member of the clergy, a pastor, never ceases being an apprentice, learner, and disciple on par with everyone else who confesses the name of Christ. God is equitable when it comes to meting out gifts and calling all people of God to serve. A few are gifted to train and lead and build up others, but the muscle of the church is found in the people who engage in ministry in the world of home, work, and service.

Division of Labor in the Priesthood of All Believers

A reading of the gospel of Luke shows that only John the Baptist came from the priestly class. Jesus, his cousin, did not. Jesus learned in the temple, studied in the synagogue; yet as Jesus begins his public ministry, he calls fishermen and tax collectors as his team in mission. There is not a religious professional in sight. Luke 8 describes Jesus as surrounded by the twelve named disciples and a circle of other disciples that included men and women who had been called, healed, and invited to follow. As they traveled with Jesus they learned on the road. And soon "the seventy-two," not a priest or ordained clergy member among them either, as far as we know, were sent out to all the towns and villages to preach the kingdom of God by engaging with those they met, to do what Jesus had showed them (Luke 10:2). When they returned they continued on with Jesus who declares that the way to inherit eternal life is to fulfill the great command: "Love the Lord your God with all your heart, and with all your soul, and with all your strength, and with all your mind; and your neighbor as yourself" (v. 27). Jesus tells the story of the Good Samaritan, highlighting the nonprofessional in the story as the one who does rightly, and saying, "Go and do likewise" (v. 37).

Throughout the New Testament the Greek word for people (*laos*), refers to people without distinction who are gathered together and jointly involved in the new and somewhat disorganized Jesus movement that would become the Christian church. The Anglicized form of *laos*, rendered as *laity*, is church language for all those who seek to be disciples of Jesus. First Peter 2:9 offers a seminal description of the role of all the people in the church: "But you are a chosen race, a royal priesthood, a holy nation, God's *own people*, in order that you may proclaim the mighty acts of him who called you out of darkness into his marvelous light" (italics mine). The laity, God's own people, are tasked with proclamation and witness. Those essential tasks of ministry are not left to any one person or group with special gifts or temperaments. They are the whole work of the laity.

Our common church distinction between clergy and lay takes a simple biblical word, *kleros* (which describes a method of drawing straws, "choosing by lots") and applies it to those who had witnessed Jesus' ministry firsthand. The early Christians used the word for assigning tasks (Acts 1:26); the concept of *kleros* (or clergy) develops over time. Often our current assumptions for clergy demand a highly professional job description and years of training for anyone who is called clergy. But a member of the clergy, in biblical terms, is simply one who has gifts recognized by the church, but who is chosen by drawing straws to perform a needed public task in the church. In the earliest expression of church, wisdom garnered from years of faithful service was seen as qualification for leadership by the elders, *presbyteros*. Spiritual maturity, wisdom, and spiritual gifts affirmed by the gathered people were the qualifications for ministry *leadership*. But the whole church ministered.

The Early Church

Over time as the church organized and institutionalized it began to educate and choose leaders in the same way leaders in other public areas were prepared or designated. What began as a fairly functional designation accrued power and stratified, making starker distinctions between the roles of clergy disciples and lay disciples in function and task. Early church accounts from the first centuries after Jesus' resurrection show that laity were engaged in liturgical[3] leadership in the first century; in the second, Irenaeus wrote, "All who are justified through Christ have the sacerdotal (priestly) order."[4] Divine worship was not conducted by a singular person or in one prescribed way. There was no singular job description for leadership in the early church. People of good character, reputation, discipline, strong faith, and obvious gifts were chosen by the people in their local bread-breaking community for leadership. It was clear that all who were baptized were "ordained" and set apart for witnessing, testifying, and ethically responding to God's love in the world. Categories among the laity were designations based on faith and baptism, not primarily by function. The baptized were set apart from those being prepared for baptism (the catechumen) who were set apart from the world (those unreconciled to Christ). The church existed to further God's mission through a shared way of life that required leadership, yes, but the church was ultimately led by the Holy Spirit and staffed by the laity. Form and function of laity and clergy was fluid. It was not yet the formal institution it would become.

When Christianity became the imperial religion of Rome in 313 under Emperor Constantine, an increasingly formalized structure led by the bishop of Rome mirrored the governmental structures for administration and discipline. (There were exceptions to this in places like North Africa where faithful elders worked with the bishop in administrative, disciplinary, and worship leadership. Lay Christians also retreated from the structured church and formed monasteries that were mostly communal worshipping communities of lay men or women.) Over time, in many places Christian priests took on a role of being the governmentally sanctioned dispensers of salvation through the formal rites of the organized church. The laity became recipients of a rite and adherents to a religious tradition. The bold vision of the full people of God, as joint-heirs in the community of faith who were sent out for mission in the world, sometimes dimmed but never flamed out.

The Reformation Period

One of the lenses through which the Protestant Reformation can be viewed is that of a movement to restore the ministry of the laity in the church. Martin Luther, a monk and priest himself before his renunciation of formal vows, advocated for the reforming of the *priesthood of all believers*. He called for the church to recall that all Christians hold the same standing before God through faith, and he championed the need for all to have access to the written Word of God in their own language. As co-heirs with Christ, he railed that Christians need no mediating priest, since all are called to obedience to bear the cross and praise God in all vocations and stations in life.

The oft-recounted story of Martin Luther is his response to his barber Peter's request for instruction on how to pray; it illustrates the Reformer's urge to reempower the laity to learn and live devoted lives. Luther counseled Peter to pray the "four-stranded garland" using the Lord's Prayer, the Psalms, the Ten Commandments, and the Apostles' Creed as a way to connect Christian teaching and personal spiritual disciplines in one's life—be it in the barber shop, at the dining room table, or in the marketplace. Vocation was not just a calling to a religious vocation of priest or nun; it was the Christian call to be "little Christs" in all places of labor and relationship from the barber's chair to the bishop's seat.

Wesley's Lay Movement

John Wesley, the eighteenth-century son and grandson of clergy and highly educated Oxford don, began his ministry in a time when the church at large was still roiling over the rights of the established Church of England and the level of freedom that would be granted to the disestablished or "free" churches that were not subsidized or fully managed by the king. Wesley was hardly a prime candidate for engineering a lay movement to empower "a genuine people of God from within the institutional Church."[5] Wesley worked from within the established church movement, albeit often at its margins. He did not set out to begin a new church or dismiss the need for institutional structures, but he had a parallel hope. While the local church and the parish priests continue to administer the sacraments and provide the place and grace of ordered worship, he asked, can the laity be empowered and freed to attend to their function: to leave the church building and witness, care and educate in their neighborhoods, humble or high, and especially in those places where people labor for little and who will never sit in polished pews?

The early Methodist laity were a highly disciplined lot that ordered their personal lives by attending church-based worship but adding much, much more. Many committed to a common life shared in small devotional societies where they prayed, read the Bible, and spoke confessionally together about matters that would both edify and hold each accountable for their lives before God and for their active ministry to their neighbors. They sought to follow the injunction in James 5:16, "Confess your sins to one another, and pray for one another, so that you may be healed," and then to enact their faith by preaching the gospel to the poor in word and deed. John and Charles Wesley had long been trained in such societies and had seen one led by their mother, Susanna, in their own home grow out of family devotions to include over two hundred persons.

Unleashing the laity often unsettles church structures and norms, and that was true in Wesley's day. Wesley challenged the established church to respond to God in faith alone and not to assume that social status or educational privilege were automatic marks of spiritual vitality. As a result, he found many pulpits were closed to him. At the behest of George Whitefield, Wesley agreed to preach outdoors in Bristol near the coal mines. Significant crowds gathered and people responded in faith. Preaching points began to spring up offering societies for edification, classes for in-depth instruction, and bands for small-group pastoral care. These "chapels" grew up outside of the structures of the Church of England in many places and were often tended to by traveling lay preachers who were often trained on the job through rigorous reading and regular "conference."[6] Coal miners, a few women (like Sarah Crosby and Mary Bosanquet Fletcher), and people from all social and economic classes were aflame with love and set out to witness to what God was doing. Lay leaders, who were not always university trained yet were rigorously disciplined and pursuing on-the-job training and accountability, moved into leadership in the Methodist movement.

Wesley's call to faith as the measure of leadership opened a door for many to step into preaching, teaching, and administrative roles that countered the model of the Oxford-qualified ordained as the singular leader in the church. Wesley's impulse to renew the church through the laity returned the people's energy to mission. While he did not set out to redefine the role of the lay preacher and leader, that is what happened as the new Methodist movement crossed the Atlantic to the New World.

The Church in North America

In Colonial America the democratic impulse to enshrine individual liberty and the eventual separation of church and state led to the necessity for members to assume the responsibility for church life. No longer did clergy receive governmental stipends or appointments as they had on the Continent. There would be no government funds. Many early clergy and ministers were itinerant or bivocational. Here, in this new land, churches would become both congregationally focused rather than nationally oriented and over time leadership would begin to take on the character of the culture around it, just as in earlier centuries. When there was finally a settled clergy, rather than circuit riders who sought to keep multiple rural, lay-led meeting-houses functioning, ministers often became civic leaders and educators as well as preachers.[7] There was a renewed emphasis and need for highly educated clergy. Then in the latter half of the twentieth century, the CEO model of leadership began to replace and usurp the expectation of clergy to be theological trainers, and clergy began to be seen as dispensers of a well-prepared worship experience on Sunday. During much of the twentieth century the laity were often treated and acted like shareholders who showed up to vote or evaluate what was happening in ministry. Churches became a place to join, as one might join a club or sports team. The understanding of church as people on a mission waned. Church programs led by professional clergy and staff for the benefit of those who attended became normal. But then some amateurs began to ask: Again, who and what is the church for?

The Logics of the Laity

In recent decades in the United States, churches have sought to grow in numbers by strategies of multiplication. Nearly all of these methods deployed the laity for taking the church outside of the church walls to invite family, friends, and coworkers to join in small groups and mission endeavors. The small-group movement initiated in many churches began to help laity discover their spiritual gifts and unleash them to serve in myriad ministries. Small groups rose up around stages of life, professional affinities, or hobbies. Laity were again building relationships of accountability and service. Some of this has led to people joining churches, but it has also led to a concurrent explosion in nonprofit, nonaffiliated ministry organizations for compassionate service, prophetic action, and community development. In many ways, in recent decades the empowered laity have gloriously left the building.

People of the Mission

Good theology always keeps the end in sight. The goal or purposes, the *telos* in Greek, of God is the reconciliation of all things. Colossians 1:19-20 reminds us that in Christ "all the fullness of God was pleased to dwell, and through him God was pleased to reconcile to himself all things, whether on earth or in heaven, by making peace through the blood of his cross." When we consider the role of the laity, we do so keeping the reconciliation of all things firmly in mind. God's mission is to reconcile all people and every purpose under heaven to the ways and will of God. God's plan to accomplish this is to call everyday people, baptize them into the ways and work of Christ, empower them through the energizing of the Spirit, so that we can participate with God as this eternal purpose becomes an ever-present reality. God picked ordinary people who have encountered love and restoration of heart, mind, and soul through Jesus and who continue to be discipled into spiritual maturity to go out and walk by the lakeside, ride buses, preach and witness outdoors, establish preaching points, start agencies, and be the kind of Christians who witness in word and practical care to the sad, sick, lonely, isolated, and unreconciled. The ministry of the laity is for ordinary, faithful people to live the mission, to be the mission, to proclaim the mission, and to staff the mission. The people of God are sent out into the world on an extraordinary everyday mission out of, for, and by the gracious love of our missionary God. We are all called to be the kind of Christians we want to be, are gifted to be, and God needs us to be for the sake of all creation that groans in expectation of full redemption and restoration (Rom. 8:22-23). We have joyful work and witness to do as the purposeful people of God's mission.

Questions for Discussion

1. What are the strengths and challenges of leaving ministry to amateurs and novices? Do you agree that this is the New Testament model for ministry? Is this what you see in your local church or congregation? Give examples.

2. List all of the expectations you have for a local church pastor. If you are in a group, brainstorm all the things the "perfect" pastor would be able to do. If "equip the laity for ministry" is the first priority on such a list, what else might better be done by others? If you were to

go back to your local church and suggest reordering roles for ministry, what do you imagine might happen?

3. Name as many of Jesus' first disciples as you can. Since none of them were religious professionals or seminary-trained, what qualified them for service? Discuss the traits and gifts of a few of the various disciples. What do you imagine Jesus saw in them?

4. How would you define the word *laity* to someone unfamiliar with the term? What synonyms or other phrases might you use instead to describe this group of people in the church? Write a job description for the laity.

5. How has the Christian church organized itself and understood leadership in varying ways through the centuries? How do differing social concepts of leadership impact expectations for the church's public leaders?

6. How do you understand God's mission in the world and your role in it? What might God be trying to do through you?

Suggestions for Further Reading

Bonhoeffer, Dietrich. "Ministry," in *Life Together*. New York: Harper and Row, 1954.

Christensen, Michael J., and Carl E. Savage. *Equipping the Saints: Mobilizing Laity for Ministry*. Nashville: Abingdon, 2000.

Garlow, Jim. *Partners in Ministry: Laity and Pastors Working Together*. Kansas City: Beacon Hill Press of Kansas City, 1986.

Mallory, Sue. *The Equipping Church: Serving Together to Transform Lives*. Grand Rapids: Zondervan, 2001.

Trueblood, Roy W., and Jackie B. Trueblood. *Partners in Ministry: Clergy and Laity*. Nashville: Abingdon, 1999.

eighteen
UNIFYING THE CHURCH
A THEOLOGICAL UNDERSTANDING OF ORDINATION

Brent Peterson

Christians familiar with the term *ordination* probably think this has something to do with priests or pastors. Of course this is true, but are priests and pastors the only persons that God by the power of the Spirit ordains in the church? As one looks back across the history of God's people, it is noteworthy that God calls and equips many persons, often persons outside the clerical leaders of the church. This chapter has two primary and interrelated theses: *First, Christian ordination is a gift God gives for the further healing and maturing of the church, which is united as the body of Christ. Second, the primary function and purpose of the church is to participate in the redemption of all creation into the fullness of the kingdom of God.* While more attention in this chapter is given to the first thesis, the second is potently latent in the extrapolation of the first. It is also important that this chapter be read in conversation with the chapters that precede and follow. This chapter will spend most of its time on those who are ordained from among the laity for leadership in the church as elders. This chapter will *first* suggest a Christian theology and purpose of ordination. *Second,* in light of such an understanding, it will be suggested that all Christians are ordained into the office of laity at their baptism. *Third,* God also calls, equips, and empowers those from among the baptized laity for specific leadership in the church. *Fourth,* the chapter considers some things that ordination is not. Finally, the chapter suggests that ordained clergy are primarily consecrated to preach the Word, administer the sacraments, and provide order in the local church in order to be in communion with the church universal.

Ordination as Empowered and Consecrated Order

As the conversation of this entire book develops, it is crucial to recognize that the understanding and gift of ordination fall completely within the realm of the church and is thus part of an adequate ecclesiology. Moreover, a conversation on ordination cannot be had apart from a robust entanglement with Christology, pneumatology, Trinitarian theology, eschatology, and beyond. While all of that cannot be done in this short chapter, it is dangerous when ordination becomes segmented from the fullness of the Christian tradition. Hopefully the reader will also view this chapter as a multifaceted conversation with various categories of theology.

At a very basic level ordination is about *order*, as opposed to *chaos*. To ordain means to appoint, invest, or consecrate something or someone with a specific purpose, often for a specific place and for a specific time. William Willimon notes that ordination should be celebrated as "*a creative act of God, not unlike the creation of the world or the call of Israel, that brings order out of chaos, a world out of the void.*"[1] While some things can be ordained for eternity, most things or persons are ordained for specific contexts. When a law is decreed, it is ordained with certain implications. Similarly, when persons are ordained, they are set apart; they are consecrated with specific roles and responsibilities that are often very contextual (more will be said about this below). Moreover, in the act of ordaining someone or something, power is invested and placed onto that which is ordained, such as a law or person. So in light of God's creative act of birth and order, who exactly is ordained?

Priesthood of All Believers

To begin, priests and pastors (aka those paid to go to church) are not the only persons in the church ordained. Recall one of the main emphases of Martin Luther and the Protestant Reformation was the celebration of the "priesthood of all believers." One of the themes present in the Protestant Reformation was the celebration that a person can connect to God and can do so without the aid of a priest. However, the primary affirmation is not that each person is his or her own priest but that each Christian can be a priest, advocate, intercessor, and evangelist to others.[2] However, in this celebration that all Christians can connect with God, the role of being a priest also implies that *all* Christians are called, charged, and empowered to preach the gospel at all times and in all places the Holy Spirit provides. Recall at Pentecost that the Spirit falls upon all, especially the marginalized, to be witnesses to all the world.[3] In fact, 1 Peter 2:9-10 asserts, "But you are a chosen race, a royal priesthood, a holy nation, God's own people, in order that you may proclaim the mighty acts of him who called you out of darkness into his marvelous light. Once you were not a people, but now you are God's people; once you had not received mercy, but now you have received mercy."

The idea of the church as a holy nation coming from those who were once not a people directly connects to God's calling, blessing, and creating the people of Israel. One can recall from Genesis that when God approached Abram and Sarai, they were old, barren, and had no future. God took, blessed, and provided life out of barrenness. Many remember God's promise to bless and curse those whom Abraham blesses and curses, but we must also remember that such a vocation to be God's people implies a commission of responsibility. "And in you all the families of the earth shall be blessed" (Gen. 12:3). Just like Abram and Sarai, who were wandering, aimless nomads without a people and future, the Christian church emerges from a ragtag group of followers of Jesus. By the power of the Holy Spirit they are ordained (charged, called, and equipped) to spread the kingdom of God to the nations.[4] Persons are rescued from sin and isolation, into a people who are receiving grace and mercy, who have been brought from darkness to light, from death to life. Within the Abrahamic covenant to be a blessing to all the world, the church as a chosen royal priesthood has a calling (Latin, *vocare*—"vocation") to proclaim the mighty acts of what God has done for them and what God is doing in the world.

Therefore, while there is not adequate space to make the case in full, Christians should consider that all Christians are ordained into the office of laity at their baptism. Martin Luther affirmed that at one's baptism one also enters into the priesthood of believers.[5] As baptism is one's entrance into God's covenant people, the church, being a part of God's people entails a missional vocation to proclaim God to the nations.[6] Reflecting on the life of Jesus, whose ministry begins after his baptism, Willimon notes that "ministry is a gift of baptism."[7] To be brought into God's covenant people is also to be empowered to live into the mission of God's people, as an act of worship to God to become broken and spread out before the lost and broken. In light of all Christians ordained in the office of laity, the focus now shifts to those ordained, from among the laity, for leadership in the church.

Ordained for Leadership in the Church

While the Abrahamic covenant to be a blessing to all the peoples of the earth pertained to all the tribes and just as all Christians are to live into the vocation of the Great Commission, God by the power of the Spirit calls, equips, sets apart, and empowers persons for leadership within God's people. Recall that ordination is about order, refusing chaos. Similarly, God called the Levites, as one of the Twelve tribes, for leadership over the people, largely for their cultic and worship practices.[8] When considering the ordination of priests and pastors, it is curious to note the specificity of purpose and function the Levites played in regard to communal worship. Unfortunately, it is often the case that those ordained as priests and pastors (at least among evangelical Protestants) do not see their calling as located primarily for leadership in communal worship.

The New Testament is a bit messy in regard to titles for those given leadership in the church. Some churches refer to "bishops" (*episkopoi*—"overseers"), who were also called pastors. In other churches there was a council of elders (*presbuteroi*) who were given distinct duties by the congregation. It appears that after the apostolic era bishops were given charge over a number of congregations while elders were those who presided over individual congregations.[9] There is also a wonderful history to those raised up by the church as deacons, for the helping ministry of the church both in and outside the congregation. The following chapter will deal with the role of the episcopacy as superintendents/bishops (overseers) who have responsibilities beyond those of the local church. This chapter will focus specifically on those called to the office of elder, who have a primary focus on leadership in a local church.

The Purpose of the Ordained Supports the Purpose of the Church—Unity in Christ

The apostle Paul offers a powerful exposition that illumines the gift and purpose of the ordination of clergy imagined within the full scope of the kingdom of God. Paul has just reminded the Ephesians that unity is the ground of hope and confidence in Christianity. As there is "one Lord, one faith, one baptism, one God and Father of all" (4:5-6), it seems that Paul would also affirm that which was confessed with the Council of Nicaea, there is one church.[10] Yet this unity also celebrates the diversity of God's creation.

While there are other Pauline passages celebrating the gifts of the body of Christ outside clergy in the church, this passage focuses on the purpose of those who are ordained into leadership positions in the church.[11]

> The gifts he gave were that some would be apostles, some prophets, some evangelists, some pastors and teachers, to equip the saints for the work of ministry, for building up the body of Christ, until all of us come to the unity of the faith and of the knowledge of the Son of God, to maturity, to the measure of the full stature of Christ. We must no longer be children, tossed to and fro and blown about by every wind of doctrine, by people's trickery, by their craftiness in deceitful scheming. But speaking the truth in love, we must grow up in every way into him who is the head, into Christ, from whom the whole body, joined and knit together by every ligament with which it is equipped, as each part is working properly, promotes the body's growth in building itself up in love. (Eph. 4:11-16)

This rich passage celebrates the diversity of gifts of those who are given responsibility in leadership over the church. It is crucial to affirm there is not a hierarchy of gifts, but unique *charisms*—gifts to each one as the Spirit works. Ordination into the priesthood is not primarily about authority, but about order and service. Each one is gifted to serve, not to lord their gifts over the other.[12] Verse 12 provides a primary purpose of those who are ordained for leadership in the church: "to equip the saints." What is then the purpose of equipping the saints: that that body of Christ—the church—may be built up? What is such a journey of growth aiming for? The church is to be united by faith and in such unity a deeper and fuller encounter with Jesus Christ enables the church to become more fully what it is—the body of Christ. At a very basic level an explanation of ordination is that it is a gift of God in order that the church may more fully become united. In verse 14 Paul speaks about the challenges to unity in the body of Christ. At the core, the opposite of unity is a deceptive relational chaos of discord. As opposed to such chaos God calls and the Spirit empowers leaders in the church, in order to facilitate the church having a more fit and healthy body, built by and into the love of God.

Ordination is about *order* that runs against and countermands the chaos and disease of sin. Before moving forward it is necessary to clarify what ordination is not.

Bad Ideas and Practices of Ordination

In affirming the gift and celebration of ordination into leadership in the church, some cautions and boundaries need attention. Most of these are obvious but are important to keep in mind.

Not the Most Holy

One of my brilliant undergrad professors, who later became a colleague, offered some sage advice to a group of young undergrad ministers in training. While the specific context escapes me, he essentially looked at us future ministers and said with great intensity and seriousness, "Friends, after many years in the ministry I have become convinced that God often calls persons into full-time ministry because their faith is probably not strong enough otherwise." Of course he said this with a smile, but after all these years as I have been privileged to pastor, shepherd, and teach as one of the ordained, what becomes clear very quickly is that the clergy are largely not the most holy or righteous persons in the congregation. This is not to excuse sin by any persons in the church, but for the laity and ordained clergy it is an important reminder that ordained clergy are not the "super-righteous" ones simply because of their ordination into leadership. However, throughout the Christian tradition it is to be the case that the ordained elder is to be an exemplar and spiritual leader to the congregation.

Not the Smartest

While in seminary I entered into my first full-time ministry assignment. This congregation was located in a town that had a denominational university, seminary, and headquarters. As such, the congregation I was privileged to serve had over 140 ordained elders who attended. On my fourth Sunday on staff, I was invited to preach. I was very aware of the wisdom in these elders and my immaturity as a preacher and theologian. Of course the congregation was very gracious and supportive. The longer I remained in that congregation, not only did wisdom flow from those ordained elders, but vast amounts of wisdom and care came from farmers, teachers, social workers, single moms and dads, bankers, construction workers, and on and on. Even though I was pursuing a master's degree in theology, it also became apparent that there were many in the congregation who had life and theological expertise that could teach and form me. The ordained elder, therefore, has a charge to be a theologian of the congregation. Yet this does not mean the ordained elder is automatically the best theologian in the congregation or is right on all theological matters.

Not CEO of an NGO

One of the challenges for many persons considering their call into full-time leadership ministry is to discern what is precisely one's role and task. Below, this chapter will outline some of the basic callings and *charisms* given and placed upon those ordained as elders. While ordained elders are tasked to do many things that fall outside the specific *charisms* given to them, it is important that the ordained do not image themselves as the executive officers of not-for-profit organizations. Part of the concern is some clergy fail to recall the primary focus of their calling and become busy doing important work that falls outside what the church universal and God actually called and empowered them to do. While ordained elders need to be very well versed in many fields, including leadership and fiscal jurisprudence, they may not be the best skilled at those aspects. The ordained elder is not primarily the boss that is running a corporation. For those ordained as elders and those in congregations who have clergy, too often there is a lack of clarity and focus about the expectations of those ordained as elders.

Not Institutional Hoop Jumping or Credentialing

It is curious to me that with the age of the Internet and the loss of "authority" many of my students find the process of seeking to be ordained, and ordination itself, as simply playing the corporate ladder game to get ahead. Moreover, many students (often Protestant) have a difficult time affirming that the very act of ordination really does anything more than offer a nice sentimental prayer of affirmation. The process of ordination affirms that simply because one feels called into ministry does not mean one is actually called and gifted by God for ministry. With many persons this is a long process of discernment both for the person seeking ordination and those prayerfully considering whether or not to ordain. Of course, these processes of discernment can feel like hoop jumping, and clearly all processes could be improved. Yet the process of seeking ordination can also be envisioned as a means of grace whereby a local community of faith and other ordained elders can affirm and celebrate one's call into ministry. Moreover, as Christians who believe in the power of prayer, we should also affirm that the church's presentation of the ordinand to be ordained by the episcopacy (bishops/superintendents) affirms that God provides extra *charisms* to those who are ordained. In other words, the entire process and the very act of ordination are occasions where the Spirit equips and empowers those called for the specific tasks and responsibilities to which they were called. Moreover, remembering that all Christians are ordained into the office of laity at their baptism, those among the baptized who are then set apart for leadership in the church have unique gifts and *charisms* that only the elders are called, authorized, and empowered to do. Recall Paul's analogy of the church as the body of Christ. Each part is called and equipped to do its part. Just as the Levites were set apart for leadership for the Israelites' worship, so, too, the ordained elders were set apart by God and the church for specific tasks that only they have been authorized and equipped to perform. This is not about hierarchy but about a proper discerning of the unique gifts of service in the body. After considering some of what ordination is not, let's now briefly consider the gift of ordination.

The Gift of Ordination

As stated above, in the process of discernment and in the very act of ordination the church authorizes and the Spirit empowers the ordinand with specific gifts (*charisms*) for ministry. With the laying on of hands (1 Tim. 4:14; 2 Tim. 1:6), the act celebrates "the gift of the Holy Spirit and the bestowal of authority by those who have preceded the candidate in ministry."[13] It is also essential that such an ordination is done in the presence of the gathered assembly. The act of ordination is *not* done *by* and *for* the elites, but as all ordained are called by God and empowered, the local church plays a crucial role in nurturing, testing, and affirming the call to clerical ministry. As such, ordination is an act of Christ, by the power of the Spirit, and of the church as the body of Christ. Part of the challenge is to remember the unique *charisms* that apply to one's ordination and remember that limitations and boundaries of one's *charisms* as an ordained elder. Moreover, within this discernment process it was stated above the danger of the elder thinking that the ordination was a personal possession to be used in a multiplicity of contexts. Not only are the *charisms* of the elder specific, historically a person is ordained for a certain place and people. While there is certainly diversity within the practice of ordination, it was often the case that someone who was raised in a place would be noticed to have unique gifts for leadership in the church. As this person would also testify to such a calling, those people in that place with that person would nurture those gifts. As both the person and community affirmed such gifts, those from the episcopacy would also be invited to train and discern a person's fitness for ministry. In this discerning process it was often recognized that persons not only are called and equipped with unique gifts for leadership in the church but also were uniquely gifted for a unique place to a unique people.

When John Wesley was asked what defines a true church, he drew upon the Anglican Articles of Faith, which he largely copied for the Methodist's Articles of Faith. "Our twentieth Article defines a true church, 'a congregation of faithful people, wherein the true Word of God is preached and the sacraments duly administered.'"[14] Communal worship and specifically the celebration of the Lord's Supper define the church's chief performance according to Wesley. As such the primary *charisms* offered to the elder revolve around preaching the Word, administering the sacraments, and providing order to the church. In this charge and *charisms* there is a great deal of diversity. It is often under this charge where the temptation to envision the elder as CEO arises. The Nicene Creed confesses and proclaims the "one, holy, catholic, and apostolic church." One of the celebrations of the church's apostolicity is the celebration that each ordained elder has faithfully been transformed and can properly teach and lead persons into the orthodox kerygma of the faith. While contextualization is continuous, like the apostle Paul, the elders are charged to faithfully pass on what they have received.[15] Moreover, each elder represents the local church's connection to other Christians present, past, and future. The ordained elder becomes a physical celebration and connection to the church universal for each local church. A proper ordering of the church calls for the elder to pastor and guide the local church to be a faithful mission outpost, a faithful expression of the body of Christ. The elder is to assist and orchestrate the diverse *charisms* and ministries to bring them into great unity of service.

Questions for Discussion

1. What do you think of the idea that all Christians are ordained into the office of laity at baptism?

2. How does thinking about ordination as a gift from God, building unity and preventing chaos, shape your view of ordination?

3. What do most laity and clergy think are the clergy's "primary tasks"?

4. What did you find helpful or unhelpful in this chapter regarding ordination?

5. What are the biggest areas that the church needs to grow and mature in regard to the ordination of elders and their function in the body?

Suggestions for Further Reading

Pelzel, Morris. *Ecclesiology: The Church as Communion and Mission.* Chicago: Loyola Press, 2002.

Peterson, Brent. *Created to Worship: God's Invitation to Become Fully Human.* Kansas City: Beacon Hill Press of Kansas City, 2012.

Willimon, William. *Pastor: A Theology and Practice of Ordained Ministry.* Nashville: Abingdon Press, 2002.

nineteen
THE "DESIGNATED READER"
AN ECCLESIOLOGICAL METAPHOR FOR PASTORAL LEADERSHIP

Jeff Crosno

To paraphrase the dilemma reported by the German novelist Thomas Mann, a writer is someone for whom writing proves to be *more difficult* than it is for other people. Presumably Mann had in mind the myriad of creative obstacles to writing *well* rather than the physical challenge of successfully manipulating a computer keyboard or fountain pen and legal pad. But perhaps his wry observation also suggests a predicament familiar to many working pastors. For in recognizing the occasional distance many pastors attempt to navigate between stated ecclesiological commitments and vocational responsibilities, some may be tempted to abandon any pretense of theological rigor and integrity. Under pressure to find "something that will work" in this task of leading a congregation (which may often seem like an exercise in herding cats), who could blame the pastor for casting jealous eyes toward more authoritarian or even manipulative leadership strategies? But keeping ordination vows in mind, maybe such tempted ministers will instead confess like Mann that learning to be a truly pastoral leader is a journey by which leadership becomes more difficult than it is for other people.

Consider, for instance, the recent "Statement of Ecclesiology" offered within the "Nazarene Future Report" as an implied job description for those who serve as elders in the Church of the Nazarene: "Elders are ordained to shape the body of Christ through preaching the gospel, administering the sacraments, nurturing the people in worship, and *ordering congregational life*" (italics mine).[1] It might easily be assumed that most elders would be able to offer articulate descriptions of the first three ministerial actions named. After all, what part of our "body life" is more routinely on display than these practices of Christian ministry performed through the preaching, sacramental observances, and public celebration of congregational worship? But how are pastors to understand and explain the fourth expectation that elders will nurture the body of Christ by ordering congregational life? One suspects that for at least some elders of the church, this fourth imperative might easily be something of an "unfunded mandate" for which pastors may lack a cogent and coherent theological rationale. And in the absence of such ecclesiological underpinnings, is it hard to imagine that a primary point of emphasis for too many pastors degenerates into considerations of ministerial *technique*? How odd it would be for Wesley's heirs to devalue their birthright by devoting so much attention to pastoral techniques and methods at the expense of deeper commitments required for the formation of Christlike character evidenced by the holy *affections* and *tempers* Wesley often described.

In speaking about ecclesial roles in a culture with apparently limitless energy and appetite for developing methods and technologies, we should probably affirm that our pastors are an extremely inventive group who seem quite capable of ordering and reordering congregational life through the application of allegedly cutting-edge spiritual knowledge and ministry techniques. So with truly impressive predictability, wave after wave of these attractively packaged religious goods and services wash over and into our congregations. But after riding the tide of an endless succession of congregational emphases, our pastors and laypeople may be forgiven for growing skeptical regarding the latest promise that the kingdom will come in its fullness just as soon as everybody signs up for the class and buys a hardback copy of *The DaVinci-Purpose-Driven-Left-Behind-Prayer-Shack-of-Jabez*.[2] One suspects (and hopes) that congregations are now waiting for something deeper and more substantial than a sugary and insubstantial diet of so-called gospel sweetmeats[3] that appears at least partially responsible for the alarming rise of attention deficit disordered congregations littering the North American religious landscape.[4] Simultaneously overstimulated and malnourished, such churches pose a significant challenge to Holiness pastors responsible for ordering congregational life toward ministry outcomes consistent with their stated ecclesiological commitments.[5]

To the degree I am correct in my hunch that many pastors discern a gap between their responsibilities and the available resources of their *functional ecclesiology*, we can anticipate a common response to any sense of inadequacy they may be experiencing in their ministerial role. Often we respond with practical theology resources heavily devoted to the development of more effective ministry *techniques*.[6] But such pastoral self-help materials also demonstrate what Heifetz described as *technical* rather than *adaptive* work.[7] And as Willimon recently observed while reflecting upon the "technical work" evident across his ministerial career, there are clear shortcomings to this approach:

> Technical work Heifetz defined as the search for the right application of technique to solve known problems—our earlier application of the insights of the church growth movement (which I eagerly and rather naively applied to my inner-city parish in the early 1980s), congregational transformation (those workshops that I led in churches during the late 1980s), and leadership development (district seminars helping clergy retool their skills to lead in the 1990s). For all the good in these efforts . . . "they didn't get us all the way to where we wanted to go."
>
> More than problem solving and platitudes, we needed conversion of beliefs and assumptions. I love technical work because it focuses upon action. But now—if what was needed was a change of beliefs and assumptions—more than a commander, I needed to be a more curious learner, a constant questioner, and a creative teacher. That's what Heifetz calls "adaptive work"—helping an organization adapt to its environment on the basis of its purposes and values by facing the painful realities and then mobilizing new attitudes and behaviors. . . . *Adaptive change is deep change because it aims at the modification of an organization's culture rather than discarding a few of its practices.* (Italics mine)[8]

Reading Willimon's assessment, it is sobering to think of the implications for any tradition emphasizing primarily technical approaches to ecclesiology and leadership. In my North American context, this approach can be particularly dangerous given cultural preferences for leadership models focusing upon "expert resources" of managerial competency. With the "Jesus CEO" as a dominant christological image, André Resner recently asked, "What is to prevent the capitalistic, consumer-oriented Church from desiring and selecting a minister to function partly as buoyant master of ceremonies and entertainer and partly as Wal-Mart style manager and motivator?"[9] But at the risk of provoking a minor theological fistfight among my leadership peers, the shortest answer may be that there is little within the functional ecclesiology of many pastors to avoid such an outcome. Yet warnings from other professions make it obvious that reliance on purely technical approaches is inadequate given the complexity of adaptive challenges that defy solutions of technique. In a Harvard Medical School commencement address, surgeon Atul Gawande described the changing face of modern medical practice in which doctors can no longer mentally retain all necessary information or master every skill needed to care effectively for patients. He went on to observe that "we train, hire, and pay doctors to be [solitary, autonomous] cowboys . . . [when it is high-functioning and interdependent auto racing] pit crews people need" when entering the hospital:

> [You need an essential skill] that you must have but haven't been taught—the ability to implement at scale, the ability to get colleagues along the entire chain of care functioning like pit crews for patients. There is resistance, sometimes vehement resistance, to the efforts that make it possible. Partly, it is because the work is rooted in different values than the ones we've had. They include *humility*, an understanding that no matter who you are, how experienced or smart, you will fail. (Italics mine)[10]

Taking seriously these cautionary warnings, it is this essential note of humility highlighted by Gawande that I want to push forward as the dominant concern for the remainder of this chapter. Drawing again from earlier distinctions between the technical and adaptive work of the leader outlined by Heifetz,[11] let me suggest that our pastors need a new ecclesiological metaphor to guide them through the bewildering array of congregational choices clamoring for attention and allegiance.[12] But I suspect that a truly helpful metaphor will also exert an ecclesiological counterbalance, namely an appropriate sense of pastoral restraint in addressing the challenges to be faced by leaders responsible to faithfully order congregational life. For it is the humility of effective leaders, the recognition of our propensity for *hubris* and overreaching that we often seem to miss when assuming that the pastor is by virtue of ordination endowed with the *Spiritual Gift of Immaculate Perception*. Knowing this, I have been looking to the Scriptures to find a metaphor describing that Christlike character representative of the Holiness emphasis we profess to admire in our pastors. But I am also struck by the fact that we do not always affirm those embodying the costly, cruciform values we espouse. As David Brooks notes:

> [When] you read a biography of someone you admire, it's rarely the things that made them happy that compel your admiration. *It's the things they did to court unhappiness*—the things they did that were arduous and miserable, which sometimes cost them friends and aroused hatred. It's excellence, not happiness that we admire most. . . . *Doing your job well often means suppressing yourself* . . . Most of us are egotistical and most are self-concerned most of the time, but it's nonetheless true that life comes to a point only in those moments when the self dissolves into some task. *The purpose in life is not to find yourself. It's to lose yourself.* (All italics mine)[13]

Assuming that Brooks is right, is it too much for us to hope for a biblical metaphor that might help us focus and sustain our attention upon the cultivation of a leader's character?

Let me propose one such candidate for our consideration: the so-called kingship law narrated in Deut. 17:14-20. The English translation of the NRSV reads as follows:

> When you have come into the land that the LORD your God is giving you, and have taken possession of it and settled in it, and you say, "I will set a king over me, like all the nations that are around me," you may indeed set over you a king whom the LORD your God will choose. One of your own community you may set as king over you; you are not permitted to put a foreigner over you, who is not of your own community. Even so, he must not acquire many horses for himself, or return the people to Egypt in order to acquire more horses, since the LORD has said to you, "You must never return that way again." And he must not acquire many wives for himself, or else his heart will turn away; also silver and gold he must not acquire in great quantity for himself. When he has taken the throne of his kingdom, he shall have a copy of this law written for him in the presence of the levitical priests. It shall remain with him and he shall read in it all the days of his life, so that he may learn to fear the LORD his God, diligently observing all the words of this law and these statutes, neither exalting himself above other members of the community nor turning aside from the commandment, ei-

ther to the right or to the left, so that he and his descendants may reign long over his kingdom in Israel.

Although this text has often become a lightning rod for scholarly debate, the apparent function of its location within the larger literary structure of Deuteronomy has been helpfully explained by Lohfink and McBride as a "statement of polity" regarding Israel's divided powers of governance.[14] Many scholars also notice "the explicit literary structure of the book . . . [and] its self-presentation as a series of Mosaic speeches" given the insertion of four "editorial superscriptions" (1:1-5; 4:44-49; 29:1; 33:1).[15] But Olson also thinks that the literary sequence of Deuteronomy 12—26 perhaps follows the order of the Decalogue, offering a meditation on the limits of human power:

> The statutes and ordinances of 16:18—18:22 share with the commandment honoring parents a basic set of values concerning the role and purpose of authority, whether exercised in a smaller family context (5:16) or in a larger community or national context (16:18—18:22). In ancient Israel, parents were primary holders of authority within the family context and warranted honor and respect. But parents were not gods, and they were not to be worshiped . . . The primary thrust of the *commandment* concerning parents is that authorities are to be honored. The primary thrust of the *statutes and ordinances* that explicate the parents commandment is that authorities are to be worthy of the honor they receive. Leadership brings responsibilities. Deuteronomy thus moves beyond what ethicist Paul Lehman describes as the false opposition between hierarchy and equality to a model of "reciprocal responsibility" involving both those who hold authority and those who are led.[16]

Now it is precisely this apparent modesty and humility regarding the exercise of human power envisioned by this call for reciprocal responsibility that highlights the most obvious and surprising characteristic of the kingship law. As Crüsemann notes, within the neighborhood of the ancient Near East a monarch was routinely understood to mediate between the earthly and heavenly realms, and Israel "generally participated in this view" as we see in the royal psalms.[17] However, something quite different is in view within the kingship law. Grant comments that while Israel was not alone in offering written advice to the reigning monarch, the law of the king remains extraordinary in the context of the ancient Near East in that "we find no other ancient texts which seek to limit the power of the king in this way."[18] Levinson's evaluation summarizes the text:

> [The] paragraph devoted to the king [suppresses] just those royal attributes that arguably represented the monarch's greatest source of dignity. Indeed, the depiction of the functions of the king in this unit serves far more to hamstring him than to permit him to exercise any meaningful authority whatsoever. After the introductory specification that the king should not be a foreigner (vv. 14-15), five prohibitions specify what the king should *not* do (vv. 16-17). There remains for the king but a single positive duty: while sitting demurely on his throne to "read each day of his life" from the very Torah scroll that delimits his powers (vv. 18-20).[19]

And Knoppers concludes in very similar fashion by noting that apart from the obligation to be what I have termed the designated reader, this law of the king "contains only restrictions on the monarchy and monarchical power, disqualifying non-Israelites from holding this office and limiting the number of a king's horses, the number of his wives, and the amount of his wealth."[20]

What exactly is the point of this perspective on Israel's monarchy? Given that the introductory rationale for seeking a king effectively denies the distinctive identity of the people of Israel (in that they are making the potentially dubious request to be like those peoples who live around them),[21] it is easy to discern an implicit critique of royal power and prerogatives within the text.[22] But explaining these criticisms regarding the standard operating procedures of Israel's kings, Grant quotes Christopher J. H. Wright:

> These three restrictions (vv 16f.) are remarkable because they quite explicitly cut across the accepted pattern of kingship throughout the ancient Near East. Military power, through the building up of a large chariot force (the point of having great numbers of horses), the prestige of a large harem of many wives (frequently related to international marriage alliances), and the enjoyment of great wealth (large amounts of silver and gold)—these were the defining marks of kings worthy of the title. Weapons, women, and wealth: why else be a king?[23]

As Grant makes clear in balancing the presumably negative rationale of Israel's request for a king against the affirmation that Israel is nonetheless free to have the king who has been *chosen* by Yahweh, this text is not really focused on whether or not there is any real point for a king to exist. The crucial question of the text is rather, "What should Israel's king be like?"[24]

And seeing that the only positive command of the kingship law envisions the monarch internalizing Torah on a daily basis as the designated reader just as the Shema (Deut. 6:4-9) previously called for all to be engaged in uninterrupted, daily listening before God, Nelson draws an elegant conclusion: "The king becomes the ideal citizen, a model Israelite, more a student of the law than a ruler."[25] He is now the one who embodies absolute dependence upon God by refusing to be self-deceived by the accoutrements of concentrated human power. Serving as the designated reader, the king becomes a public and visible reminder of the trust and piety to which all his subjects are called. Grant concludes:

> It is a powerful image of one who is committed to do more than learn from his "assigned text"—he seeks to shape and form his whole life and outlook based around that text. Torah, according to Deut. 17:14-20, is vital to the king's vertical and horizontal relationships. If the king is to know the blessing of Yahweh (v 20), he is to live by the torah. If he is to relate properly to his fellows (v 20), he must live by the torah. So we see that the instruction of Yahweh is absolutely essential to every aspect of the king's exercise of monarchic rule. In fact, we can observe a principle of intensification at work here. The king is to be characterized by a typically [Deuteronomistic] attitude towards the torah, reflecting that which is to be expected of all Israelites. According to Deuteronomy, *all of the people* are to absorb the divine instruction into their inner beings so that their lives and attitudes are shaped by it (e.g. Deut. 6:1-9). . . . However, the essence of the kingship law is that the king is expected to do so *all the more*—this is the principle of intensification. The people are to follow the torah, to keep the torah, not to forget the torah, but the king is to *excel* in these areas.[26]

Giving attention to these words about a king embodying true *excellence* in serving his constituents as the designated reader of a *book*, Eugene Peterson reminds me that "the Hebrew word for Bible is *Miqra*, a noun formed from the verb "to call," *qara* . . . [the] Bible is not a book to carry around and read for information on God, but a voice to listen to."[27] In fact, I am asserting that this daily reading, which is actually a profound and humble *listening,* is perhaps an essential ecclesiological restraint that can help save our leaders from themselves.[28] Certainly we can see how Deuteronomy attempts in its law of the king to curb the avaricious appetites of any monarch tempted to act in ways that are completely consistent with the neighbors but utterly corrosive of covenantal faithfulness. But perhaps our church could also appropriate this image of the designated reader to reaffirm priorities that value the formation of holy character above mere competency in pastoral technique or method. After all, can we doubt that our pastors may be tempted, like kings, to do whatever seems right in their own eyes when leading the church?

Questions for Discussion

1. Early in this chapter, the author suggested that church leaders may at times experience some discomfort regarding the underlying theological convictions that are foundational to their "functional ecclesiology" in ministry. To what degree do you think this is true, and what available evidence leads you to draw such a conclusion?

2. From your own perspective, how do you assess the author's assertion that too much attention within the discipline of what is often called "practical theology" is at present focused upon the development of new ministry *techniques* rather than "core questions of pastoral vocation, formation, and character"?

3. As you evaluate your own ministry, how does the distinction between *technical* and *adaptive* work inform the way you assess your experience and effectiveness as a leader?

4. What do the limitations and restrictions of the "kingship law" of Deuteronomy 17 suggest to you regarding your own approach to leadership at the present time?

5. What practice(s) should you develop and strengthen as a leader committed to serve as the kind of designated reader envisioned by the kingship law of Deuteronomy 17?

Suggestions for Further Reading

Barnes, Craig M. *The Pastor as Minor Poet: Texts and Subtexts in the Ministerial Life.* Grand Rapids: Eerdmans, 2009.

Brower, Kent E., and Andy Johnson, eds. *Holiness and Ecclesiology in the New Testament.* Grand Rapids: Eerdmans, 2007.

Lischer, Richard. *Open Secrets: A Spiritual Journey Through a Country Church.* New York: Doubleday, 2001.

Neumark, Heidi B. *Breathing Space: A Spiritual Journey in the South Bronx.* Boston: Beacon Press, 2003.

Peterson, Eugene H. *Practice Resurrection: A Conversation on Growing Up in Christ.* Grand Rapids: Eerdmans, 2010.

Willimon, William H. *Pastor: The Theology and Practice of Ordained Ministry.* Nashville: Abingdon Press, 2002.

twenty
PASTORING PASTORS
A FUNCTIONAL THEOLOGY OF SUPERINTENDENCY

Jeren Rowell

Returning from a recent sabbatical, I was delighted to receive this note from a pastor who serves on the staff of one of the congregations under my oversight:

> Though I don't often call you or see you on a regular basis, I was stunned at how much I really missed you during this sabbatical. I didn't even realize the feeling of security and stability your presence imparts to me simply by being our "pastor of pastors" here on the district.

Aside from the boost to my personal esteem, this note demonstrates what I believe to be most essential about the role of overseers in the church. When pastors do their work well, the value of that ministry goes much deeper than services rendered to a people. The heart of pastoral life is to so live among a people while following Jesus that the pastor becomes a living sign of the Good Shepherd. When this is done well it is life-giving to the people of God. In the same way, I propose that a functional theology of superintendency, while necessarily practical, must lay first on this foundation of a pastoral theology that provides the truest kind of leadership for the church.

Leadership

While the word suffers from gross overuse, the necessity of leadership is recognized in many areas of life. In communities of all kinds, congregations, families, and even in relationships between just two people we usually need someone to take the lead. At times this leadership is assigned but often it emerges naturally. Sometimes it remains located in an office or individual, but regularly it moves from person to person as needed.

I remember when this leadership realization dawned on me. I cannot describe all of the particulars now, this many years removed, but I distinctly remember the feelings and the thoughts of those moments. Elementary school was the setting, perhaps the fourth or fifth grade. A group comprised of me and several peers had been given an assignment to work on together. I can distinctly remember thinking, "Someone needs to guide this group." It was clear to me that this would be a frustrating and futile exercise without some sense of leadership, although I am sure I would not have articulated it just that way at the time. It was an intuitive sense that in a situation where several people are seeking to accomplish a common mission, leadership is critical. My next thought after "Someone needs to guide this group" was "Why not me?" Why not me indeed, so I led. I did not lead by announcing, "I am the leader now," or by suggesting an election. I think I led simply by providing a framework from which each participant could make his or her best contribution. I do not think I was fully aware at the time of what I was doing. I was simply responding naturally from the shaping contexts in my own life (primarily family and congregation) where I saw and sensed the impact of good leadership.

In my role as overseer (*superintendent* in the language of my church family), I have often noticed the communal anxiety that arises when a congregation is without pastoral leadership. This is true even in congregations where leadership is shared and leadership skills are abundant. A key component of our social agreements is knowing who can and will give vision, direction, correction, and care. Thinking of leadership in the church, however, takes us beyond social agreements to thinking about how the Spirit of God gathers and forms the people of God. The biblical story of God doing this demonstrates the critical nature of leadership as a component of healthy communities of faith. From Abraham to Moses to David and throughout the New Testament, God consistently calls and equips leaders as a sign of God's love and care for the world. So thinking about how leadership should work in the church is indeed theological as well as functional.

Overseers in the Church

Given the essential nature of leadership, then, it is especially important to think of it rightly when talking about how leadership works in the church. Our failure to think well in this area may have contributed to the modern adoption of models for ecclesial leadership rooted more in commerce and less in relationship of love. Too often the role of superintendent in the church has been conceived and executed in practical terms around the ideas of judicial administration or business management. To begin rightly with a functional theology suggests that a superintendent must first know who he or she is and what in the world he or she is trying to do in response to the call of God through the church. This identity could (and no doubt does) derive from a number of sources, but the present focus is on how superintendency functions in a Wesleyan theological framework. This way of thinking about it places Scripture at the center of all conceptions.

William H. Willimon noted recently that the Bible "seldom bothers with bishops."[1] This is true in terms of the handful of occurrences in the New Testament, but even a brief survey of the texts suggests that the idea of *episkope*, like other ideas borrowed from the culture of the time, finds its way into the language of the church with special application. First Timothy 3:1-7 and Titus 1:6-9 give the fullest descriptions of an overseer but focus especially on the character and lifestyle of persons who would hold the office. Most other references not only make mention of the role of overseer but do so in a way that presses the weight of responsibility in on those who would take this place of service in the church.[2] The texts that may be most shaping in terms of a theology of superintendency are those that attach the idea of *episkope* not to an office in the church, nor to a particular Christian, but to God. First Peter 2:25 uses the word in reference to the crucified and risen Jesus, saying to the church, "but now you have returned to the Shepherd and Overseer [*episkopon*] of your souls" (NIV). Earlier in that passage Peter exhorts the church, using a verb form of the word: "Live such good lives among the pagans that, though they accuse you of doing wrong, they may see your good deeds and glorify God on the day he visits [*episkopes*] us" (v. 12, NIV). Additionally, a verb form is used in Luke 19:44 as Jesus weeps over Jerusalem saying, "You did not recognize the time of God's coming [*episkopes*] to you" (NIV). These texts give some motion to the idea of *episkope* as it is used to describe overseers, suggesting that the actions of *going, visiting,* and *seeing* may be viewed not only in terms of the practices of oversight and accountability but also especially in terms of an oversight that is informed by God's initiating movement toward us in love. Moving from this recognition, then, the idea of an *itinerant* superintendency seems essential to a functional theology of superintendency.[3] As God moves toward us in love, so those called to and charged with oversight in God's church should move toward the people of God in love rather than employing models of leadership that become hierarchical and deferential.

Superintendents as Pastors

In current conversations one way the whole idea of superintendency seems to be justified goes something like, "Well, even pastors need a pastor." This is certainly true. However, it is critical to understand clearly what this actually means. Without biblical moorings the idea of oversight can either soften to a rather bland form of cheerleading or harden to the all-too-common notions of superintendents whose job it is to put the squeeze on pastors and congregations to grow more and pay more or suffer the unceremonious closing of the local church. In my work as a district superintendent, I have certainly sensed my share of resistance to "the district" (which I eventually figured out meant me) when the role was obviously being understood in these ways. I have also witnessed a melting of suspicion and a warming of esteem when the role of spiritual overseer begins to be seen as one who comes alongside to help restore a sense of hopeful imagination by rearticulating the rich missional vision to which our Lord has called us.

Unfortunately the modern idol of church growth (which too often had little to do with mission) placed superintendents as middle managers who were to spend their time primarily as organizational consultants and human resource administrators. These are not necessarily bad activities, and at times are very much needed in a particular context. The problem becomes acute when superintendents are not able or willing to offer much more than this. In my own recent study of the relationship between pastors and superintendents,[4] it was clear that pastors desire deeply the pastoral leadership of the person(s) who have been placed by the church in authority over them. Unfortunately, this relationship is fraught with peril given that superintendents often exercise their ministries in times of conflict between pastor and congregation or in times when discipline must be applied to the ill-advised or sinful actions of a pastor. Consequently, the superintendent often finds himself or herself in a tension between the responsibility to pastor the pastor and yet the equal responsibility to care for the congregation. When emotions run high and facts elude clear focus, this can be something of a tightrope on which the overseer seeks to navigate the relational chasm of a conflicted congregation.

So what does it mean for superintendents to function as pastors? Some argue that this cannot be done, suggesting that the entire notion of the superintendent as "pastor to the pastors" is misplaced and dangerous. This may be true when the idea of pastor is coming from recent domesticated notions of what pastors are to be and do. By this I mean to critique the common contemporary image of the pastor as not much more than an experience director, a kind of religious concierge serving up events that dazzle and an empathetic posture that soothes the troubled soul. The expected carriage and activities of pastoral care (as popularly understood) are certainly important, but in no way are they all of what it means to be a pastor. Good pastoral life and work means living from rich and prayerful study of the Scriptures so as to become in the whole of one's life a sign of the presence of the Good Shepherd in the midst of God's people. This living sign is known not only through the activities of presence, listening, and counsel but also especially through the pastor's ability to articulate and model a biblical vision for discipleship and mission.

The thoughts on this point of N. T. Wright, who knows the life of episcopacy personally, continue to challenge me in the exercise of my calling. Bishop Wright recognizes and models in his own work that the essential role of bishops is found not in administrative leadership but in the study and teaching of the Bible. He rightly notes that ecclesial leaders are often so consumed with the relentless tasks of administration that "though they still preach sermons and perhaps even give lectures, *they do not give the Church the benefit of fresh, careful, and prayerful study of the text.*"[5] As this happens not only is the church robbed of this teaching but also the pastoral office suffers from the poor modeling of its leaders. A truly functional theology of superintendency must begin with the core identity of superintendents or bishops as pastors and not first as organizational managers or chief executive officers. In my denomination all of the superintendents have been local pastors and most move directly from parish ministry to the superintendency. We know the rhythms of pastoral work especially of moving each week from text to sermon. And yet in the role of overseer, that motion of biblical study to teaching and proclamation often gives way to the urgencies of polity and program.

This is not an either/or proposition. I am simply arguing that we need superintendents to be less *managers* and more *teachers*. Whether it is a church/pastoral review, meeting with a board in pastoral transition, preaching to a congregation, or seeking to guide church leaders through a time of conflict, the role of the bishop is to try and call out a community that orders its life around the values and priorities, not of this world, but of the kingdom of God as expressed when God's people live together in a covenant of self-sacrificing love.

Pastoring Pastors

As already noted, the relationship of overseer and pastor is relatively complex. On the one hand, most people recognize as a matter of common sense that pastors also need a pastor. It is not hard to imagine that even pastors need someone to come to the rescue when the stress becomes unbearable and the vocation is in danger of being lost. Bishops and superintendents are the logical and rightful people to provide this relationship for local pastors, but research exposes across denominational groups that there is considerable angst about this relationship. A significant study of pastors by Dean Hoge and Jacqueline Wenger noted that "half of our respondents said they could not speak openly with their denominational officials."[6] In their study, just 39 percent of currently active pastors report that they felt supported by their overseers, while only 18 percent of those who recently left active ministry felt that they were supported. They also noted that "many ex-pastors speak with considerable passion about . . . the insensitivity and lack of support that they received from the denominational officials."[7] Richard Gilbert expressed well this strain of relational trust that explains in part the hesitancy of pastors to bring troubles to their overseer:

> How do I say, "I am tired of this ministry, the people don't cooperate, my family is complaining, and I have more and more doubts about God's effectiveness in my life?" What if we say that to the wrong parishioner? *We dare not tell our bishop or judicatory leader.* He or she may be my pastor, at least in theory, but how can you have this person as your pastor when he or she is also your boss? (Italics mine)[8]

Therein is the proverbial rub. No matter how much an overseer may desire to function pastorally for those under his or her charge, there is no escaping the fact that in most church groups there is, to varying degrees, a hierarchical reality. In addition to the nature of the relationship there is also the consuming administrative work that typically defines much of the role of bishop or superintendent. Consequently, pastors looking for help from their leaders are often looking to people who are as stressed out and overloaded as they are. This observation only deepens the sense of urgency for superintendents to learn how to avoid getting utterly swamped by the details and to keep first focus on the core pastoral works of prayer, Scripture study, and theological reflection. Superintendents in the church need to understand and conduct their work more from a pastoral theology that remembers and prefers the essential work of spiritual direction and keeps in proper perspective the secondary work of administration. The real work of the office is to cast a biblical and theological framework for the work of the church rather than to default to a pragmatic consumer orientation that concerns itself mostly with attendance and finances. This is not to suggest that certain metrics and systems for accountability to the measures of mission effectiveness are not important. Willimon makes a very strong case for this in *Bishop* and modeled it in the oversight of his Methodist Conference. To the degree, however, that pastors believe these are the things superintendents *really* care about, we have our work before us to help the church reimagine the role of overseer as pastor in the truest sense of the word.

In my study of pastors and superintendents, four things emerged that pastors desire from their overseer. These qualities could stand in answer to the negative ways that pastors sometimes assess their relationship with the superintendent. Some narrative responses from the study illustrate the potential for growth in the relationship between pastor and superintendent (DS in these comments):

- "DS seems disconnected from real life and giving practical support."
- "See him as a boss more than a friend; don't get to speak with him very often."
- "My DS is great but I'm responsible; he's busy."
- "Didn't want to add to his stress load; he is aware of our situation; hate to complain."
- "I was ashamed and felt I had failed."[9]

I propose that this obvious relational strain is real but not inevitable. It need not be this way if and when superintendents recover the true pastoral nature of their work. The particular point of focus in my study was the crisis of decision for pastors regarding persistence in active vocational ministry. In other words, will the pastor continue in this work or has the damage been done and the vocation lost? Regardless of the circumstances that precipitate such a decision point, these moments in any pastor's life expose what may be the most poignant opportunity for superintendents to work as pastors. This is true not only in terms of expressing care and concern, but especially in terms of guiding a pastor in spiritual discernment through the disciplines of prayer, careful reading of the Scriptures, and the grace of Christian conference that begins to bring clear perspective and fresh vision. Practically, then, pastors report wishing for or needing especially the following four things from their overseer.[10]

Communication is the most desired component in the relationship between pastors and superintendents. This expansive category includes the particular ideas of communication that is regular, initiated by the superintendent, and has as its evident motivation a concern for the pastor rather than the promotion of the organization's agenda for growth or success.

Trust is significantly related to communication and has to do particularly with whether the pastor feels that he or she has access to the superintendent. It especially appears when an expectation violation has occurred in the relationship. That is, the pastor expected or assumed things about how the superintendent might respond to a critical situation and then was disappointed that the response was different from what the pastor expected. The concern in this area is first a relational concern but it is also an institutional concern in terms of fear of potential negative consequences if a pastor were to reveal areas of personal struggle or congregational conflict.

Conflict management assistance or even decisive intervention of a superintendent in times of congregational conflict is the third key thing that pastors desire from superintendents. However, what pastors seem to need at this point, more than simple solutions or policy application, is the pastoral presence of one who understands and appreciates what these kinds of experiences mean for pastor, family, and congregation. Another significant component in this is what I call *church-pastor preference* that has to do with whether the congregation or the pastor receives the best support of the superintendent during times of disagreement. In my study, several respondents commented that when faced with this tension, superintendents (at least in the pastor's view) tended to side with congregational leadership. This very point of tension is an opportunity for overseers to do significant pastoral work in terms of teaching lay congregational leaders what *pastor* really means from the perspective of a biblical pastoral theology. Too often laypersons view the pastoral office mostly in terms of organizational function. Even worse, congregations often assume that they have "hired" a pastor and therefore the pastor is an employee of the church. Legal definitions aside, this is a dangerous mindset for a people who are called to submit to the spiritual authority, not of a particular individual, but of the pastoral office (see Heb. 13:17, for example). Superintendents have an obligation to teach the church at this point, binding our functional understandings of pastor to a clear and biblical understanding of pastor as a reflection of the offices of Christ.

Fourth, the thread of *resourcing* is a repeated theme from pastors in what they desire from superintendents. This has to do with pastors desiring opportunities for continuing education and mentoring or coaching that is initiated and enabled by leadership. Superintendents are in a strong position to encourage, model, and facilitate mentoring relationships, accountability relationships among pastors, and resource partnerships between congregations. Another component of resourcing is located in the superintendent's ability to provide renewal strategies such as the planning and execution of retreats, the connection of pastors to retreat and renewal ministries for individual or family use, and the promotion and assistance for times of sabbatical leave for pastors and their families.

These practical ministries are certainly not the whole or even the center of a bishop's work, but they do begin to build a culture of relational trust on which the core works of pastoral oversight can find carriage. Wherever superintendents may have allowed their work to be formed mostly by administrative responsibilities or by popular business models of leadership, I hope that more overseers will recover a framework for the office that is biblically grounded, theologically reflective, and relationally rich in love. Under the positive influence of superintendents, may the congregations and pastors under our care live together and toward the world as an authentic expression of the kingdom of God.

Questions for Discussion

1. What are some implications of thinking of the role of superintendents in the church first from a biblical perspective rather than an organizational perspective?

2. In view of contemporary culture and our particular church tradition, what is the meaning of submission to the authority of the church? If this remains a valid idea, what is its foundation?

3. What positive outcomes for the church may emerge in response to biblically informed and healthy relationships between superintendents and pastors?

Suggestions for Further Reading

The Holy Rule of Saint Benedict. Located at http://www.ccel.org/ccel/benedict/rule2/files/rule2.html.

Lathrop, Gordon W. *The Pastor: A Spirituality.* Minneapolis: Fortress Press, 2006.

Richey, R. *Episcopacy in the Methodist Tradition.* Nashville: Abingdon Press, 2004.

Willimon, William. *Bishop: The Art of Questioning Authority by an Authority in Question.* Nashville: Abingdon Press, 2012.

NOTES

Chapter 1

1. John Wesley, Sermon 74, "Of the Church," para. 1, in *The Sermons of John Wesley*, Wesley Center Online, http://wesley.nnu.edu/john-wesley/the-sermons-of-john-wesley-1872-edition/sermon-74-of-the-church/.

2. Approximately forty thousand.

3. Gwang Seok Oh, *John Wesley's Ecclesiology* (Lanham, MD: Scarecrow Press, 2008), xvi-xvii.

4. Wesley, "Of the Church," para. 18. He is quoting from the Anglican Article of Faith.

5. Ibid.

6. Ibid., para. 19.

7. Ibid.

8. See Brent Peterson, *Created to Worship: God's Invitation to Become Fully Human* (Kansas City: Beacon Hill Press of Kansas City, 2012).

9. See Colossians 3:12-14.

10. Wesley, "Of the Church," para. 20.

11. Ibid., para. 21.

12. Ibid., para. 26-27.

13. See James 5:16.

Chapter 2

1. Thomas Hobbes, *Leviathan* (Cambridge, UK: Cambridge University Press, 1904), 84.

2. *Catechism of the Catholic Church* (Vatican City: Libreria Editrice Vaticana, 1994), 210.

3. Dan Kimball, *They Like Jesus but Not the Church: Insights from Emerging Generations* (Grand Rapids: Zondervan, 2007).

4. See Luke 10:29-37.

5. Mark 12:41-44 and Luke 21:1-4.

6. Matthew 5:40.

7. Karl Barth, *Church Dogmatics*, vol. 4, pt. 2 (Louisville, KY: Westminster John Knox Press, 1994), 682.

8. Ibid.

9. Jonathan Trigg, *Baptism in the Theology of Martin Luther* (Leiden, Netherlands: Brill, 1994), 174.

10. Dietrich Bonhoeffer, *Christ the Center* (New York: Harper and Row, 1978), 50-51.

11. See Matthew 25:31-46.

12. See Matthew 18:12-14 and Luke 15:3-7.

Chapter 3

1. "Preambles and Articles of Faith," Official Site of the International Church of the Nazarene, http://nazarene.org/ministries/administration/visitorcenter/articles/display.html (accessed January 7, 2013).

2. *The Catechism of the Catholic Church* (New York: Doubleday/Image Book, 1995, 233 (Article 9, para. 3, I).

3. Dietrich Bonhoeffer, "What Is the Church?" *Berlin: 1932-1933*, Vol. 12, ed. Larry I. Rasmussen, trans. Isbel Best and David Higgins (Minneapolis: Fortress Press, 2009), 262.

4. Robert Jenson, *Systematic Theology*, vol. 2, *The Works of God* (New York: Oxford University Press, 1999), 227.

5. David Bentley Hart, *The Beauty of the Infinite: The Aesthetics of Christian Truth* (Grand Rapids: Eerdmans, 2003), 155.

6. Ibid.

7. "Preambles and Articles of Faith," article XI.

8. Karl Barth, *Church Dogmatics*, Vol. II.I, secs. 28-30, ed. G. W. Bromiley and T. F. Torrance (New York: T&T Clark, 2009), 13.

9. Ibid., 4.

10. Ibid., 16.

11. Robert Jenson, *Systematic Theology*, vol. 1, *The Triune God* (New York: Oxford University Press, 1997), 65.

12. For an excellent exposition of the *analogia entis* see Erich Przywara's *Analogia Entis: Metaphysics: Original Structure and Universal Rhythm* (Grand Rapids: Eerdmans, 2013).

13. Dietrich Bonhoeffer, *Creation and Fall* (Minneapolis: Fortress Press, 1997), 64-65.

14. Ibid., 67.

15. Pierre Bourdieu, *The Logic of Practice*, trans. Richard Nice (Stanford, CA: Stanford University Press, 1980), 52.

16. Roger D. Haight, *Christian Community in History*, vol. 3: *Ecclesial Existence* (New York: Continuum, 2008), 60.

17. Ibid., 61.

18. Augustine, *The Trinity* (New York: New City Press, 1991), 173.

19. Ibid., 174.

20. See Samuel Wells, *God's Companions: Reimagining Christian Ethics* (Malden, MA: Blackwell, 2006).

21. Christopher L. Heuertz and Christine D. Pohl, *Friendship at the Margins: Discovering Mutuality in Service and Mission* (Downers Grove, IL: IVP, 2010), 34.

22. Jenson, *Systematic Theology*, 2:322.

23. Jenson, *Systematic Theology*, 1:11.

24. Christopher Morse, *The Difference Heaven Makes: Rehearsing the Gospel as News* (New York: T&T Clark, 2010), 17.

25. Jenson, *Systematic Theology*, 2:222.

26. John Milbank, *Theology and Social Theory: Beyond Secular Reason*, 2nd ed. (Malden, MA: Blackwell Publishing, 1990, 2006), 389.

27. *Manual*, article XI.

Chapter 4

1. Significant revisions were made at the 2009 General Assembly.

2. The language of the Church of the Nazarene as a "voluntary association" does not enter into the *Manual* until 1928 (28) but this language is present in the 1908 *Manual* when speaking of "The Churches Severally"—they are "composed" of "regenerate persons" who have "become associated together for holy fellowship and ministries" (27). However, the language goes back to the pre-merger 1898 Nazarene *Manual* in which the first Nazarenes declared themselves to "associate themselves together as a Church of God" (13).

3. The statement on "The General Church" that serves as the preamble to the further statement on the church has remained unchanged from 1908 until today: "The Church of God is composed of all spiritually regenerate persons, whose names are written in heaven." Note that there is no christological reference here. The church is a community of persons who happen all to be regenerate.

4. Cf. Stan Ingersol, "Christian Baptism and the Early Nazarenes: The Sources that Shaped a Pluralistic Baptismal Tradition," *Past and Prospect: The Promise of Nazarene History* (San Diego: Point Loma Press/Wipf and Stock, 2013).

5. Cf. Jeffrey Knapp, "Throwing the Baby out with the Font Water: The Development of Baptismal Practice in the Church of the Nazarene," *Worship*, 76:3 (May 2002): 225-44.

6. The Nazarene Article of Faith on Baptism (XII) says this quite explicitly: "Christian baptism . . . is a sacrament *signifying acceptance of the benefits* of the atonement . . . *declarative of their faith* in Jesus Christ" (32) (italics mine).

7. This was my own experience, and that of many of my friends, growing up in the Church of the Nazarene. Although I could testify to having received salvation from the age of five, I was encouraged only many years later to become

baptized when I was "ready." I would finally be baptized at the age of eighteen during my first year at Eastern Nazarene College, despite having been taken into church membership with all of my peers at the age of twelve and even serving on the church board.

8. Despite their profound influence on the development of evangelical Christianity, Anabaptists have often been marginalized in the history of Christianity, often identified with the variety of oddities that make up the so-called Radical Reformation, a term definitely not preferred by contemporary Anabaptists, many of whom are pacifists and have little in common with other so-called radicals of a violent and apocalyptic bent, such as Thomas Müntzer and the polygamous Münsterites. For a standard history of the movement written from this perspective, see George Huntston Williams, *The Radical Reformation*, 3rd ed. (Kirksville, MO: Truman State University Press, 2000). For a more sympathetic "insiders'" perspective on the movement, see William R. Estep, *The Anabaptist Story* (Grand Rapids: Eerdmans, 1995).

9. For one introduction to Pietism, see Carter Lindberg, ed., *The Pietist Theologians: An Introduction to Theology in the Seventeenth and Eighteenth Centuries* (Hoboken, NJ: Wiley-Blackwell, 2004). I was fortunate enough to have studied under Lindberg in graduate school.

10. Cf. Arthur Wilford Nagler's classic *Pietism and Methodism: Or, The Significance of German Pietism in the Origin and Early Development of Methodism* (Nashville: Methodist Publishing House, 1918).

11. See Ingersol, *Past and Prospect*.

12. That early Nazarenes understood themselves as but one expression or denomination of the larger church is evident in their careful distinction between "the general church," the "churches severally," and their own particular denomination (1898, 27). This exact distinction continues to be made in the most recent *Manual* (2009, 37).

13. The Foreword to the *Manual* reads as follows: "The primary objective of the Church of the Nazarene is to advance God's kingdom by the preservation and propagation of Christian holiness" (2009, 5). This language did not appear until the 1985 edition (5), but its roots are in the introduction to the 1898 *Manual*.

14. This is not to say that Pietists and Anabaptists are necessarily individualistic or, as we will later discuss, necessarily think of the church in essentially nonchristological ways, or put individual faith *before* the church. Indeed, Pietists typically see their call to piety as a call to the already-existent church, thus the idea of the *ecclesiola in ecclesia*. And, there are many Anabaptist groups that would say that one is *not* truly part of the body of Christ by virtue of personal faith but also *must* be baptized into the church.

15. Sociologist Christian Smith has spoken of the theology of the youth of today—the fastest-growing sector of the nones—in terms of a "moral therapeutic deism" for which God is vaguely a kind of personal friend who only requires that we all be good people and who is always there to help me when I am in need. I would side with Drew Underwood, who has suggested that this is not actually deism but a kind of watered-down Christian theism. I would also want to suggest that it is deeply rooted in a believers' church ecclesiology. For Smith's work, see especially Christian Smith and Melina Lundquist Denton, *Soul Searching: The Religious and Spiritual Lives of American Teenagers* (New York: Oxford University Press, 2005). Underwood's response can be found in "Moralistic Therapeutic . . . Theism?" *Springfield Deism Examiner* (9/22/2011).

16. Cf. Reuben Welch, *We Really Do Need Each Other: A Call to Community* (Grand Rapids: Zondervan, 1981). Welch was one of the first within the Church of the Nazarene to sense the deep dangers of our overly individualistic ecclesiology, though his work also betrays some of the same assumptions about the fundamental nature of the church as essentially an instrument for the growth of individual Christians.

17. During the height of the Arian controversy, it appears that nearly the entire population of the Roman Empire was caught up in the debates, that one could even find common people debating whether the relationship between Father and Son was one *homoousias* (of one substance) or *homoiousias* (of similar substance).

18. This is one of the chief points of divergence between Eastern and Western Christians and why each has its own version of the Nicene Creed. The Eastern church affirms that the Holy Spirit "proceeds from the Father" while the Western church—including Catholics and Protestants—affirms that the Holy Spirit "proceeds from the Father *and the Son*" thus more explicitly identifying a christological and Christocentric role to the Spirit.

19. Colleague and New Testament scholar Kara Lyons-Pardue suggested to me this image during a personal conversation about Pauline ecclesiology. A similar point is made by Jesus when he calls himself the "vine" and believers the "branches" in John 15:5. There is no life apart from the body of Christ, the church.

20. I like to tell my students that, when it comes to salvation, we do have a role, but God does 99.999999999999999 percent of the work!

21. Cf. John A. T. Robinson's beautiful little book *The Body: A Study in Pauline Theology* (Philadelphia: Westminster John Knox Press, 1977).

22. This was the core conviction about the fundamental nature of the church for most of the history of the church, even among Anabaptists and Pietists. Although I am not absolutely certain of this, I believe that the first theologian of significance to think otherwise about the church is Friedrich Schleiermacher, the

father of Protestant liberalism. Schleiermacher's magisterial systematic theology *The Christian Faith* importantly *begins* with conceptions about the nature of the church drawn from philosophical reflection about (what he considers) the universal nature of human experience. Schleiermacher was, it is important to note, a child of German Pietism, but he was also in other ways a child both of the Enlightenment and of the romantic movement. My sense is, then, that by seeking to ground all of Christian theology in universal experience (albeit communal experience), Schleiermacher made a significant contribution to dislodging traditional ecclesiology in its rootedness in God's self-revelation in Jesus Christ—that is, Christology. Put another way, theology became a bottom-up (anthropocentric) enterprise, rather than a top-down (Christocentric), and ecclesiology from a bottom-up perspective looks like an association of believers, while from a top-down perspective is the body of Christ.

23. See, for instance, Hans Küng, *The Church* (Garden City, NY: Image Books, 1976), 266-74.

24. Rob L. Staples first suggested this to me while I was his student at Nazarene Theological Seminary in 1991. Cf. *Outward Sign and Inward Grace: The Place of the Sacraments in Wesleyan Spirituality* (Kansas City: Beacon Hill Press of Kansas City, 1991).

25. John Wesley makes this point no more strongly than in his sermon "The Scripture Way of Salvation"—salvation comes *only* by grace through faith!

26. See especially chapter 9 by Brent Peterson.

Chapter 5

1. This is especially true of the more Reformed tradition. As the Church of the Nazarene has taken in Reformed theology in the form of fundamentalism, its pneumatology, I would argue, has suffered.

2. While supportive of the attempts of feminism to "de-masculinize" the Godhead, I would reject strongly the identification of the Holy Spirit as the "female" expression of God, for if understood in a Western model, it simply serves to resubordinate femaleness, and thus consequently, women.

3. It is key for Wesley and Wesleyans that this second aspect of repentance is only possible *after* faith and only through the assistance of God. Otherwise, we would inappropriately connect salvation to our own efforts at righteousness. It is only grace, through faith, that enables us to repent in this second sense.

4. This can be summarized using Wesley's concept of the "analogy of faith." Each passage should be interpreted in light of the whole, and in light of the specific doctrines of: original sin, justification and new birth, and inward and outward holiness. Wesley would not be sidetracked by other issues in finding the meaning and purpose of Scripture; although he certainly comments on these other issues, he strongly maintains the purpose of Scripture is God's revelation

to humankind about God's nature—through Old Testament events and in the incarnation, crucifixion, and resurrection of Christ—and about God's intention to save and restore us in God's image, which expresses itself in holiness, perfect love.

5. A personal note: when I ask my students why they read the Bible, it is often articulated as an act of obedience. It is rare to hear any expression resembling that of spiritual nourishment or that the Holy Spirit presently inspires our hearts and connects us to God. For them, the Bible has the right answers and tells us what we are supposed to believe. There is little comprehension of spiritual formation gained from Scripture.

6. I would assert that sacrifice without first experiencing the liberating work in God, which gives us a truly renewed self, can reinforce structures of oppression. And yet, a renewed self can then pour out itself in sacrificial living. See my book for elaboration, *Singleness of Heart: Gender, Sin, and Holiness in Historical Perspective* (Scarecrow, 2001).

7. It would serve us well if every Nazarene was required to read Donald Dayton's book *Discovering an Evangelical Heritage,* where he traces this incredible involvement of holiness folks in issues such as abolitionism, the rights of women, and advocacy for the poor.

8. Stanley Hauerwas is an example of such a voice.

Chapter 7

1. Taken from Kevin Corcoran, ed., *Church in the Present Tense* (Grand Rapids: Brazos Press, 2011). I am aware that I oscillate between the church as "it" (a collective object) and "she" (a collective subject).

2. H. Richard Niebuhr, *Christ and Culture* (New York: Harper, 1956).

3. Correlationalism here means taking the truth of the gospel to a particular culture, which often requires some sort of "translation" work. In other words, the truth does not change, but the language and strategies of communication may need to change in order to effectively deliver its message.

4. Of course, the shorthand depiction of Wesley's theological bias means that he is also formed by Scripture, tradition (mediated in particular ways by particular people and traditions), reason (to the extent available), and experience (carefully understood and guarded by fruit-bearing evidence and witness).

5. See Diogenes Allen and Eric O. Springsted, *Philosophy for Understanding Theology* (London: Westminster John Knox Press, 2007), chaps. 12–13. The following marks are a synthesis developed from reading a range of sources and thinkers. The recommended reading list points toward the ones most helpful to understanding the marks as I am developing them.

6. See Stanley Grenz, *A Primer on Postmodernism* (Grand Rapids: Eerdmans, 1996), and James K. A. Smith, *Who's Afraid of Postmodernism?* (Grand Rapids: Baker Academic, 2006).

7. See Scot McKnight, "Scripture in the Emerging Movement" in *Church in the Present Tense,* for a discussion of this; 105-22, especially 111-14.

8. For an interesting analysis of listening, see Aaron Perry, "The Phenomenological Role of Listening in Shaping the Church into a Leading Community," in *Wesleyan Theological Journal* 47, 2 (2012), 165-78.

9. There is—in some versions of postmodern thinking—an emphasis on apophatic theology as a result of such epistemic humility. A reflection that there is more unsayable than sayable. I am not developing that here but am inclined to think that a helpful balance may be struck between the kataphatic and apophatic as theology is drawn upon to talk of/about/with God.

10. Anthony Thiselton, *The Two Horizons: New Testament Hermeneutics and Philosophical Description* (Exeter, UK: Paternoster, 1980).

11. H. G. Gadamer, *Truth and Method,* 2nd rev. ed., trans. J. Weinsheimer and D. G. Marshall (New York: Crossroad, 2004).

12. Helen Cameron, Deborah Bhatti, Catherine Duce, James Sweeney, and Clare Watkins, *Talking About God in Practice: Theological Action Research and Practical Theology* (London: SCM, 2010), 54.

13. For a full explanation of the voices, see Cameron, et al., *Talking about God in Practice,* part 2, chap. 4.

14. See John D. Caputo, *What Would Jesus Deconstruct?* (Grand Rapid: Baker Academic, 2007), for a good example of such an understanding of deconstruction.

15. I am aware, of course, that there is a sense in which others argue equally strongly for fragmentation. That is, multiple identities held in hermetically sealed ways as manifest (for example) in Facebook or multiple blogs or online churches. I am not arguing against that but am suggesting that only as the emphasis on wholeness and integral witness is developed by the church as a mark of postmodern engagement will the church have the capacity to counter the more fragmented, but powerful, legions of the empire.

16. See Kimball, *They Like Jesus but Not the Church*; David Kinnaman, *unChristian* (Grand Rapids: Baker Books, 2007); Graham Tomlin, *The Provocative Church* (London: SPCK, 2002).

17. It is possible that this area is one that demonstrates most fully that postmodern marks are inseparable from relative wealth, education, and Western cultural norms. People who are victims, starving, raped, on the run don't have the luxury of Sabbath, caring for the other when starving becomes a short-cut to mutual death and survival means you probably do cut the last tree down.

18. I suspect that here our contexts will frame our considerations very differently. In the US setting Wallis, Hauerwas, and McLaren speak into this drive. In the UK setting Murray, Williams, Tomlin, Cray, and others consider what this means for the established church.

Chapter 8

1. It is important to acknowledge that no one comes to the Scriptures or the study of worship without presuppositions. Despite my best efforts to read Scripture communally and to listen to alternate readings, I come as a white, male, Western Christian. This reality does not dismiss my reading but invites further conversation and reflection among fellow pastors, liturgists, musicians, and others.

2. The use of the term *ecclesia* throughout this essay will refer to the "called out ones." The ecclesia's identity, rooted and grounded in God, differentiates them for living God's way in the world. This is not a move toward exclusivity. Rather, as the ecclesia bear witness to God in the world, all of creation is invited into God's life.

3. James F. White, *Introduction to Christian Worship*, 3rd ed. (Nashville: Abingdon Press, 2000), 68.

4. See Philippians 2:5-11. Paul's use of the kenosis hymn describes the self-emptying movement of Christ. Humility, obedience, and sacrifice mark the life of Christ, and these are to be the hallmarks of Christ's church. The sacrificial nature of self-emptying is most evident in the Eucharist.

5. Peterson, *Created to Worship*, 32.

6. John Wesley, Preface to *Sermons on Several Occasions,* vol. 1 (1746), sec. 5, in *The Bicentennial Edition of the Works of John Wesley* (Nashville: Abingdon, 1984—), 1:104-5, hereafter cited as *Bicentennial Edition.*

7. Samuel E. Balentine, *The Torah's Vision of Worship* (Minneapolis: Fortress Press, 1999), 123.

8. Eugene Peterson, *Practicing Resurrection: A Conversation on Growing Up in Christ* (Grand Rapids: Eerdmans, 2010), 89.

9. The role and function of the sacraments will be considered in another chapter. It is the author's conviction that the sacraments render visible the invisible by naming the church's belief about God's action in the world on behalf of God's people. In lower sacramental traditions, worship necessitates a deep commitment to the reading and interpretation of the Christian Scriptures. The biblical text must center the worshipping community.

10. The following summary is drawn primarily from White, *Introduction to Christian Worship*, 22-23.

11. White, *Introduction to Christian Worship*, 23-24.

12. John Wesley, *The Works of John Wesley*, ed. Thomas Jackson, 14 vols. (Kansas City: Beacon Hill Press of Kansas City, 1978), 10:102, hereafter cited as *Works* (Jackson).

13. See Lester Ruth's chapter "A Rose by Any Other Name" in *The Conviction of Things Not Seen: Worship and Ministry in the 21st Century* (Ada, MI: Brazos Press, 2007).

14. A third classification introduced by Ruth identifies a congregation's denominational connection. Some are independent congregations. This element invites those maintaining a denominational connection to name this affiliation and give voice to the denominational/theological commitment in how God's story is remembered in worship. The voice of this denominational/theological affiliation seems increasingly important in the absence of a formal book of worship.

15. Ruth, "A Rose by Any Other Name," 47.

Chapter 9

1. James F. White, *The Sacraments in Protestant Practice and Faith* (Nashville: Abingdon, 1999), 109.

2. See Peterson, *Created to Worship*, 151-53. Here I discuss how the sacraments are both a command and promise of God where God transforms common actions of bathing and eating to help persons become more fully human as a participation in the further coming of the kingdom of God.

3. Wesley, Sermon 16, "The Means of Grace," sec. 1.1, in *Sermons I*, in *Bicentennial Edition*, 1:378.

4. See Mildred Bangs Wynkoop, *A Theology of Love: The Dynamic of Wesleyanism* (Kansas City: Beacon Hill Press of Kansas City, 1972).

5. See Randy Maddox, *Responsible Grace* (Nashville: Abingdon Press, 1994). Maddox suggests that John Wesley's entire theological framework could be viewed through the lens of God's grace coming to persons, wooing and empowering them to respond to God's healing power.

6. Wesley, Sermon 74, "Of the Church," sec. 16, in *Sermons III*, in *Bicentennial Edition*, 3:51. Concerning this statement, footnote 28 remarks that it is "the first half of the first sentence of Art. XIX which, in turn, had been borrowed from Art. VIII of the Augsburg Confession (1530)."

7. Ole Borgen, *John Wesley on the Sacraments* (Grand Rapids: Francis Asbury Press of Zondervan Publishing House, 1985), 96.

8. Wesley, "An Earnest Appeal to Men of Reason and Religion," sec. 76, in *Addresses, Essays, Letters*, in *Works* (Jackson), 8:31.

9. Howard Snyder, *The Radical Wesley and Patterns of Church Renewal* (Downers Grove, IL: InterVarsity, 1980), 74.

10. Wesley, "Large Minutes 1744 to 1789," sec. Q.3, in *Works* (Jackson), 8:299.

11. See Wesley, Sermon 121, "Prophets and Priests," sec. 8, in *Bicentennial Edition*, 4:78; and A Letter to Mr. Hall, December 27, 1745, in *Bicentennial Edition*, 20:110.

12. See Wesley, "A Treatise on Baptism," sec. I.1, in *Works* (Jackson), 10:188.

13. Ibid.

14. See Staples, *Outward Sign and Inward Grace*, 119-200.

15. Ibid., 130.

16. See Acts 2:38 and Romans 6:3.

17. See Romans 6:4-5.

18. Wesley, "A Treatise on Baptism," sec. I.4, in *Works* (Jackson), 10:189.

19. Michael G. Witczak, *The Sacrament of Baptism: Lex Orandi Series* (Collegeville, MN: Liturgical Press, 2011), 5.

20. With the celebration of what infant baptism is, considering what infant baptism is not may also be helpful. See my book *Created to Worship*, 159-69, for a fuller conversation on infant baptism.

21. Wesley, Sermon 101, "The Duty of Constant Communion," sec. II.5, in *Bicentennial Edition*, 3:432.

22. For a fuller discussion of presence, sacrifice, and mission see *Created to Worship*, 184-200.

Chapter 10

1. Avery Dulles, *Models of the Church* (Garden City, NY: Doubleday, 1974).

2. Richard P. McBrien, *Church: The Continuing Quest* (New York: Newman, 1970), 11, cited in Dulles, *Models of the Church*, 71-72.

3. Wesley wrote this entry in his journal on July 28, 1757 (*Works* [Jackson], 2:420).

4. Stuart Andrews, *Methodism and Society* (London: Longman Group, 1970), 37.

5. Wesley, "Minutes of Several Conversations Between the Rev. Mr. Wesley and Others," in *Works* (Jackson), 8:310.

6. John Wesley, *Explanatory Notes upon the New Testament* (1754; repr., Kansas City: Beacon Hill Press of Kansas City, 1981), Acts 6:2.

7. "XIX. Of the Church," *The Book of Common Prayer*, 870 (New York: Seabury Press, 1979). When John Wesley produced a prayer book for ME Church in America, he retained the first part of this article almost verbatim but deleted entirely the section that spoke of the errors of the church at Rome. It was not an indication that Wesley thought that church to be *without* error but rather a reflection of his "catholic spirit" that sought the unity of the church.

8. For the text of the Augsburg Confession, see Philip Schaff, *The Creeds of Christendom*, 4th ed. (New York: Harper & Brothers, 1919), 3:3-73.

9. For further discussion of the nuanced views, see James N. Fitzgerald, "Weaving a Rope of Sand: The Separation of the Proclamation of the Word and the Celebration of the Eucharist in the Church of the Nazarene," Ph.D. diss. (Nashville: Vanderbilt University, 1999), 3-12.

10. Wesley, "An Earnest Appeal to Men of Reason and Religion," in *Works* (Jackson), 8:31.

11. Ibid., 8:30.

12. Wesley, A letter to Charles Wesley, August 19, 1785, in *Works* (Jackson), 13:254. He also repeats this distinction between *essence* and *properties* in "A Farther Appeal to Men of Reason and Religion," *Works* (Jackson), 8:76.

13. While in Georgia, Wesley refused to baptize a child because the parents wanted baptism by pouring, and Wesley said the rubrics only allowed that mode of baptism if the child was weak. He also insisted on rebaptizing dissenters before allowing them to receive the Eucharist, and he refused Communion to the Lutheran minister Johann Bolzius because Bolzius had not been baptized by a minister with episcopal ordination. See *Bicentennial Edition*, 18:157; *Journal*, 1:370. Wesley later apologized to Bolzius (1749) and later still spoke of being "delivered" from "this zeal for the Church" (sec. 1.4-5 and fn. 17, in *Bicentennial Edition*, 3:582-83).

14. Wesley, "Prophets and Priests," in the *Bicentennial Edition*, 4:79.

15. Albert Outler, ed., *John Wesley* (New York: Oxford University Press, 1964), 307.

16. Adrian Burdon, *The Preaching Service, the Glory of the Methodists: A Study of the Piety, Ethos, and Development of the Methodist Preaching Service* (Bramcote, Nottingham: Grove Books, 1991).

17. *Minutes of the Methodist Conferences* (London: Conference Office, 1812), 1:58.

18. Dulles, *Models of the Church*, 78.

19. Ibid., 71.

20. Ibid., 79.

21. Hughes Oliphant Old, *The Reading and Preaching of the Scriptures in the Worship of the Christian Church*, vol. 1: *The Biblical Period* (Grand Rapids: Eerdmans, 1998), 7.

22. Dulles, *Models of the Church*, 77.

23. In the *Manual*s issued in 1908 and 1911, these three statements stood at the beginning of the section that had the heading "Part I: The Church." They preceded the "Agreed Statement of Belief" and the "Doctrinal Statement." In 1915 and 1919, the statements on "The General Church" and "The Churches Severally" were included at the end of the Doctrinal Statement. Immediately following that, but under a separate heading, was the statement on "The Church of the Nazarene."

24. In 1923 the General Assembly approved a constitution for the first time, and the "Doctrinal Statement" became "Articles of Faith." The constitution that was approved by the assembly included the three statements about the church as Articles of Faith XVI, XVII, and XVIII. *Journal of the Sixth General Assembly of the Church of the Nazarene* (1923), 284.

25. When the 1923 *Manual* was published, the three statements on the church had been moved out of the Articles of Faith. They were placed under a separate heading, just before the shorter Agreed Statement of Belief. No record is given of exactly whose editorial decision it was to remove the statements from the Articles of Faith, but the move probably did best reflect the nature of the statements as they existed. They were not so much doctrinal statements on the nature of the church as they were a statement of the raison d'être for the Church of the Nazarene and a justification for denominationalism.

26. *Manual* (1989), 35.

27. Ibid.

Chapter 11

1. John Westerhoff, "A Discipline in Crisis," *Religious Education* 74:1 (1979), 13.

2. John Westerhoff, *Learning Through Liturgy* (New York: Seabury Press, 1978), 285.

3. For a further discussion about the means of grace, which includes formation, discernment, and transformation, see Dean Blevins, "John Wesley and the Means of Grace: An Approach to Christian Education," Ph.D. diss., Claremont School of Theology (Ann Arbor, MI: UMI, 1999).

4. Wesley, "The Means of Grace," in *Bicentennial Edition*, 1:381.

5. Dean G. Blevins and Mark A. Maddix, *Discovering Discipleship: Dynamics of Christian Education* (Kansas City: Beacon Hill Press of Kansas City, 2010), 86. Also see Blevins, *John Wesley and the Means of Grace*.

6. Blevins and Maddix, *Discovering Discipleship*, 87.

7. Charles R. Foster, *Congregational Education: The Future of Christian Education* (Nashville: Abingdon Press, 1994), 70-76.

8. For a more complete reading, see Mark A. Maddix, "John Wesley and a Holistic Approach to Christian Education," *Wesleyan Theological Journal* 44:2 (Fall 2009): 76-93.

9. Wesley, Sermon 95, "On the Education of Children," in *Bicentennial Edition*, 3:352.

10. Wesley, "A Treatise on Baptism," in *Works* (Jackson), 10:188-201.

11. Wesley, Sermon 45, "The New Birth," in *Works* (Jackson), 6:74.

12. John Wesley Prince, *Wesley on Religious Education: A Study of John Wesley's Theories and Methods of the Education of Children in Religion* (New York: Methodist Book Concern, 1926), 96.

13. Ibid.

14. Ibid., 87-88.

15. David I. Naglee, *From Font to Faith: John Wesley on Infant Baptism and the Nurture of Children* (New York: Peter Lang, 1987), 228-37.

16. See Mark A. Maddix, "John Wesley's Small Groups: A Model of Christian Community," *Holiness Today* (November-December 2009), 20-21.

17. D. Michael Henderson, *A Model for Making Disciples: John Wesley's Class Meeting* (Nappanee, IN: Evangel Publishing House, 1997).

18. John Westerhoff, *Living the Faith Community: The Church that Makes a Difference* (Minneapolis: Winston Press, 1985), 23.

19. Ibid., 25.

20. Ibid., 85.

21. Debra Dean Murphy, *Teaching that Transforms: Worship as the Heart of Christian Education* (Grand Rapids: Brazos, 2004), 10.

22. Wesley, Sermon 51, "The Duty of Constant Communion," sec. I.3, in *Works* (Jackson), 7:148.

23. Sandra Schneiders, "Biblical Spirituality," *Interpretation* 56.2 (2002): 137.

24. Marva M. Dawn, *Reaching Out without Dumbing Down: A Theology of Worship for the Turn-of-the-Century Culture* (Grand Rapids: Eerdmans, 1995), 211.

25. Murphy, *Teaching that Transforms*, 145.

26. See Mark A. Maddix and Richard Thompson, "Scripture as Formation: The Role of Scripture in Christian Formation," in *Wesleyan Theological Journal* 46(1) (Spring 2011), 134-49.

27. Blevins and Maddix, *Discovering Discipleship*, 88.

28. See Maddix and Thompson, "Scripture as Formation."

29. Blevins and Maddix, *Discovering Discipleship*, 91-92.

30. Ibid., 91.

31. For a complete discussion, see Mark A. Maddix and Jay R. Akkerman, eds., *Missional Discipleship: Partners in God's Redemptive Mission* (Kansas City: Beacon Hill Press of Kansas City, 2013).

32. Henry Abelove, *The Evangelist of Desire: John Wesley and the Methodists* (Stanford, CA: Stanford University Press, 1990), 8.

33. Ibid., 9.

34. Ibid.

Chapter 12

1. Richard P. Heitzenrater, *Wesley and the People Called Methodists* (Nashville: Abingdon Press, 1995); Henry H. Knight III, *The Presence of God in the Christian Life: John Wesley and the Means of Grace* (Metuchen, NJ: Scarecrow Press, 1992), 92-95.

2. David Lowes Watson, *The Early Methodist Class Meetings* (Nashville: Discipleship Resources, 1985/1987), 68-91.

3. Heitzenrater, *Wesley and the People Called Methodists*, 33-95.

4. Rupert E. Davies, Introduction to *The Methodist Societies: History, Nature, and Design*, in *Bicentennial Edition*, 9:11.

5. Ibid., 10-11.

6. Ibid., 12; Watson, *Early Methodist Class Meetings*, 93-133.

7. Watson, *Early Methodist Class Meetings*, 93-94.

8. Heitzenrater, *Wesley and the People Called Methodists*, 122-23, 146, 180.

9. Wesley, "Of the Church," in *Bicentennial Edition*, 3:48-52.

10. Ibid., 46.

11. Wesley, Sermon 92, "On Zeal," in *Bicentennial Edition*, 3:313-14.

12. Wesley, "Of the Church," in *Bicentennial Edition*, 3:53-56.

13. Blevins and Maddix, *Discovering Discipleship*, 78-80; Matthaei, *Making Disciples*, 19-54.

14. Gregory S. Clapper, *John Wesley on Religious Affections* (Metuchen, NJ: Scarecrow Press, 1989); Randy Maddox, "Reconnecting the Means to the End: A Wesleyan Prescription for the Holiness Movement," *Wesleyan Theological Journal* 33, 2 (1998): 29-66.

15. Blevins, *John Wesley and the Means of Grace*.

16. Dean G. Blevins, "Practicing the New Creation: Wesley's Eschatological Community Formed by the Means of Grace," *Asbury Theological Journal* 57, no. 2 and 58, no. 1 (Fall 2002/Spring 2003), 81-104.

17. Clifford W. Dugmore, *Eucharistic Doctrine in England from Hooker to Waterland* (London: SPCK, 1942), 41.

18. Wesley, "The Means of Grace," in *Bicentennial Edition*, 1:381.

19. Wesley, *Journal*, in *Journals and Diaries*, eds. W. Reginald Ward and Richard P. Heitzenrater, in *Bicentennial Edition*, 18:218-20, 19:116-18, 20:131-39. See also W. Stephen Gunter, *The Limits of Love Divine: John Wesley's Response to Antinomianism and Enthusiasm* (Nashville: Kingswood Books, 1989), 83-117.

20. *The Book of Common Prayer and Administration of the Sacraments and Other Rites and Ceremonies of the Church* (England, 1663; Ann Arbor, MI: UMI, 1986), microfilm; Albert Outler, Introduction to *John Wesley: Sermons*, in *Bicentennial Edition*, 1:377; Edward H. Sugden, ed., *Wesley's Standard Sermons* (London: Epworth Press, 1921), 1:242. Outler notes that the original source of the contribution was probably Bishop Edward Reynolds of Norwich, which Outler

describes as "a former Nonconformist and still something of a 'puritan' in his theology."

21. David Lowes Watson, *Covenant Discipleship: Christian Formation through Mutual Accountability* (Nashville: Discipleship Resources, 1991), 43-58.

22. Heitzenrater, *Wesley and the People Called Methodists*, 175-76; Wesley, "Minutes of Several Conversations between the Rev. Mr. Wesley and Others," in *Works* (Jackson), 8:322-24.

23. Wesley, "Minutes of Several Conversations," in *Works* (Jackson), 8:323.

24. Dean Blevins, "Faithful Discipleship: A Conjoined Catechesis of Truth and Love," in *Considering the Great Commission: Evangelism and Mission in the Wesleyan Spirit*, eds. W. Stephen Gunter and Elaine Robinson (Nasvhille: Abingdon Press, 2005), 197-210; Wesley, *Journal* extract, Thursday, February 21, 1740, in *Journals and Diaries*, in *Bicentennial Edition*, 19:139. In his dispute with the Moravians Wesley writes in his journal, "I had a long conference with those whom I esteem highly in love. But I could not yet understand on one point, 'Christian openness and plainness of speech.' They pleaded for reservedness and closeness of conversation I could in no wise reconcile with St. Paul's direction, 'by manifestation of the truth to commend ourselves to every man's conscience in the sight of God.'"

25. Wesley, "Earnest Appeal to Men of Reason and Religion," in *Bicentennial Edition*, 11:67-68; "A Farther Appeal to Men of Reason and Religion part I," in *Bicentennial Edition*, 11:189.

26. Thomas R. Albin, "An Empirical Study of Early Methodist Spirituality," in *Wesleyan Theology Today*, ed. Theodore Runyon (Nashville: Kingswood Books, 1985), 275-90.

27. Randy L. Maddox, "Social Grace: The Eclipse of the Church as a Means of Grace in American Methodism," in *Methodism in Its Cultural Milieu*, ed. Tim Macquiban (Oxford, UK: Applied Theology Press, Westminster College, 1994), 131-34.

28. Lester Ruth, *Early Methodist Life and Spirituality: A Reader* (Nashville: Kingswood Books), 257-59.

29. Mary Elizabeth Moore, *Teaching as a Sacramental Act* (Cleveland, OH: Pilgrim Press, 2004), 153-69.

30. John W. Drakeford, *People to People Therapy, Self Help Groups: Roots, Principles, and Processes* (San Francisco: Harper and Row, 1978), 3-24.

31. Paul Wesley Chilcote, *Recapturing the Wesleys' Vision* (Downers Grove, IL: InterVarsity Press, 2004), 45-52.

32. Paul N. Markham, *Rewired: Exploring Religious Conversion* (Eugene, OR: Pickwick Books, 2007).

33. Charles R. Foster, *Educating Congregations: The Future of Christian Education* (Nashville: Abingdon Press, 1994); C. Ellis Nelson, ed., *Congrega-*

tions: Their Power to Form and Transform (Atlanta: John Knox Press, 1988); John Westerhoff, "Fashioning Christians in Our Day," in *Schooling Christians: "Holy Experiments" in American Education,* eds. Stanley Hauerwas and John Westerhoff (Grand Rapids: Eerdmans, 1992).

34. Blevins and Maddix, *Discovering Discipleship,* 106-12.

35. Ibid., 197-99.

36. Philip Pfatteicher, *The School of the Church: Worship and Christian Formation* (Valley Forge, PA: Trinity Press International, 1995); Murphy, *Teaching that Transforms,* 117-219.

37. Blevins, "Practicing the New Creation"; Dean Blevins, "On Earth as (if) It Were in Heaven: Practicing a Liturgical Eschatology," *Wesleyan Theological Journal* 40, no. 1 (Spring 2005), 69-92.

38. Dean Blevins, "A Wesleyan View of the Liturgical Construction of the Self," *Wesleyan Theological Journal* 38, no. 2 (Fall 2003), 7-29.

39. Drakeford, *People to People Therapy,* 10-20; Henderson, *Model for Making Disciples,* 83-126. Drakeford emphasizes relationship by stating Methodist societies provided a framework for associations, while class meetings provided behavioral change, bands were opportunities to be motivated, and penitent bands were for reclamation. Henderson follows an educational framework where societies focus on cognitive learning, class meetings on behavioral learning, bands on affective change, and penitent bands again on reclamation.

40. Watson, *Covenant Discipleship.*

41. Drakeford, *People to People Therapy,* 18-19; Henderson, *Model for Making Disciples,* 121-25.

42. Chilcote, *Recapturing the Wesleys' Vision,* 55-63.

43. Foster, *Educating Congregations,* 51-62; Donald E. Miller, *Story and Context: An Introduction to Christian Education* (Nashville: Abingdon, 1987), 103-82.

44. Foster, *Educating Congregations,* 62-67.

45. Watson, *Covenant Discipleship,* 69-74.

46. Blevins and Maddix, *Discovering Discipleship,* 245-46.

47. Craig Dykstra and Dorothy C. Bass, "Times of Yearning, Practices of Faith," in *Practicing Our Faith,* 2nd ed., ed. Dorothy C. Bass (San Francisco: Jossey-Bass, 1997, 2010), 6-7.

48. Ibid., 7-9.

49. Murphy, *Teaching that Transforms,* 209-16; Alexander Schmemann, *For the Life of the World: Sacraments and Orthodoxy* (Crestwood, NY: St. Vladimir's Seminary Press, 1973).

50. Wesley, "The Means of Grace," in *Bicentennial Edition,* 1:394.

Chapter 14

1. Walter Brueggemann, *Peace* (St. Louis: Chalice, 2001), 13.

2. Carol J. Dempsey, *Justice: A Biblical Perspective on Justice* (St. Louis: Chalice, 2008), 98.

3. Desmond Tutu, *No Future Without Forgiveness* (New York: Image/Doubleday, 1999), 31.

Chapter 16

1. See Richard P. Thompson, "Gathered at the Table: Holiness and Ecclesiology in the Gospel of Luke," in *Holiness and Ecclesiology in the New Testament*, ed. Kent E. Brower and Andy Johnson (Grand Rapids: Eerdmans, 2007), 76-94.

2. See the comment on 2 Timothy 3:16 by John Wesley, *Explanatory Notes upon the New Testament* (London: Epworth, 1958), 794: "The Spirit of God not only once inspired those who wrote it, but continually inspires, supernaturally assists, those that read it with earnest prayer." Cf. Richard P. Thompson, "Inspired Imagination: John Wesley's Concept of Biblical Inspiration and Literary-Critical Studies," in *Reading the Bible in Wesleyan Ways: Some Constructive Proposals*, ed. Barry L. Callen and Richard P. Thompson (Kansas City: Beacon Hill Press of Kansas City, 2004), 62-65.

3. This issue of the development in thought holds whether one considers the Ephesian and Colossian letters to have been written by a deutero-Pauline author (as do most biblical scholars) or by the apostle Paul. However, the extended time available in the first option makes that possibility more likely, as will be indicated later in this essay.

4. See, e.g., Peter Lampe, "Theological Wisdom and the 'Word About the Cross': The Rhetorical Scheme in I Corinthians 1—4," *Interpretation* 44, no. 2 (Apr. 1990): 117-31; and Victor Paul Furnish, *The Theology of the First Letter to the Corinthians*, New Testament Theology (Cambridge, UK: Cambridge University Press, 1999), 28-48.

5. See James D. G. Dunn, *The Theology of Paul the Apostle* (Grand Rapids: Eerdmans, 1998), 537-40. It should be noted that Paul is not alone among New Testament writers in borrowing *ekklēsia* language to refer to the church as the people of God, as the book of Acts similarly appropriates this terminology. See Richard P. Thompson, *Keeping the Church in Its Place: The Church as Narrative Character in Acts* (New York: T&T Clark International, 2006), esp. 241-48.

6. A common understanding of the literal meaning of *ekklēsia* as "called out ones" or those called to be separate (i.e., from the world) mistakenly assumes that the prefix/preposition *ek* ("out") connotes separation when, in this instance, the emphasis may likely be on the source of the call.

7. Cf. Paul D. Hanson, *The People Called: The Growth of Community in the Bible* (San Francisco: Harper and Row, 1986), 69-78.

8. Furnish, *Theology of the First Letter to the Corinthians*, 32-33.

9. Menenius Agrippa first told this famous fable in the midst of a volatile standoff between aristocrats and commoners in the fifth century B.C. The story is about the hands, mouth, and teeth of a man's body revolting against the belly. Since the hands, mouth, and teeth thought it unfair that they provided everything for the belly and that the belly did nothing but enjoy their provision, they conspired to starve the belly into submission. But while they did this, these members as well as the rest of the body were also severely weakened. Thus, it became clear to the whole body that even the belly had an important task to do. Because of Agrippa's wisdom, the people understood the parallels between the story and their dire situation, and the crisis was averted (Livy, *History* 2.32; and Dionysius of Halicarnassus, *Roman Antiquities* 6.86). Cf. also Plato, *Republic* 5.462c-d; and Aristotle, *Politics* 5.2.7. See Margaret M. Mitchell, *Paul and the Rhetoric of Reconciliation: An Exegetical Investigation of the Language and Composition of 1 Corinthians* (Louisville, KY: Westminster/John Knox, 1991), 157-64.

10. See Eckhard J. Schnabel, "The Community of the Followers of Jesus in 1 Corinthians," in *The New Testament Church: The Challenge of Developing Ecclesiologies*, ed. John Harrison and James D. Dvorak, McMaster Biblical Studies Series (Eugene, OR: Wipf and Stock, 2012), 117-18; and Furnish, *Theology of the First Letter to the Corinthians*, 90-91.

11. See Dunn, *Theology of Paul the Apostle*, 558-59.

12. See Richard B. Hays, *The Moral Vision of the New Testament: A Contemporary Introduction to New Testament Ethics* (San Francisco: HarperSanFrancisco, 1996), 35.

13. See, e.g., Wesley, "A Plain Account of Christian Perfection," in *Works* (Jackson), 9:420. Cf. Wynkoop, *A Theology of Love;* Diane Leclerc, *Discovering Christian Holiness: The Heart of Wesleyan-Holiness Theology* (Kansas City: Beacon Hill Press of Kansas City, 2010), 273-87.

14. Wesley, Preface to *Sermons on Several Occasions*, in *Bicentennial Edition*, 1:104-5.

15. This statement recognizes differences in perspective regarding the authorship of Ephesians and Colossians (i.e., whether Paul or perhaps one of his followers wrote these letters). However, regardless of the particular position regarding the authorship of these two letters (whether Pauline or deutero-Pauline), these perspectives agree that the two letters originated *after* 1 Corinthians and reflect later developments in thought and usage.

Chapter 17

1. Barbara Brown Taylor, *The Preaching Life* (Boston: Cowley Publications, 1993), 25.

2. The *Manual of the Church of the Nazarene* states, "All Christians should consider themselves ministers of Christ and seek to know the will of God concerning their appropriate avenues of service" (para. 400 [Kansas City: Nazarene Publishing House, 2009], 183).

3. The Greek root for liturgy, *leitourgia*, means work or service of the *laos*, the people.

4. See Stephen Charles Neill and Hans-Ruedi Weber, eds., *The Layman in Christian History* (Philadelphia: Westminster, 1963), 33.

5. Snyder, *Radical Wesley and Patterns for Church Renewal*, 3.

6. In eighteenth-century terms, "to conference" referred to two or more people meeting together to discuss and discern over matters of mutual concern. Christian conference was a reference to Matthew 18:20, trusting that where two or more were gathered, Christ's Spirit would be present to edify and guide.

7. United Methodist churches today continue to elect "lay leaders" who represent the congregation on all committees and in district functions. The clergy remain itinerant, and long-term leadership officially rests with the lay leader.

Chapter 18

1. Willimon, *Pastor*, 33.

2. Ibid., 44.

3. See Acts 2:17-21.

4. One of the clearest expressions of the power of the Holy Spirit is to consider the Twelve in the Gospels compared to Acts. While there were still struggles, the power of the Holy Spirit is evident. The church today must never neglect the importance and necessity of the Spirit in all the church does.

5. Luther states, "Whoever comes out of the water of baptism can boast that he is already consecrated priest, bishop, and pope, although of course it is not seemly that just anybody should exercise such office. . . . There is no true, basic difference between laymen and priests . . . Except for the sake of office and work, but not for the sake of status" ("To the Christian Nobility of the German Nation," *Luther's Works*, vol. 44, trans. Charles M. Jacobs and James Atkinson [Philadelphia: Fortress Press, 1966], 129).

6. See Peterson, *Created to Worship*, 157-58.

7. Willimon, *Pastor*, 28.

8. See Numbers 3:1-20; 8:1-26.

9. Willimon, *Pastor*, 29.

10. See Ephesians 4:4-6.

11. In many places Paul affirms the bounty of God's *charisms* given to the body for many ministries outside of those charged to the episcopal leaders in the church. (For some examples see Rom. 12:4-8; 1 Cor. 16:1-3; 12:4-31; 2 Cor. 5:18-21.)

12. See Morris Pelzel, *Ecclesiology: The Church as Communion and Mission* (Chicago: Loyola Press, 2002), 37-41.

13. Willimon, *Pastor*, 32.

14. Wesley, February 6, 1740, *Journal and Diaries II*, 19:138. Actually, John was incorrect; it is the Anglican article 19. The Methodist Article of Religion 13 "Of the Church" was adopted virtually verbatim with the Church of England's Article 19 "Of the Church." Article 19 states, "The visible Church of Christ is a congregation of faithful men, in the which the pure Word of God is preached, and the Sacraments be duly ministered according to Christ's ordinance in all those things that of necessity are requisite to the same. As the Church of Jerusalem, Alexandria, and Antioch have erred; so also the Church of Rome hath erred, not only in their living and manner of Ceremonies, but also in matters of Faith." The Methodist Article 13 states, "The visible Church of Christ is a congregation of faithful men in which the pure Word of God is preached, and the Sacraments duly administered according to Christ's ordinance, in all those things that of necessity are requisite to the same."

15. See 1 Corinthians 15:3-5.

Chapter 19

1. Board of General Superintendents, Church of the Nazarene, "Nazarene Future Report: A Sustainable System of Global Mission"—"Statement of Ecclesiology"; denominational records available at http://nazarene.org/files/docs/BGS%20NAZARENE%20FUTURE%20REPORT%20February%202013%20-%20English.pdf (accessed June 11, 2013).

2. For the benefit of global church leaders serving beyond my immediate pastoral context, here I am critiquing the way the discipleship agenda of many North American congregations is easily hijacked by the well-financed mass marketing of religious books, films, and other multimedia productions purporting to strengthen credentials regarding the "cultural relevance" of our ministry. One may also argue that North American evangelical church life is dominated by the outsized influence of *megachurches* that exploit zeitgeist trends, amplifying the effectiveness of such marketing campaigns. For reviews regarding the relevance and impact of megachurches, see Scott L. Thumma, "The Kingdom, the Power, and the Glory: The Megachurch in Modern American Society" (Ph.D. diss., Emory University, 1996); and Nancy L. Eiesland, *A Particular Place: Urban Restructuring and Religious Ecology in a Southern Exurb* (New Brunswick, NJ: Rutgers University Press, 2000). For discussions of these dynamics in the most influential North American megachurch, see Kimon Howland Sargeant, "Willow Creek and the Future of Evangelicalism" (Ph.D. diss., University of Virginia, 1996); Gregory A. Pritchard, "The Strategy of Willow Creek Community Church: A Study in the Sociology of Religion" (Ph.D. diss., Northwest-

ern University, 1994); and James Mellado, "Willow Creek Community Church" (1991 case study for Harvard Business School prepared under the supervision of Professor Leonard A. Schlesinger, revised February 23, 1999; Harvard Business School Publishing, Boston).

3. For the origin of this "sweetmeats" analogy, readers are referred to John Wesley, *Letter on Preaching Christ,* London; December 20, 1751. In this correspondence, Wesley complains about the long-term impact of so-called gospel preaching that is neglecting essential aspects of formation in holiness: "Why, this is the very thing I assert: That the gospel Preachers, so called, corrupt their hearers; they vitiate their taste, so that they cannot relish sound doctrine; and spoil their appetite, so that they cannot turn it into nourishment; they, as it were, feed themselves with *sweetmeats,* till the wine of the kingdom seems quite insipid to them. They give them *cordial* upon cordial, which make them all life and spirit for the present; but meantime, their appetite is destroyed, so that they can neither retain nor digest the pure milk of the word." For further comment on this correspondence and its significance for the developing Methodist societies, see Heitzenrater, *Wesley and the People Called Methodists,* 185. Given my own early ministerial experience following the thirty-seven-year tenure of the founding pastor in a 2,600-member congregation, I can affirm Wesley's concerns regarding the formative influence of preaching with this observation: *over time, the shape of the pastor's preaching* (and we might add, the core emphases of that pastor's ministry) *will decisively shape the faith of the congregation, for good or ill.*

4. A perceptive treatment of the disaster resulting from this kind of congregational overstimulation comes from novelist Georges Bernanos, whose young priest and narrator comments that his parish is "bored stiff" but always "on the go." See Georges Bernanos, *The Diary of a Country Priest,* trans. Pamela Morris (New York: Carroll and Graf, 1983), 1-2.

5. Listening recently to journalist Michael Pollan, I heard him suggest that a first rule for reforming the disastrous diet that North Americans have developed in the practice of their industrialized approach to agriculture can be reduced to a deceptively simple but profound proposal: *only eat real food!* By analogy, I wonder about the degree to which we may be able to assist our satiated, self-indulgent congregations by simply weaning ourselves from cleverly marketed programming that detracts from the "nutritional value" of a more balanced diet of Word, Table, and redemptively sacrificial lives. See Michael Pollan, *The Omnivore's Dilemma: A Natural History of Four Meals* (New York: Penguin Press, 2006).

6. I will cite a single example of this trend: the recent publishing collaboration between Leadership Network and Jossey-Bass that has thus far generated forty-six titles intended to provide "thought leadership" for more effective ministry praxis. Having served as a senior pastor to large churches within two dissimilar denominations, I have profound gratitude and respect for the collegial

support and resources offered to me over my nearly three decades of association with Leadership Network. This association of entrepreneurial, megachurch pastors generously seeks "to help leaders of innovation navigate the future by exploring new ideas together to find application to their own unique contexts." But any close review of the new leadership literature published as a result of this joint venture should also demonstrate convincingly that the attention of these megachurch "thought partners" is very heavily skewed toward matters of ministry technique and method rather than core questions of pastoral vocation, formation, and character. The Leadership Network Mission Statement is available at http://leadnet.org/about/page/mission (accessed June 6, 2013).

7. See Ronald A. Heifetz, *Leadership Without Easy Answers* (Cambridge, MA: Harvard University Press, 1994); and Ronald Heifetz, Alexander Grashow, and Marty Linsky, *The Practice of Adaptive Leadership* (Boston: Harvard Business School Publishing, 2009).

8. William H. Willimon, *Bishop: The Art of Questioning Authority by an Authority in Question* (Nashville: Abingdon Press, 2012), 130.

9. André Resner Jr., "Eighth Sunday after the Epiphany, Year A—Second Lesson: 1 Corinthians 4:1-5," *The Lectionary Commentary: Theological Exegesis for Sunday's Texts*, vol. 2, *Acts and the Epistles*, ed. Roger E. Van Harn (Grand Rapids: Eerdmans, 2001), 179.

10. Atul Gawande, "Cowboys and Pit Crews," *New Yorker* (May 26, 2011); available online at http://www.newyorker.com/online/blogs/newsdesk/2011/05/atul-gawande-harvard-medical-school-commencement-address.html (accessed June 11, 2013).

11. For a concise discussion distinguishing between adaptive and technical work, see Heifetz, *Leadership Without Easy Answers*, 73-76.

12. The problem for many ministers is not that we lack methods and techniques that we might like to try within our congregations, *but that the sources of ecclesiological authority for discernment and implementation within our ministries are often impoverished.* As a result, the concentration of power that occurs as our churches grow larger (and as our pastoral tenures lengthen) makes it easier to accomplish almost anything we can imagine *even if we should not!* For a discussion of sociological dynamics as congregations become *functionally diffuse* instead of *functionally specific,* particularly within North American churches, see R. Stephen Warner, *New Wine in Old Wineskins: Evangelicals and Liberals in a Small-Town Church* (Berkeley, CA: University of California Press, 1988), 63. Warner notes that as churches grow functionally diffuse, the burden of proof falls upon those who would exclude a potential activity as illegitimate since the institution "will tend to absorb activities that are feasible given available resources." We might call such results the *metastases* of ill-advised technical work.

13. David Brooks, "It's Not About You," *New York Times,* May 30, 2011; available at http://www.nytimes.com/2011/05/31/opinion/31brooks.html?_r=0 (accessed June 11, 2013).

14. See Norbert Lohfink, "Distribution of the Functions of Power: The Laws Concerning Public Offices in Deuteronomy 16:18-18:22," and S. Dean McBride Jr., "Polity of the Covenant People: The Book of Deuteronomy," in *A Song of Power and the Power of Song: Essays on the Book of Deuteronomy,* ed. Duane L. Christensen, vol. 3 of *Sources for Biblical and Theological Study* (Winona Lake, IN: Eisenbrauns, 1993), 336-54 and 62-77.

15. Patrick D. Miller, *Deuteronomy* (Louisville, KY: John Knox Press, 1990), 10. As Miller explains elsewhere, the presentation of Deuteronomy as a "speech event" ostensibly voiced by Moses carries great importance for interpreters of the text: "The introductory verses of the book, reinforced constantly by the rest of the chapters, say in effect to readers of any time: Read these words as the Lord's instruction taught and explained by the prophet Moses, *and you will know what force and authority they are to have*" (italics mine). See Patrick D. Miller, "'Moses My Servant': The Deuteronomic Portrait of Moses," in *A Song of Power and the Power of Song,* 307.

16. Dennis T. Olson, *Deuteronomy and the Death of Moses: A Theological Reading* (Minneapolis: Fortress Press, 1994), 80-81. For a more modest appraisal of this perceived correspondence, see also Georg Braulik, "The Sequence of the Laws in Deuteronomy 12-26 and in the Decalogue," in *A Song of Power and the Power of Song,* 321.

17. Frank Crüsemann, *The Torah: Theology and Social History of Old Testament Law,* trans. Allen W. Mahnke (Minneapolis: Fortress Press, 1996), 234. For a review of how these royal expectations line up with the immediate context of the ancient Near East, see Ronald E. Clements, "The Book of Deuteronomy," in *The New Interpreter's Bible,* vol. 2 (Nashville: Abingdon Press, 1998), 426; and Gary N. Knoppers, "The Deuteronomist and the Deuteronomic Law of the King: A Reexamination of a Relationship," *Zeitschrift für die Alttestamentliche Wissenschaft,* vol. 108, no. 3 (1996), 329. In addition, six features of the royal ideology shared by Israel and its neighbors across the ancient Near East are outlined in Bernard M. Levinson, "The Reconceptualization of Kingship in Deuteronomy and the Deuteronomistic History's Transformation of Torah," *Vetus Testamentum,* vol. 51, no. 4 (2001), 511-34.

18. Jamie A. Grant, *The King as Exemplar: The Function of Deuteronomy's Kingship Law in the Shaping of the Book of Psalms* (Atlanta: Society of Biblical Literature, 2004), 192.

19. Bernard M. Levinson, *Deuteronomy and the Hermeneutics of Legal Innovation* (New York: Oxford University Press, 1998), 141.

20. Knoppers, "The Deuteronomist and the Deuteronomic Law of the King," 330-31.

21. For evaluations of the worrisome nature of this request for a king, see David M. Howard, "The Case for Kingship in Deuteronomy and the Former Prophets," *Westminster Theological Journal*, vol. 52, no. 1 (Spring 1990), 107; and Gerhard von Rad, *Deuteronomy*, trans. Dorothea Barton (Philadelphia: Westminster Press, 1966), 118-20.

22. See, for instance, J. A. Thompson, *Deuteronomy* (Downers Grove, IL: InterVarsity Press, 1974), 205; J. G. McConville, *Deuteronomy* (Downers Grove, IL: InterVarsity Press, 2002), 293; and Mark E. Biddle, *Deuteronomy* (Macon, GA: Smith & Helwys Publishing, 2003), 289.

23. Grant, *King as Exemplar*, 201.

24. Ibid., 197.

25. Richard D. Nelson, *Deuteronomy* (Louisville, KY: Westminster John Knox Press, 2002), 222.

26. Grant, *King as Exemplar*, 207-8.

27. Eugene H. Peterson, *Practice Resurrection: A Conversation on Growing Up in Christ* (Grand Rapids: Eerdmans, 2010), 33.

28. In a recent lecture delivered to the plebe class at the United States Military Academy at West Point, William Deresiewicz draws a significant distinction between *accomplishment* and *leadership:* "Does being a leader, I wondered, just mean being accomplished, being successful? Does getting straight As make you a leader? I didn't think so. Great heart surgeons or great novelists or great shortstops may be terrific at what they do, but that doesn't mean they're leaders. Leadership and aptitude, leadership and achievement, leadership and even excellence have to be different things, otherwise the concept of leadership has no meaning. . . . We have a crisis of leadership in America because our overwhelming power and wealth, earned under earlier generations of leaders, made us complacent, and for too long we have been training leaders who only know how to keep the routine going. Who can answer questions, but don't know how to ask them. Who can fulfill goals, but don't know how to set them. Who think about *how* to get things done, but not whether they're worth doing in the first place. What we have now are the greatest technocrats the world has ever seen, people who have been trained to be incredibly good at one specific thing, but who have no interest in anything beyond their area of expertise. What we *don't* have are leaders. What we don't have, in other words, are *thinkers*. People who can think for themselves . . . Multitasking . . . is not only not thinking, it impairs your ability to think. *Thinking means concentrating on one thing long enough to develop an idea about it.* Not learning other people's ideas, or memorizing a body of information, however much those may sometimes be useful. Developing your own ideas. In short, thinking for yourself. You simply cannot do that in

bursts of 20 seconds at a time, constantly interrupted by Facebook messages or Twitter tweets, or fiddling with your iPod, or watching something on YouTube. . . . So why is reading books any better than reading tweets or wall posts? Well, sometimes it isn't. Sometimes, you need to put down your book, if only to think about what you're reading, what *you* think about what you're reading. But a book has two advantages over a tweet. First, the person who wrote it thought about it a lot more carefully. The book is the result of *his* solitude, *his* attempt to think for himself. Second, most books are old. This is not a disadvantage: this is precisely what makes them valuable. They stand against the conventional wisdom of today simply because they're not *from* today. Even if they merely reflect the conventional wisdom of their own day, they say something different from what you hear all the time. But the great books, the ones you find on a syllabus, the ones people have continued to read, don't reflect the conventional wisdom of their day. *They say things that have the permanent power to disrupt our habits of thought*" (italics mine). See William Deresiewicz, "Solitude and Leadership," in *The American Scholar* (Spring 2010); available online at http://theamericanscholar.org/solitude-and-leadership/ (accessed December 24, 2010).

Chapter 20

1. Willimon, *Bishop,* 12.
2. Note especially Paul's charge to the Ephesian elders in Acts 20:28.
3. Russell E. Richey has done excellent work on this idea, including *Episcopacy in the Methodist Tradition* (Nashville: Abingdon, 2004).
4. Jeren Rowell, "Clergy Retention in the Church of the Nazarene, the Role of the District Superintendent in Clergy Decision Making Regarding Persistence in Active Vocational Ministry," unpublished doctoral diss. (Bourbonnais, IL: Olivet Nazarene University, 2010).
5. N. T. Wright, *Scripture and the Authority of God* (New York: HarperCollins Publishers, 2005), 137 (italics mine).
6. Dean R. Hoge and Jacqueline Wenger, *Pastors in Transition: Why Clergy Leave Local Church Ministry* (Grand Rapids: Eerdmans, 2005), 99.
7. Ibid., ix.
8. Richard B. Gilbert, "Healing the Holy Helpers, Healthy Clergy for the Third Millennium," doctoral diss. (Oxford, UK: Oxford University, 2003), 47.
9. Rowell, "Clergy Retention in the Church of the Nazarene," 82-83.
10. These are summations of the survey results in my previously mentioned study of pastors and superintendents.

WESLEYAN PARADIGM SERIES

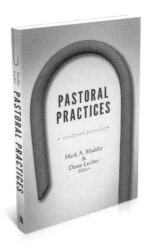

Pastoral Practices
Whatever the task may be—preaching, discipling, evangelizing, or administrating—this book sheds light on the way Wesleyan theology refines, informs, and enhances the theories and methods of each pastoral practice.

Pastoral Practices
Mark A. Maddix, Diane Leclerc (Editors)
978-0-8341-3009-8

Essential Church
Contributing pastors and educators explore the meaning, purpose, and function of the church as well as its structure. They address topics such as the kingdom of God, worship, and mission in relation to the body of Christ, and give special attention to Wesleyan theological concerns.

Essential Church
Diane Leclerc, Mark A. Maddix (Editors)
978-0-8341-3242-9

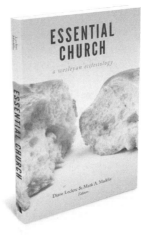

Spiritual Formation
People have a deep hunger and thirst for something that transcends them. This book focuses on how people can grow in Christlikeness while also providing guidance on self-care, spiritual direction, and mentoring.

Spiritual Formation
Diane Leclerc, Mark A. Maddix (Editors)
978-0-8341-2613-8

Also available in ebook formats

BEACON HILL PRESS
OF KANSAS CITY

Available online at BeaconHillBooks.com